DEIN COACH ZUM ERFOLG!

Dein ActiveBook auf MySTARK:

Du kannst auf alle digitalen Inhalte (Prüfung 2022, Hördateien, interaktive Aufgaben, Videos, „MindCards") online zugreifen. Registriere dich dazu unter **www.stark-verlag.de/mystark** mit deinem persönlichen Zugangscode:

D4W8-M3J8-M2H7

Die Inhalte dieser Auflage stehen bis 31.7.2024 zur Verfügung.

Das ActiveBook bietet dir:

- Viele interaktive Übungsaufgaben zu prüfungsrelevanten Kompetenzen
- Tipps zur Bearbeitung der Aufgaben
- Sofortige Ergebnisauswertung und detailliertes Feedback
- „MindCards" und Lernvideos zum gezielten Wiederholen zentraler Inhalte

MySTARK

DEIN COACH ZUM ERFOLG!

So kannst du interaktiv lernen:

Interaktive Aufgaben

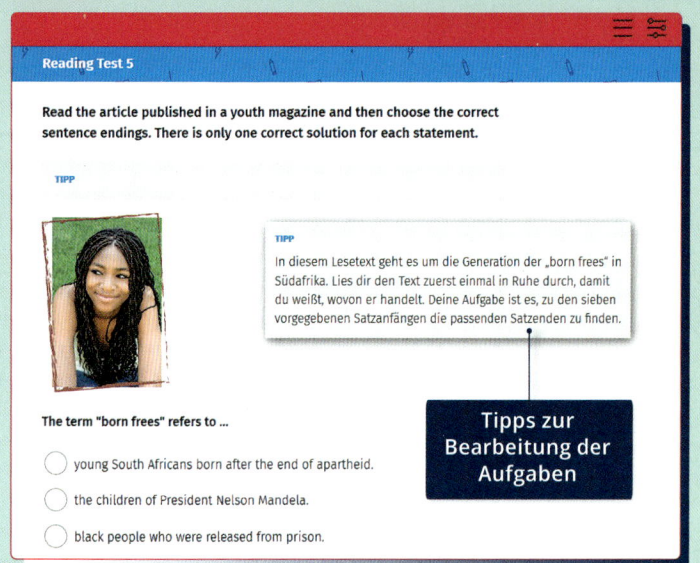

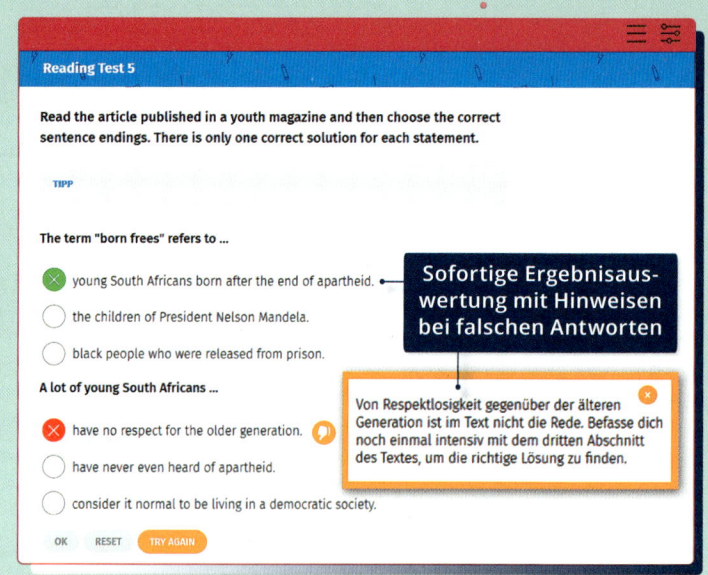

Tipps zur Bearbeitung der Aufgaben

Sofortige Ergebnisauswertung mit Hinweisen bei falschen Antworten

Lernvideos

Anschauliche Erklärungen zur Grammatik und Tipps zum Vokabellernen

Lernvideos

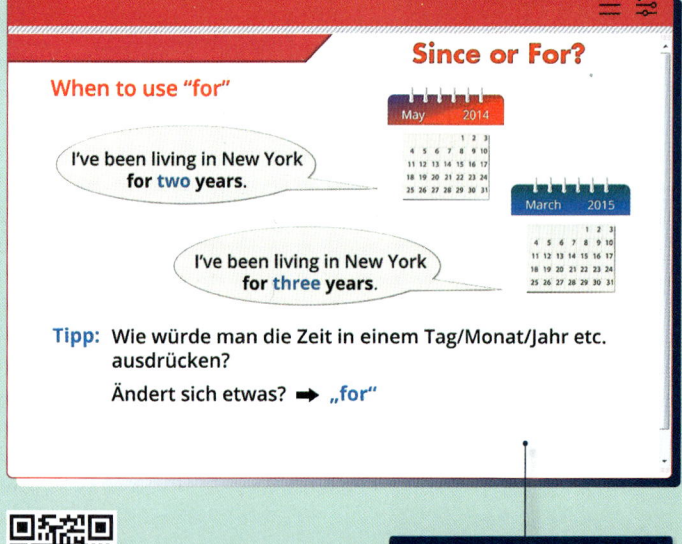

Web-App „MindCards"

Nützliche Wendungen mit Übersetzung

Individuelles Lernen nach dem Karteikartensystem

Speaking

Writing

Systemvoraussetzungen:
- Mindestens 1024×768 Pixel Bildschirmauflösung
- Chrome, Firefox oder ähnlicher Webbrowser
- Internetzugang
- Adobe Reader oder kompatibler anderer PDF-Reader

2023

Training
Abschlussprüfung

Realschule Baden-Württemberg

Englisch

Mila 10B

STARK

Bildnachweis

Deckblätter
- S. 1 Deckblatt „Kurzgrammatik" © Africa Studio. Shutterstock
- S. 31 Deckblatt „Hinweise, Tipps und Übungsaufgaben" © 123rf.com
- S. 185 Deckblatt „Aufgaben im Stil" © Splendens | Dreamstime.com
- S. 197 Deckblatt „Original-Aufgaben" © wavebreakmedia. Shutterstock

Listening
- S. 38 Flugzeug © farang. 123rf.com
- S. 39 Edinburgh Castle © jan kranendonk. Shutterstock
- S. 40 Spinne © James van den Broek. Shutterstock; Tintenfisch © 1608407. Shutterstock; Salzwasserkrokodil (Tabelle) © Dr. J. Beller. Shutterstock; Krokodil © nattanan726. Shutterstock
- S. 41 Robben Island © Bernhard Richter | Dreamstime
- S. 42 Poster „Free Nelson Mandela" © HelenSTB/flickr.com, CC BY-SA 2.0
- S. 43 Skyline London © pcruciatti. Shutterstock; Goldnugget © Steffen Foerster. Shutterstock
- S. 44 Bild „California Gold Rush" © 2733991. Shutterstock
- S. 45 Kind © Nikol Senkyrikova | Dreamstime
- S. 46 John © Studio 8. Pearson Education Ltd; Olivia © Jon Barlow. Pearson Education Ltd; Hailey © East. Shutterstock; Carter © Monkey Business Images. Shutterstock
- S. 49 Jugendliche beim Abschlussball © Monkey Business Images. Shutterstock

Reading – Text-based Tasks
- S. 55 Mädchen © Can Stock Photo Inc. | keeweeboy
- S. 59 „Welcome to Canada"-Schild © Becky Stares. Shutterstock; Niagarafälle © Chawalit S. Shutterstock
- S. 60 Blätter © Smileus | Dreamstime.com
- S. 62 Nationalpark © kavram. 123rf.com
- S. 63 Mädchen mit Handy © Ian Allenden | 123rf
- S. 67 Fußballspielerinnen mit Ball © Wavebreak Media Ltd. 123rf.com
- S. 68 Fußball © Pincarel. Shutterstock
- S. 71 Mädchen © Studio 8. Pearson Education Ltd
- S. 72 Schülergruppe © Studio 8. Pearson Education Ltd
- S. 74 Kürbis © Yellowj. Shutterstock
- S. 77 Hummel © Ian Grainger. 123rf.com
- S. 81 Roboter © Sarah Holmlund. Shutterstock

Use of Language
- S. 92 Familie auf Campingplatz © Landd09 | Dreamstime.com
- S. 94 Lehrerin © Multiart61 | Dreamstime.com
- S. 95 Eisverkäufer © Paul Jenkinson
- S. 97 Mädchen © Luminis | Dreamstime.com
- S. 74 Klettern © Olivier Tuffé – Fotolia.com; Windsurfen © Can Stock Photo Inc./3355m; Reiten © Krzyssagit | Dreamstime.com
- S. 100 Hintergrund „Party Night" © Janski | www.photocase.de
- S. 101 Pokal © zentilia | 123RF; Teddybär © AM-STUDIO. Shutterstock
- S. 102 Disney-Figuren © Anthony Totah Jr. | Dreamstime.com
- S. 103 Schild eines Obdachlosen © Digitalpress | Dreamstime.com
- S. 109 Noten © 123rf.com
- S. 110 Stegosaurus © Ozja. Shutterstock
- S. 111 Herz © Dalibor Sevaljevic. Shutterstock
- S. 112 Mann mit Hut © Stephanie Horrocks | iStockphoto
- S. 117 Band © Poznyakov. Shutterstock
- S. 120 Uluru © Csld | Dreamstime.com

Writing
- S. 132 Junge nach Mobbingvorfall © mandy godbehear | 123RF
- S. 135 Piloten im Cockpit © Tea | Dreamstime.com
- S. 138 Dorf © Jennifer Brown. 123rf.com
- S. 140 Schnipsel © 123rf.com
- S. 140/145 Hintergrund Brief © 123rf.com
- S. 141 Smartphone © flydragon. Shutterstock
- S. 142 Frau © PathDoc. Shutterstock; Baustelle © Devin Pavel. Shutterstock; Hotelzimmer © Dreamshot | Dreamstime.com; Kakerlake © 607708. Shutterstock
- S. 148 Tagebuch © Dana Rothstein | Dreamstime.com
- S. 149 Mädchen mit Smartphone © Syda Productions | Dreamstime.com

Interpreting
- S. 154 Lehrer © Jon Barlow. Pearson Education; Cameron © Tracy Whiteside. Shutterstock
- S. 157 Begrüßung © Jules Selmes. Pearson Education Ltd
- S. 158 Vater mit Tochter © Ron Chapple | Dreamstime.com
- S. 159 Fenster © Jürgen Fälche – Fotolia.de; München © Stefan Kühn, lizensiert unter CC BY-SA 3.0; Mädchen beim Schaukeln © Pavel Lysenko – Fotolia.de Restaurant © Sebastian Czapnik | Dreamstime.com
- S. 160 Sonne © LEWEB. Shutterstock
- S. 161 Flugzeug © elenathewise. 123rf.com
- S. 163 Vancouver © MAFord. Shutterstock; Totempfähle © Regien Paassen. Shutterstock; Steam Clock © Jpldesigns | Dreamstime.com
- S. 166 Mount Rushmore © Francesco Dazzi. Shutterstock; Schild „South Dakota" © Wellesenterprises | Dreamstime.com

Speaking
- S. 175 Sprung ins Wasser © Sk Elena. Shutterstock; Mädchen beim Klettern © marilyn barbone. Shutterstock; Mädchen mit Mountainbike © Gennadiy Poznyakov. 123rf.com; Junge vor Zelt © Dmitry Naumov. Shutterstock; Rom © Pavel K. Shutterstock; Strand © lauraslens. Shutterstock; Schwein © Alexander Raths. Shutterstock
- S. 176 Notizzettel © amasterphotographer. Shutterstock; Mädchen im Klassenzimmer © Emil Kudahl Christensen | Dreamstime.com; World AIDS Day © Allies Interactive Services Private Limited | Dreamstime.com; Holzzug © Ntcandrej | Dreamstime.com; Hund © Susan Schmitz. Shutterstock Umweltschützer © Wavebreakmedia Ltd | Dreamstime.com
- S. 177 Babysitter © Anita Patterson Peppers. Shutterstock.com; Nachhilfe © Dan Race. Shutterstock; Einkaufshelfer © dglimages. 123rf.com; Kellnerin © CREATISTA. Shutterstock; Zeitungsausträger © Daisy Daisy. Shutterstock; Hundesitterin © Skumer. Shutterstock; Erntehelfer © Kaca Skokanova. Shutterstock
- S. 178 Schild „Tourist Information" © Sterling Images. Shutterstock
- S. 179 Mädchen und Junge mit Stadtplan © Gareth Boden. Pearson Education Ltd

© 2022 Stark Verlag GmbH
17. ergänzte Auflage
www.stark-verlag.de

Das Werk und alle seine Bestandteile sind urheberrechtlich geschützt. Jede vollständige oder teilweise Vervielfältigung, Verbreitung und Veröffentlichung bedarf der ausdrücklichen Genehmigung des Verlages. Dies gilt insbesondere für Vervielfältigungen, Mikroverfilmungen sowie die Speicherung und Verarbeitung in elektronischen Systemen.

Inhalt

Vorwort
Häufige Fragen zur Abschlussprüfung

Kurzgrammatik		1
1	Besonderheiten einiger Wortarten	3
1.1	Adjektive und Adverbien – *Adjectives and Adverbs*	3
1.2	Artikel – *Article*	6
1.3	Pronomen – *Pronouns*	8
1.4	Präpositionen – *Prepositions*	9
1.5	Konjunktionen – *Conjunctions*	10
1.6	Modale Hilfsverben – *Modal Auxiliaries*	11
2	Finite Verbformen	12
2.1	Zeiten – *Tenses* ▶	12
2.2	Passiv – *Passive Voice* ▶	18
3	Infinite Verbformen	19
3.1	Infinitiv – *Infinitive*	19
3.2	Gerundium (-*ing*-Form) – *Gerund*	21
3.3	Infinitiv oder Gerundium? – *Infinitive or Gerund?*	22
3.4	Partizipien – *Participles*	23
4	Der Satz im Englischen	25
4.1	Wortstellung – *Word Order*	25
4.2	Bedingungssätze – *Conditional Sentences* ▶	26
4.3	Relativsätze – *Relative Clauses*	27
4.4	Indirekte Rede – *Reported Speech* ▶	29
Hinweise, Tipps und Übungsaufgaben zu den Prüfungsbereichen		31
1	Listening	33
1.1	Strategien zum Bereich „Listening"	33
1.2	Häufige Aufgabenstellungen zum Bereich „Listening"	35
1.3	Übungsaufgaben zum Bereich „Listening"	38
	Listening Test 1: Announcement on board	38
	Listening Test 2: Booking a hotel room	39
	Listening Test 3: Dangerous Australians	40
	Listening Test 4: Robben Island	41
	Listening Test 5: Things you didn't know about London	43
	Listening Test 6: The California Gold Rush	43
	Listening Test 7: The Stolen Generations	45

Inhalt

	Listening Test 8: Talking about the environment	45
	Listening Test 9: Couchsurfing or wilderness?	46
	Listening Test 10: Part-time jobs	47
	Listening Test 11: What's on your plate?	48
	Listening Test 12: Integrated prom	49
2	**Reading – Text-based Tasks**	**51**
2.1	Strategien zum Bereich „Reading"	51
2.2	Häufige Aufgabenstellungen zum Bereich „Reading"	51
2.3	Übungsaufgaben zum Bereich „Reading"	55
	Reading Test 1: "We may be 'born free', but…"	55
	Reading Test 2: Getting to know Canada	59
	Reading Test 3: Cyberbullying	63
	Reading Test 4: Young refugees learn about U.S. on the soccer field	67
	Reading Test 5: A year in England	71
	Reading Test 6: The history of Halloween	74
	Reading Test 7: Scientists say many "good" insects are disappearing	77
	Reading Test 8: How will machines and AI change the future of work?	81
3	**Use of Language**	**85**
3.1	Strategien zum Bereich „Use of Language"	85
3.2	Häufige Aufgabenstellungen zum Bereich „Use of Language"	89
3.3	Übungsaufgaben zum Grundwissen	92
	Grammatik ▶	92
	Wortschatz ▶	104
3.4	Prüfungsähnliche Aufgaben zum Bereich „Use of Language"	113
	Use of Language – Test 1	113
	Use of Language – Test 2	116
	Use of Language – Test 3	119
4	**Writing**	**123**
4.1	Strategien zum Bereich „Writing"	123
4.2	Häufige Aufgabenstellungen zum Bereich „Writing"	125
4.3	Hilfreiche Wendungen zum Bereich „Writing"	127
4.4	Übungsaufgaben zum Bereich „Writing"	132
5	**Interpreting**	**151**
5.1	Häufige Aufgabenstellungen zum Bereich „Interpreting"	151
5.2	Übungsaufgaben zum Bereich „Interpreting"	152

6	Speaking – Kommunikationsprüfung	167
6.1	Strategien zum Bereich „Speaking"	167
6.2	Die Kommunikationsprüfung	168
6.3	Hilfreiche Wendungen zum Bereich „Speaking"	170
6.4	Übungsaufgaben zum Bereich „Speaking"	174

Aufgaben im Stil der Abschlussprüfung 185

Original-Aufgaben der Abschlussprüfung 197
Abschlussprüfung 2021 2021-1

> Abschlussprüfung 2022 .... www.stark-verlag.de/mystark
> Sobald die Original-Prüfungsaufgaben 2022 freigegeben sind, können sie als PDF auf der Plattform MyStark heruntergeladen werden (Zugangscode vgl. Farbseiten vorne im Buch).

MP3-Dateien

Listening Test 1: Announcement on board

Listening Test 2: Booking a hotel room

Listening Test 3: Dangerous Australians

Listening Test 4: Robben Island

Listening Test 5: Things you didn't know about London

Listening Test 6: The California Gold Rush

Listening Test 7: The Stolen Generations

Listening Test 8: Talking about the environment

Listening Test 9: Couchsurfing or wilderness?

Listening Test 10: Part-time jobs

Listening Test 11: What's on your plate?

Listening Test 12: Integrated Prom

Aufgaben im Stil der Abschlussprüfung

Abschlussprüfung 2021

Abschlussprüfung 2022

Hinweis: Auf die MP3-Dateien kannst du online zugreifen. Den Zugangscode zur Plattform MyStark findest du zu Beginn des Buches.

Sprecherinnen und Sprecher:
Eva Adelseck, Daniel Beaver, Blair Gaulton, Esther Gilvray, Clare Gnasmüller, Daniel Holzberg, Rees Jeannotte, Daria Kozlova, Barbara Krzoska, Jennifer Mikulla, Julian Powell, Veronica Stivala, Rachel Teear, Ben Tendler

Die **Hintergrundgeräusche** in den Tracks stammen von Freesound, Pacdv und Soundsnap.

Inhalt

Autorinnen und Autoren

Übungsaufgaben: Patrick Charles, Walter Düringer, Heinz Gövert, Paul Jenkinson, Brigitte Katzer, Dr. Jasmin Kurz, Elke Lüdeke, Caroline Neu-Costello, Gerhard Philipp, Wencke Sockolowsky, Redaktion

Aufgaben im Stil der Abschlussprüfung: Dr. Jasmin Kurz

Lösungen der Original-Abschlussprüfungen: Dr. Jasmin Kurz

Sollten nach Erscheinen dieses Bandes noch wichtige Änderungen in der Abschlussprüfung vom Ministerium für Kultus, Jugend und Sport bekannt gegeben werden, findest du aktuelle Informationen dazu auf der Plattform **MyStark**.

Vorwort

Liebe Schülerin, lieber Schüler,

dieses Buch eignet sich **ab der 9. Klasse** zur Vorbereitung auf **Klassenarbeiten** und die **Prüfung zum Erwerb des Realschulabschlusses** im Fach Englisch.

- In der **Kurzgrammatik** werden wichtige grammatische Themen knapp erläutert und an Beispielsätzen veranschaulicht.
- Zu einigen grammatischen Strukturen, mit denen erfahrungsgemäß viele Lernende Schwierigkeiten haben, gibt es zusätzlich **Lernvideos**.
  Ein weiteres Video zeigt dir, wie du mithilfe von **Lernstrategien** deinen **Wortschatz** erweitern und festigen kannst. Scanne mithilfe deines Smartphones oder Tablets den nebenstehenden QR-Code oder gib den folgenden Link ein – so gelangst du schnell und einfach zu den Lernvideos:
  http://qrcode.stark-verlag.de/lernvideos-englisch-1
- Jedes Kapitel in diesem Buch widmet sich einem **Prüfungsbereich**. In den ersten Abschnitten erfährst du jeweils, welche Anforderungen auf dich zukommen können und wie du dich am besten darauf vorbereitest. Anhand der **Übungen** kannst du dann trainieren, wie man mit möglichen Aufgabenstellungen umgeht und sie erfolgreich löst.
- Neben vielen Aufgaben findest du das Symbol für „interaktive Aufgabe". Diese Aufgaben kannst du auch am Computer oder Tablet bearbeiten.
- Am Ende des Buches findest du **Aufgaben im Stil der Abschlussprüfung** sowie die **Original-Aufgaben** der Abschlussprüfung **2021**. Die **Original-Prüfung 2022** kannst du auf der Plattform MyStark herunterladen. Anhand dieser Aufgaben kannst du deine Kenntnisse „unter Prüfungsbedingungen" testen.
- Das beiliegende **Lösungsheft** enthält ausführliche Lösungsvorschläge mit vielen hilfreichen Hinweisen und Tipps zum Lösen der Aufgaben.
- Alle **Hörtexte** stehen dir als **MP3-Dateien** online zur Verfügung.
- Mit der Web-App „**MindCards**" kannst du am Smartphone **hilfreiche Wendungen** zu den Kompetenzen „Schreiben" und „Sprechen" wiederholen.
  Scanne dazu einfach die QR-Codes oder verwende folgende Links:
  https://www.stark-verlag.de/mindcards/writing-1
  https://www.stark-verlag.de/mindcards/speaking-1

Viel Spaß beim Üben und viel Erfolg in den Klassenarbeiten und in der Prüfung!

Auf alle **digitalen Inhalte** (Prüfung 2022, MP3-Dateien, Lernvideos, MindCards und ActiveBook) kannst du online über die Plattform **MyStark** zugreifen. Deinen persönlichen **Zugangscode** findest du auf den Farbseiten vorne im Buch.

Häufige Fragen zur Abschlussprüfung

Wie ist die Abschlussprüfung aufgebaut?

Die **schriftliche Abschlussprüfung** im Fach Englisch besteht aus fünf Teilen und wird folgendermaßen bewertet: In Teil A *(Listening Comprehension)* kannst du max. 20 Punkte erlangen, in den Teilen B bis E *(Text-based Tasks, Use of Language, Writing, Interpreting)* gibt es max. 90 Punkte. Alle Prüfungsbereiche bestehen aus mehreren Aufgaben, sodass du in der Prüfungssituation vielen verschiedenen Themen und Aufgabenformaten begegnen wirst.
Vor der schriftlichen Prüfung legst du außerdem eine mündliche Prüfung ab, die sog. **Kommunikationsprüfung**. Sie besteht aus drei Teilen, in denen du jeweils 10 Punkte erreichen kannst.

Wann findet die schriftliche Prüfung statt?

Der Prüfungstermin ist voraussichtlich der **17. Mai 2023**.

Wie lange dauert die schriftliche Abschlussprüfung?

Insgesamt dauert die Prüfung **150 Minuten**. Für Teil A *(Listening Comprehension)* hast du 30 Minuten Zeit. Für die Teile B bis E stehen dir insgesamt 120 Minuten zur Verfügung. Nach Teil A findet eine 20-minütige Pause statt.

Darf ich in der schriftlichen Prüfung ein Wörterbuch benutzen?

In **Teil A** ist **kein Wörterbuch** erlaubt. Für die **Teile B bis E** steht ein **zweisprachiges Wörterbuch** zur Verfügung. Du solltest aber nicht alle unbekannten Wörter nachschlagen, denn das würde zu viel Zeit kosten. Versuche grundsätzlich, wichtige Wörter aus dem Sinnzusammenhang zu erschließen. Nur wenn du nicht weiterkommst, solltest du auf das Wörterbuch zurückgreifen.

Sind die Aufgabenformate immer gleich?

Zu den verschiedenen Prüfungsbereichen gibt es eine ganze Reihe von möglichen Aufgabenformaten, wobei bestimmte Aufgaben immer wieder vorkommen. Die häufigsten Aufgabentypen werden dir jeweils am Anfang der Kapitel in diesem Buch vorgestellt. Wenn du dir diese Informationen durchliest, die Übungsaufgaben, die Aufgaben im Stil der Prüfung und die Aufgaben der Original-Prüfungen bearbeitest, kennst du bereits eine große Bandbreite möglicher Aufgabenformate.

Wie kann ich mich noch auf die schriftliche Prüfung vorbereiten?

Das Buch „Original-Prüfungen – Englisch – BaWü" (Bestell-Nr. C08150K) enthält eine Sammlung von Aufgaben im Stil der Prüfung sowie die Original-Prüfungsaufgaben 2018, 2019, 2021 und 2022 mit Lösungsvorschlägen zu allen Aufgaben. Es eignet sich besonders für die **Vorbereitungsphase unmittelbar vor der Abschlussprüfung**. Mit diesen Aufgaben kannst du die Prüfungssituation optimal simulieren und für den „Ernstfall" trainieren.

▶ Kurzgrammatik

Kurzgrammatik

Damit du die für deine Klassenarbeiten und für deine Prüfung relevanten Grammatikbereiche noch einmal wiederholen kannst, findest du hier die wichtigsten Grammatikregeln mit prägnanten Beispielen. Zu einigen Themen stehen dir zusätzlich Lernvideos ▶ zur Verfügung. Die mit * gekennzeichneten Bereiche der Grammatik musst du nicht aktiv beherrschen. Sie werden hier erklärt, damit du sie leichter verstehen kannst, falls sie einmal in einem Lese- oder Hörtext auftauchen sollten. Im Kapitel „Use of Language" erhältst du weitere Tipps, wie du mit dieser Kurzgrammatik arbeiten kannst (vgl. Kapitel 3.1).

Lernvideos

1 Besonderheiten einiger Wortarten

1.1 Adjektive und Adverbien – *Adjectives and Adverbs*

Bildung und Verwendung von Adverbien – *Formation and Use of Adverbs*

Bildung Adjektiv + *-ly*	glad →	gladly
Ausnahmen:		
• in mehrsilbigen Adjektiven wird *-y* am Wortende zu *-i*	easy → funny →	easily funnily
• stummes *-e* entfällt bei *due, true, whole*	true →	truly
• auf einen Konsonanten folgendes *-le* wird zu *-ly*	simple → probable →	simply probably
• *-ic* wird zu *-ically*	fantastic →	fantastically
Ausnahme:	public →	publicly
Beachte		
• Unregelmäßig gebildet wird:	good →	well
• Endet das Adjektiv auf *-ly*, so kann kein Adverb gebildet werden; man verwendet deshalb: *in a* + Adjektiv + *manner/way*.	friendly →	in a friendly manner
• In einigen Fällen haben Adjektiv und Adverb dieselbe Form.	daily, early, fast, hard, long, low, weekly, yearly	
• Manche Adjektive bilden zwei Adverbformen, die sich in der Bedeutung unterscheiden, z. B.:		

Adj./Adv.	Adv. auf *-ly*		
hard schwierig, hart	*hardly* kaum	The task is hard. (adjective) *Die Aufgabe ist schwierig.*	
late spät	*lately* neulich, kürzlich	She works hard. (adverb) *Sie arbeitet hart.*	
near nahe	*nearly* beinahe	She hardly works. (adverb) *Sie arbeitet kaum.*	

Kurzgrammatik

Verwendung

Adverbien bestimmen

- Verben,

  She <u>easily</u> <u>found</u> her brother in the crowd.
  Sie fand ihren Bruder leicht in der Menge.

- Adjektive,

  This band is <u>extremely</u> <u>famous</u>.
  Diese Band ist sehr berühmt.

- andere Adverbien oder

  He walks <u>extremely</u> <u>quickly</u>.
  Er geht äußerst schnell.

- einen ganzen Satz näher.

  <u>Fortunately</u>, <u>nobody</u> <u>was hurt</u>.
  Glücklicherweise wurde niemand verletzt.

Beachte

Nach bestimmten Verben, die einen **Zustand** ausdrücken, steht nicht das Adverb, sondern das Adjektiv, z. B.:

to be	sein
to seem	scheinen
to stay	bleiben

Everything <u>seems</u> <u>quiet</u>.
Alles scheint ruhig (zu sein).

Nach manchen Verben kann entweder ein Adjektiv oder ein Adverb folgen (z. B. nach *to feel, to look, to smell, to taste*). Mit Adverb beschreiben diese Verben eine **Tätigkeit**, mit Adjektiv eine **Eigenschaft** des Subjekts.

Harry <u>looks</u> <u>happy</u>. (Eigenschaft)
Harry sieht glücklich aus.
↔ Harry <u>looks</u> <u>happily</u> at his cake. (Tätigkeit)
Harry schaut glücklich auf seinen Kuchen.

Steigerung des Adjektivs – *Comparison of Adjectives*

Bildung

Man unterscheidet:

- Grundform/Positiv *(positive)*

  Peter is <u>young</u>.

- 1. Steigerungsform/Komparativ *(comparative)*

  Jane is <u>younger</u>.

- 2. Steigerungsform/Superlativ *(superlative)*

  Paul is <u>the youngest</u>.

Steigerung auf *-er, -est*

- einsilbige Adjektive

  old, old<u>er</u>, old<u>est</u>
  alt, älter, am ältesten

- zweisilbige Adjektive, die auf *-er, -le, -ow* oder *-y* enden

  clever, cleve<u>rer</u>, cleve<u>rest</u>
  klug, klüger, am klügsten

  simple, simp<u>ler</u>, simp<u>lest</u>
  einfach, einfacher, am einfachsten

  narrow, narrow<u>er</u>, narrow<u>est</u>
  eng, enger, am engsten

  funny, funn<u>ier</u>, funn<u>iest</u>
  lustig, lustiger, am lustigsten

Handwritten notes:

adverbs — adjectives — sentence — verbs

I am really nervous.
Suddenly I got ill.
extremly dangerous, very cold

Kurzgrammatik

Beachte
- stummes -e am Wortende entfällt
- nach einem Konsonanten wird -y am Wortende zu -i-
- nach betontem Vokal wird ein Konsonant am Wortende verdoppelt

simpl*e*, simpl*e*r, simpl*e*st
funn*y*, funn*i*er, funn*i*est

fi*t*, fi*tt*er, fi*tt*est

Steigerung mit *more ..., most ...*
- zweisilbige Adjektive, die nicht auf -er, -le, -ow oder -y enden
- Adjektive mit drei und mehr Silben

useful, more useful, most useful
nützlich, nützlicher, am nützlichsten

difficult, more difficult, most difficult
schwierig, schwieriger, am schwierigsten

Steigerungsformen im Satz – *Sentences with Comparisons*

Bildung
Es gibt folgende Möglichkeiten, Steigerungen im Satz zu verwenden:

- **Grundform:**
  Zwei oder mehr Personen oder Sachen sind **gleich oder ungleich**:
  (not) as + Grundform des Adjektivs + *as*

  Anne is as tall as John.
  Anne ist genauso groß wie John.

  John is not as tall as Steve.
  John ist nicht so groß wie Steve.

- **Komparativ:**
  Zwei oder mehr Personen oder Sachen sind **verschieden** (größer/besser/ ...):
  Komparativ des Adjektivs + *than*

  Steve is taller than Anne.
  Steve ist größer als Anne.

- **Superlativ:**
  Eine Person oder Sache wird **besonders hervorgehoben** (der/die/das größte/beste/ ...):
  the + Superlativ des Adjektivs

  Steve is one of the tallest boys in class.
  Steve ist einer der größten Jungen in der Klasse.

Steigerung des Adverbs – *Comparison of Adverbs*

Adverbien können wie Adjektive auch gesteigert werden.
- Adverbien auf -ly werden mit *more, most* bzw. mit *less, least* gesteigert.
- Adverbien, die dieselbe Form wie das Adjektiv haben, werden mit -er, -est gesteigert.

She talks more quickly than John.
Sie spricht schneller als John.

fast   –   faster   –   fastest
early   –   earlier   –   earliest

Unregelmäßige Steigerung – *Irregular Comparisons*

Unregelmäßig gesteigerte Formen muss man auswendig lernen. Einige wichtige Formen sind hier angegeben:	*good – better – best* *bad – worse – worst* *well – better – best* *badly – worse – worst* *little – less – least* *much – more – most*

Die Stellung von Adverbien im Satz – *The Position of Adverbs in Sentences*

Adverbien können verschiedene Positionen im Satz einnehmen:

- Am **Anfang des Satzes**, vor dem Subjekt *(front position)*

  <u>Tomorrow</u>, he will be in London.
  Morgen [betont] wird er in London sein.

  <u>Unfortunately</u>, I can't come to the party.
  Leider kann ich nicht zur Party kommen.

- **Im Satz** *(mid position)*:
  vor dem Vollverb

  She <u>often</u> goes to school by bike.
  Sie fährt oft mit dem Rad in die Schule.

  nach *to be*

  She is <u>already</u> at home.
  Sie ist schon zu Hause.

  nach dem ersten Hilfsverb

  You can <u>even</u> go swimming there.
  Man kann dort sogar schwimmen gehen.

- Am **Ende des Satzes** *(end position)*

  He will be in London <u>tomorrow</u>.
  Er wird morgen in London sein.

  Gibt es mehrere Adverbien am Satzende, so gilt die **Reihenfolge**:
  Art und Weise – Ort – Zeit
  (manner – place – time)

  The snow melts <u>slowly</u> <u>in the mountains</u> <u>at springtime</u>.
  Im Frühling schmilzt der Schnee langsam in den Bergen.

1.2 Artikel – *Article*

Der **bestimmte Artikel** steht, wenn man von einer **ganz bestimmten Person oder Sache** spricht.

<u>The</u> cat is sleeping on the sofa.
Die Katze schläft auf dem Sofa. [nicht irgendeine Katze, sondern eine bestimmte]

Beachte
Der bestimmte Artikel steht **immer** bei:
- **abstrakten Begriffen**, die näher erläutert sind

<u>The</u> agriculture practised in the USA is very successful.
Die Landwirtschaft, wie sie in den USA praktiziert wird, ist sehr erfolgreich.

Kurzgrammatik

- **Gebäudebezeichnungen**, wenn man vom Gebäude selbst spricht

  The school should be renovated soon.
  Die Schule (= das Schulgebäude) sollte bald renoviert werden.

- **Eigennamen im Plural** (z. B. bei Familiennamen, Gebirgen, Inselgruppen, einigen Ländern)

  the Johnsons, the Rockies, the Hebrides, the Netherlands, the USA

- Namen von **Flüssen** und **Meeren**

  the Mississippi, the North Sea, the Pacific Ocean

Der **unbestimmte Artikel** steht, wenn man von einer **nicht näher bestimmten Person oder Sache** spricht.

A man is walking down the road.
Ein Mann läuft gerade die Straße entlang.
[irgendein Mann]

Beachte
Der unbestimmte Artikel steht **häufig** bei:

- **Berufsbezeichnungen** und **Nationalitäten**

  She is an engineer. *Sie ist Ingenieurin.*
  He is a Scot(sman). *Er ist Schotte.*

- Zugehörigkeit zu einer **Religion** oder **Partei**

  She is a Catholic. *Sie ist Katholikin.*

Es steht **kein Artikel** bei:

- **nicht zählbaren** Nomen wie z. B. **Stoffbezeichnungen**

  Gold is very valuable.
  Gold ist sehr wertvoll.

- **abstrakten Nomen** ohne nähere Bestimmung

  Buddhism is widespread in Asia.
  Der Buddhismus ist in Asien weitverbreitet.

- **Bezeichnungen für Gruppen von Menschen**, z. B. *man* (= der Mensch bzw. alle Menschen), *society*

  Man is responsible for global warming.
  Der Mensch ist für die Klimaerwärmung verantwortlich.

- **Institutionen**, z. B. *school, church, university, prison*

  School starts at 9 a.m.
  Die Schule beginnt um 9 Uhr.

- **Mahlzeiten**, z. B. *breakfast, lunch*

  Dinner is at 8 p.m.
  Das Abendessen ist um 20 Uhr.

- *by* + **Verkehrsmittel**

  I went to school by bike.
  Ich fuhr mit dem Fahrrad zur Schule.

- **Personennamen** (auch mit Titel) oder **Verwandtschaftsbezeichnungen**, die wie Namen verwendet werden

  Tom, Mr Scott, Queen Elizabeth II, Dr Hill, Dad, Uncle Harry

- Bezeichnungen für **Straßen, Plätze, Brücken, Parkanlagen**

  Fifth Avenue, Trafalgar Square, Westminster Bridge, Hyde Park

- Namen von **Ländern, Kontinenten, Städten, Seen, Inseln, Bergen**

  France, Asia, San Francisco, Loch Ness, Corsica, Ben Nevis

1.3 Pronomen – *Pronouns*

Possessivbegleiter und -pronomen – *Possessive Determiners and Pronouns*

> „Possessiv" bedeutet **besitzanzeigend**. Man verwendet diese Formen, um zu sagen, **wem etwas gehört**.
>
> Man unterscheidet Possessivbegleiter, die mit einem Substantiv stehen, und Possessivpronomen (sie ersetzen ein Substantiv):
>
> | mit Substantiv | ohne Substantiv |
> |---|---|
> | my | mine |
> | your | yours |
> | his / her / its | his / hers / – |
> | our | ours |
> | your | yours |
> | their | theirs |

This is my bike. – This is mine.
This is your bike. – This is yours.
This is her bike. – This is hers.
This is our bike. – This is ours.
This is your bike. – This is yours.
This is their bike. – This is theirs.

Reflexivpronomen – *Reflexive Pronouns*

> Reflexivpronomen *(reflexive pronouns)*, also **rückbezügliche Fürwörter, beziehen sich auf das Subjekt** des Satzes **zurück**:
>
> myself
> yourself
> himself / herself / itself
> ourselves
> yourselves
> themselves
>
> **Beachte**
> - Einige Verben stehen ohne Reflexivpronomen, obwohl im Deutschen mit „mich, dich, sich etc." übersetzt wird.
>
> - Einige Verben können sowohl mit einem Objekt als auch mit einem Reflexivpronomen verwendet werden. Dabei ändert sich die Bedeutung, z. B. bei *to enjoy* und *to help*.

I will look after myself.
You will look after yourself.
He will look after himself.
We will look after ourselves.
You will look after yourselves.
They will look after themselves.

I apologise …
Ich entschuldige mich …

He is hiding.
Er versteckt sich.

He is enjoying the party. (Verb mit Objekt)
Er genießt die Party.

She is enjoying herself. (Verb mit Reflexivpronomen)
Sie amüsiert sich.

He is helping the child. (Verb mit Objekt)
Er hilft dem Kind.

Help yourself! (Verb mit Reflexivpronomen)
Bedienen Sie sich!

Reziprokes Pronomen – *Reciprocal Pronoun* ("each other/one another")

each other/one another ist unveränderlich. Es bezieht sich auf **zwei oder mehr Personen** und wird mit „sich (gegenseitig)"/ „einander" übersetzt.	They looked at each other and laughed. *Sie schauten sich (gegenseitig) an und lachten.* oder: *Sie schauten einander an und lachten.*
Beachte Einige Verben stehen ohne *each other*, obwohl im Deutschen mit „sich" übersetzt wird.	to meet sich treffen to kiss sich küssen to fall in love sich verlieben

1.4 Präpositionen – *Prepositions*

Präpositionen *(prepositions)* sind Verhältniswörter. Sie drücken **räumliche, zeitliche oder andere Arten von Beziehungen** aus.

The ball is under the table.
He came home after six o'clock.

Die wichtigsten Präpositionen mit Beispielen für ihre Verwendung:

- *at*
  Ortsangabe: *at home*
  Zeitangabe: *at 3 p.m.*

  I'm at home now.   Ich bin jetzt zu Hause.
  He arrived at 3 p.m.   Er kam um 15 Uhr an.

- *by*
  Angabe des Mittels: *by bike*

  She went to work by bike.
  Sie fuhr mit dem Rad zur Arbeit.

  Angabe des Verursachers (in Passivsätzen): *by a bus*

  Her car was hit by a bus.
  Ihr Auto wurde von einem Bus angefahren.

  Angabe der Ursache: *by mistake*

  He did it by mistake.
  Er hat es aus Versehen getan.

  Zeitangabe: *by tomorrow*

  You will get the letter by tomorrow.
  Du bekommst den Brief bis (spätestens) morgen.

- *for*
  Zeitdauer: *for hours*

  We waited for the bus for hours.
  Wir warteten stundenlang auf den Bus.

- *from*
  Ortsangabe: *from Dublin*

  Ian is from Dublin.
  Ian kommt aus Dublin.

  Zeitangabe: *from nine to five*

  We work from nine to five.
  Wir arbeiten von neun bis fünf Uhr.

- *in*
  Ortsangabe: *in England*

  In England, they drive on the left.
  In England herrscht Linksverkehr.

  Zeitangabe: *in the morning*

  They woke up in the morning.
  Sie wachten am Morgen auf.

- **of**
  Besitz/Zugehörigkeit/Teilmenge:
  owner of the house, north of the city, two days of the week, one bar of soap

  The village lies north of the city.
  Das Dorf liegt nördlich der Stadt.

- **on**
  Ortsangabe: *on the left, on the floor*

  On the left, you see the London Eye.
  Links sehen Sie das London Eye.

  Zeitangabe: *on Monday*

  On Monday, she will buy the tickets.
  (Am) Montag kauft sie die Karten.

- **to**
  Richtungsangabe: *to the left*

  Please turn to the left.
  Bitte wenden Sie sich nach links.

  Angabe des Ziels: *to London*

  He goes to London every year.
  Er fährt jedes Jahr nach London.

1.5 Konjunktionen – *Conjunctions*

Konjunktionen *(conjunctions)* verwendet man, um **zwei Hauptsätze oder Haupt- und Nebensatz miteinander zu verbinden**. Mit Konjunktionen lässt sich ein Text strukturieren, indem man z. B. Ursachen, Folgen oder zeitliche Abfolgen angibt.

Die wichtigsten Konjunktionen mit Beispielen für ihre Verwendung:

- *after* – nachdem

  What will you do after she's gone?
  Was wirst du tun, nachdem sie gegangen ist?

- *although* – obwohl

  Although she was ill, she went to work.
  Obwohl sie krank war, ging sie zur Arbeit.

- *as* – als (zeitlich)

  As he came into the room, the telephone rang.
  Als er ins Zimmer kam, klingelte das Telefon.

- *as soon as* – sobald

  As soon as the band began to play, …
  Sobald die Band zu spielen begann, …

- *because* – weil, da

  I need a new bike because my old bike was stolen.
  Ich brauche ein neues Rad, weil mein altes Rad gestohlen wurde.

- *before* – bevor

  Before he goes to work, he buys a newspaper.
  Bevor er zur Arbeit geht, kauft er eine Zeitung.

- *but* – aber

  She likes football but she doesn't like skiing.
  Sie mag Fußball, aber sie mag Skifahren nicht.

- *either … or* – entweder … oder

  We can either watch a film or go to a concert.
  Wir können uns entweder einen Film ansehen oder in ein Konzert gehen.

• *in order to*	– um … zu, damit	Peter is in Scotland in order to visit his friend Malcolm. *Peter ist in Schottland, um seinen Freund Malcolm zu besuchen.*
• *neither … nor*	– weder … noch	We can neither eat nor sleep outside. It's raining. *Wir können draußen weder essen noch schlafen. Es regnet.*
• *so that*	– sodass	She shut the door so that the dog couldn't go outside. *Sie machte die Tür zu, sodass der Hund nicht hinausgehen konnte.*
• *when*	– wenn (zeitlich), sobald	Have a break when you've finished painting this wall. *Mach eine Pause, sobald du diese Wand fertig gestrichen hast.*
• *while*	– während (zeitlich)	He came home while I was reading. *Er kam nach Hause, während ich gerade las.*
	– während (Gegensatz)	Belle is beautiful while the Beast is ugly. *Belle ist schön, während das Biest hässlich ist.*

1.6 Modale Hilfsverben – *Modal Auxiliaries*

Im Englischen gibt es zwei Arten von Hilfsverben: *to be, to have* und *to do* können Hilfsverben sein, wenn sie zusammen mit einem anderen Verb im Satz vorkommen:

I have read the book. *Ich habe das Buch gelesen.*

Außerdem gibt es noch die sogenannten „modalen Hilfsverben". Zu den **modalen Hilfsverben** (*modal auxiliaries*) zählen z. B.:

can, may, must

Bildung

- Die modalen Hilfsverben haben für alle Personen **nur eine Form**, in der 3. Person Singular also kein -s.

I, you, he / she / it, we, you, they } must

- Auf ein modales Hilfsverb folgt der **Infinitiv ohne *to***.

You must look at my new bike.
Du musst dir mein neues Fahrrad ansehen.

- **Frage und Verneinung** werden nicht mit *do / did* umschrieben.

"Can you hear me?" – "No, I can't."
„*Kannst du mich hören?" – „Nein, kann ich nicht."*

Ersatzformen

Die modalen Hilfsverben können nicht alle Zeiten bilden. Deshalb benötigt man **Ersatzformen**. Diese können auch im Präsens verwendet werden.

- **can** (können)
  Ersatzformen:
  (to) be able to (Fähigkeit),
  (to) be allowed to (Erlaubnis)

  Beachte
  Im *simple past* und *conditional I* ist auch *could* möglich.

- **may** (dürfen) – sehr höflich
  conditional I: might
  Ersatzform: **(to) be allowed to**

- **must** (müssen)
  Ersatzform: **(to) have to**

  Beachte
  must not/mustn't = „nicht dürfen"

  „nicht müssen, nicht brauchen"
  = **not have to, needn't**

I can sing. / I was able to sing.
Ich kann singen. / Ich konnte singen.

You can't go to the party. /
I wasn't allowed to go to the party.
Du darfst nicht auf die Party gehen. /
Ich durfte nicht auf die Party gehen.

When I was three, I could already ski.
Mit drei konnte ich schon Ski fahren.

You may go home early. /
You were allowed to go home early.
Du darfst früh nach Hause gehen. /
Du durftest früh nach Hause gehen.

He must be home by ten o'clock. /
He had to be home by ten o'clock.
Er muss um zehn Uhr zu Hause sein. /
Er musste um zehn Uhr zu Hause sein.

You must not eat all the cake.
Du darfst nicht den ganzen Kuchen essen.

You don't have to / needn't eat all the cake.
Du musst nicht den ganzen Kuchen essen. /
Du brauchst nicht … zu essen.

2 Finite Verbformen

2.1 Zeiten – *Tenses*

Simple Present

Bildung
Grundform des Verbs (Infinitiv)
Ausnahme: 3. Person Singular: Infinitiv + -s

Beachte
- Bei Verben, die auf einen Zischlaut (z. B. -s, -sh, -ch, -x und -z) enden, wird in der 3. Person Singular -es angefügt.

- Bei Verben, die auf Konsonant + -y enden, wird -es angefügt; -y wird zu -i-.

Bildung von Fragen im *simple present*
(Fragewort +) *do/does* + Subjekt + Infinitiv

I/you/we/you/they stand
he/she/it stands

kiss – he/she/it kisses
rush – he/she/it rushes
teach – he/she/it teaches
fix – he/she/it fixes
carry – he/she/it carries

Where does he live? / Does he live in London?
Wo lebt er? / Lebt er in London?

Beachte

Die Umschreibung mit *do/does* wird nicht verwendet,

- wenn nach dem Subjekt gefragt wird (mit *who, what, which*),

  <u>Who</u> <u>likes</u> pizza?
  Wer mag Pizza?

  <u>What</u> <u>happens</u> next?
  Was passiert als Nächstes?

  <u>Which</u> tree <u>has</u> more leaves?
  Welcher Baum hat mehr Blätter?

- wenn die Frage mit *is/are* gebildet wird.

  <u>Are</u> you happy?
  Bist du glücklich?

Bildung der Verneinung im *simple present*

don't/doesn't + Infinitiv

He <u>doesn't like</u> football.
Er mag Fußball nicht.

Verwendung

Das *simple present* wird verwendet:

- bei Tätigkeiten, die man **gewohnheitsmäßig** oder häufig ausführt
  Signalwörter: z. B. *always, often, never, every day, every morning, every afternoon*

  Every morning, John <u>buys</u> a newspaper.
  Jeden Morgen kauft John eine Zeitung.

- bei **allgemeingültigen** Aussagen

  London <u>is</u> a big city.
  London ist eine große Stadt.

- bei **Zustandsverben**: Sie drücken Eigenschaften/Zustände von Personen und Dingen aus und stehen normalerweise nur in der *simple form*, z. B. *to hate, to know, to like*.

  I <u>like</u> science-fiction films.
  Ich mag Science-Fiction-Filme.

Beachte

Das *simple present* kann sich auch auf die Zukunft beziehen. Siehe hierzu S. 17.

Present Progressive / Present Continuous

Bildung

am/is/are + -ing-Form (*present participle*)

read → <u>am/is/are</u> <u>reading</u>

Mehr zur Bildung des *present participle* siehe Kapitel 3.4 der Kurzgrammatik.

Bildung von Fragen im *present progressive*

(Fragewort +) *am/is/are* + Subjekt + -ing-Form

<u>Is</u> Peter <u>reading</u>? / <u>What</u> <u>is</u> he <u>reading</u>?
Liest Peter gerade? / Was liest er?

Bildung der Verneinung im *present progressive*

am not/isn't/aren't + -ing-Form

Peter <u>isn't</u> <u>reading</u>.
Peter liest gerade nicht.

Verwendung

Mit dem *present progressive* drückt man aus, dass etwas **gerade passiert** und **noch nicht abgeschlossen** ist. Es wird daher auch als **Verlaufsform** der Gegenwart bezeichnet.

Signalwörter: *at the moment, now*

Beachte
Das *present progressive* kann sich auch auf die Zukunft beziehen. Siehe hierzu S. 17.

At the moment, Peter is drinking a cup of tea.
Im Augenblick trinkt Peter eine Tasse Tee. [Er hat damit angefangen und noch nicht aufgehört.]

Simple Past

Bildung

Regelmäßige Verben: Infinitiv + *-ed*

walk → walked

Beachte
- stummes *-e* entfällt
- Bei Verben, die auf Konsonant + *-y* enden, wird *-y* zu *-i-*.
- Nach betontem Vokal wird der Schlusskonsonant verdoppelt.

hope → hoped

carry → carried

stop → stopped

Die *simple past*-Formen unregelmäßiger Verben muss man auswendig lernen. Einige wichtige Formen sind hier angegeben – weitere Beispiele sind z. B. in Wörterbüchern aufgeführt.

be → was/were
have → had
give → gave
go → went
say → said
see → saw
take → took

Bildung von Fragen im *simple past*

(Fragewort +) *did* + Subjekt + Infinitiv

Why did / Did he look out of the window?
Warum sah / Sah er aus dem Fenster?

Beachte
Die Umschreibung mit *did* wird nicht verwendet,
- wenn nach dem Subjekt gefragt wird (mit *who, what, which*),

Who paid the bill?
Wer zahlte die Rechnung?

What happened to your friend?
Was ist mit deinem Freund passiert?

Which boy cooked the meal?
Welcher Junge hat das Essen gekocht?

- wenn die Frage mit *was/were* gebildet wird.

Were you happy?
Warst du glücklich?

Bildung der Verneinung im *simple past*

didn't + Infinitiv

He didn't call me.
Er rief mich nicht an.

Verwendung

Das *simple past* beschreibt Handlungen und Ereignisse, die **in der Vergangenheit passierten** und **bereits abgeschlossen** sind.

Signalwörter: z. B. *yesterday, last week/year, two years ago, in 2012*

Last week, he helped me with my homework.
Letzte Woche half er mir bei meinen Hausaufgaben. [Die Handlung fand in der letzten Woche statt, ist also abgeschlossen.]

Past Progressive / Past Continuous

Bildung

was/were + *-ing*-Form (*present participle*)

watch → was/were watching

Verwendung

Die **Verlaufsform** *past progressive* verwendet man, wenn **zu einem bestimmten Zeitpunkt** in der Vergangenheit eine **Handlung ablief** bzw. wenn eine **Handlung** von einer anderen **unterbrochen** wurde.

Yesterday at 9 o'clock, I was still sleeping.
Gestern um 9 Uhr schlief ich noch.

I was reading a book when Peter came into the room.
Ich las (gerade) ein Buch, als Peter ins Zimmer kam.

Present Perfect (Simple)

Bildung

have/has + *past participle*

Zur Bildung des *past participle* siehe Kapitel 3.4 der Kurzgrammatik.

write → has/have written

Verwendung

Das *present perfect* verwendet man,
- wenn ein Vorgang **in der Vergangenheit begonnen** hat und **noch andauert**,
- wenn das Ergebnis einer vergangenen Handlung **Auswirkungen auf die Gegenwart** hat.

Signalwörter: z. B. *already, ever, just, how long, not … yet, since, for*

Beachte
- *have/has* können zu *'ve/'s* verkürzt werden.

He has lived in London since 2008.
Er lebt seit 2008 in London.
[Er lebt jetzt immer noch in London.]

I have just cleaned my car.
Ich habe gerade mein Auto geputzt.
[Man sieht möglicherweise das saubere Auto.]

Have you ever been to Dublin?
Warst du schon einmal in Dublin?

He's given me his umbrella.
Er hat mir seinen Regenschirm gegeben.

▶ Present perfect or Simple past?

Kurzgrammatik

Since or For?

- Das *present perfect* wird oft mit *since* und *for* verwendet, die beide „seit" bedeuten.
  - *since* gibt einen **Zeitpunkt** an:
    Ron has lived in Sydney since 2007.
    Ron lebt seit 2007 in Sydney.
  - *for* gibt einen **Zeitraum** an:
    Sally has lived in Berlin for five years.
    Sally lebt seit fünf Jahren in Berlin.

Present Perfect Progressive / Present Perfect Continuous

Bildung
have / has + been + -ing-Form *(present participle)*

write → has / have been writing

Verwendung
Die **Verlaufsform** *present perfect progressive* verwendet man, um die **Dauer einer Handlung** zu **betonen**, die in der Vergangenheit begonnen hat und noch andauert.

She has been sleeping for ten hours.
Sie schläft seit zehn Stunden.
[Sie schläft immer noch.]

Past Perfect (Simple)

Bildung
had + past participle

write → had written

Verwendung
Die Vorvergangenheit *past perfect* verwendet man, wenn ein Vorgang in der Vergangenheit **vor einem anderen Vorgang in der Vergangenheit abgeschlossen** wurde.

He had bought a ticket before he took the train to Manchester.
Er hatte eine Fahrkarte gekauft, bevor er den Zug nach Manchester nahm. [Beim Einsteigen war der Kauf abgeschlossen.]

Past Perfect Progressive / Past Perfect Continuous

Bildung
had + been + -ing-Form *(present participle)*

write → had been writing

Verwendung
Die **Verlaufsform** *past perfect progressive* verwendet man für **Handlungen**, die in der Vergangenheit **bis zu dem Zeitpunkt andauerten**, zu dem eine neue Handlung einsetzte.

She had been sleeping for ten hours when the doorbell rang.
Sie hatte seit zehn Stunden geschlafen, als es an der Tür klingelte. [Sie schlief bis zu dem Zeitpunkt, als es an der Tür klingelte.]

Will-future

Bildung
will + Infinitiv

buy → will buy

Bildung von Fragen im *will-future*
(Fragewort +) will + Subjekt + Infinitiv

What will you buy?
Was wirst du kaufen?

Bildung der Verneinung im *will-future*
will not / won't + Infinitiv

She won't come to our party.
Sie wird nicht zu unserer Party kommen.

Verwendung
Das *will-future* verwendet man, wenn ein Vorgang **in der Zukunft stattfinden** wird:
- bei Vorhersagen oder Vermutungen

The weather will be fine tomorrow.
Das Wetter wird morgen schön (sein).

- bei spontanen Entscheidungen

[doorbell] "I'll open the door."
„Ich mache die Tür auf."

Going to-future

Bildung
am/is/are + going to + Infinitiv

find → am/is/are going to find

Verwendung
Das *going to-future* verwendet man, wenn man ausdrücken will,
- was man für die Zukunft **plant** oder **zu tun beabsichtigt**,

I am going to work in England this summer.
Diesen Sommer werde ich in England arbeiten.

- dass ein **Ereignis bald eintreten wird**, da bestimmte **Anzeichen** vorhanden sind.

Look at those clouds. It's going to rain soon.
Schau dir diese Wolken an. Es wird bald regnen.

Simple Present und Present Progressive zur Wiedergabe der Zukunft – Using Simple Present and Present Progressive to Talk about the Future

Verwendung
- Mit dem *present progressive* drückt man **Pläne** für die Zukunft aus, für die bereits **Vorkehrungen** getroffen wurden.

We are flying to New York tomorrow.
Morgen fliegen wir nach New York.
[Wir haben schon Tickets.]

- Mit dem *simple present* wird ein zukünftiges Geschehen wiedergegeben, das **von außen festgelegt** wurde, z. B. Fahrpläne, Programme, Kalender.

The train leaves at 8.15 a.m.
Der Zug fährt um 8.15 Uhr.

The play ends at 10 p.m.
Das Theaterstück endet um 22 Uhr.

▶ Talking about the Future

Future Progressive / Future Continuous*

Bildung
will + be + -ing-Form (present participle)

work → will be working

Verwendung
Die **Verlaufsform** *future progressive* drückt aus, dass ein **Vorgang** in der Zukunft zu einem bestimmten Zeitpunkt **gerade ablaufen wird**.

Signalwörter: z. B. *this time next week / tomorrow, tomorrow* + Zeitangabe

This time tomorrow, I will be sitting in a plane to London.
Morgen um diese Zeit werde ich gerade im Flugzeug nach London sitzen.

Future Perfect (Future II)*

Bildung
will + have + past participle

go → will have gone

Verwendung
Das *future perfect* drückt aus, dass ein **Vorgang** in der Zukunft **abgeschlossen sein wird** (Vorzeitigkeit in der Zukunft).

Signalwörter: z. B. *by then, by* + Zeitangabe

By 5 p.m. tomorrow, I will have arrived in London.
Morgen Nachmittag um fünf Uhr werde ich bereits in London angekommen sein.

▶ Active and Passive voice

2.2 Passiv – *Passive Voice*

Bildung
Form von *(to) be* in der entsprechenden Zeitform + *past participle*

The bridge was finished in 1894.
Die Brücke wurde 1894 fertiggestellt.

Zeitformen:
- simple present

  Aktiv: Joe buys the milk.
  Passiv: The milk is bought by Joe.

- simple past

  Aktiv: Joe bought the milk.
  Passiv: The milk was bought by Joe.

- present perfect

  Aktiv: Joe has bought the milk.
  Passiv: The milk has been bought by Joe.

- past perfect

  Aktiv: Joe had bought the milk.
  Passiv: The milk had been bought by Joe.

- will-future

  Aktiv: Joe will buy the milk.
  Passiv: The milk will be bought by Joe.

Aktiv → Passiv

- Das Objekt des Aktivsatzes wird zum Subjekt des Passivsatzes.
- Soll das Subjekt des Aktivsatzes im Passivsatz angegeben werden, wird es als *by-agent* angeschlossen.
- Stehen im Aktiv **zwei Objekte**, lassen sich zwei verschiedene Passivsätze bilden. Ein Objekt wird zum Subjekt des Passivsatzes, das zweite bleibt Objekt.

Beachte
Das indirekte Objekt (wem?) muss im Passivsatz mit *to* angeschlossen werden.

Passiv → Aktiv

- Der mit *by* angeschlossene Handelnde (*by-agent*) des Passivsatzes wird zum Subjekt des Aktivsatzes; *by* entfällt.
- Das Subjekt des Passivsatzes wird zum Objekt des Aktivsatzes.
- Fehlt im Passivsatz der *by-agent*, muss im Aktivsatz ein Handelnder als Subjekt ergänzt werden, z. B. *somebody, we, you, they*.

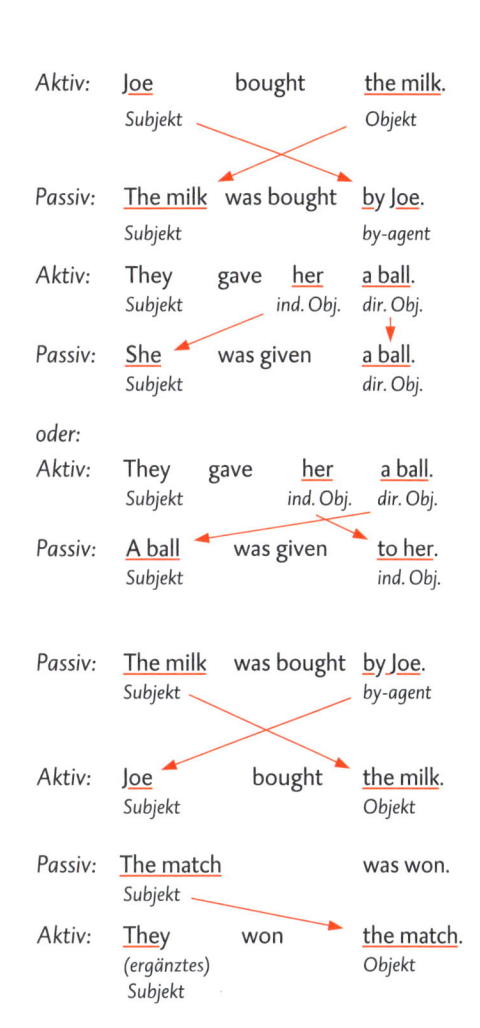

Aktiv: Joe (Subjekt) bought the milk (Objekt).
Passiv: The milk (Subjekt) was bought by Joe (by-agent).

Aktiv: They (Subjekt) gave her (ind. Obj.) a ball (dir. Obj.).
Passiv: She (Subjekt) was given a ball (dir. Obj.).

oder:
Aktiv: They (Subjekt) gave her (ind. Obj.) a ball (dir. Obj.).
Passiv: A ball (Subjekt) was given to her (ind. Obj.).

Passiv: The milk (Subjekt) was bought by Joe (by-agent).
Aktiv: Joe (Subjekt) bought the milk (Objekt).

Passiv: The match (Subjekt) was won.
Aktiv: They ((ergänztes) Subjekt) won the match (Objekt).

3 Infinite Verbformen

3.1 Infinitiv – *Infinitive*

Der **Infinitiv** (Grundform des Verbs) **mit *to*** steht z. B. **nach**:
- bestimmten **Verben**, z. B.:

to decide	(sich) entscheiden, beschließen
to expect	erwarten
to hope	hoffen
to manage	schaffen
to offer	anbieten
to plan	planen
to promise	versprechen
to seem	scheinen
to try	versuchen
to want	wollen

He decided *to wait*.
Er beschloss zu warten.

- bestimmten **Substantiven und Pronomen** (*something, anything*), z. B.:

attempt	Versuch
idea	Idee
plan	Plan
wish	Wunsch

  We haven't got anything to eat at home.
  Wir haben nichts zu essen zu Hause.

  She told him about her plan to go to Australia.
  Sie erzählte ihm von ihrem Plan, nach Australien zu reisen.

- bestimmten **Adjektiven** und deren Steigerungsformen, z. B.:

certain	sicher
difficult / hard	schwer, schwierig
easy	leicht

  Maths is often difficult to understand.
  Mathe ist oft schwer zu verstehen.

- **Fragewörtern**, wie z. B. *what, where, which, who, when, how* und nach *whether*. Diese Konstruktion ersetzt eine indirekte Frage mit modalem Hilfsverb.

  We knew where to find her. /
  We knew where we could find her.
  Wir wussten, wo wir sie finden konnten.

Die Konstruktion **Objekt + Infinitiv** wird im Deutschen oft mit einem „dass"-Satz übersetzt.

Sie steht z. B. **nach**:

- bestimmten **Verben**, z. B.:

to allow	erlauben
to get	veranlassen
to help	helfen
to persuade	überreden

  She allows him to go to the cinema.
  *Sie erlaubt ihm, dass er ins Kino geht. /
  … ins Kino zu gehen.*

- **Verb + Präposition**, z. B.:

to count on	rechnen mit
to rely on	sich verlassen auf
to wait for	warten auf

  She relies on him to arrive in time.
  Sie verlässt sich darauf, dass er rechtzeitig ankommt.

- **Adjektiv + Präposition**, z. B.:

easy for	leicht
necessary for	notwendig
nice of	nett
silly of	dumm

  It is necessary for you to study more.
  Es ist notwendig, dass du mehr lernst.

- **Substantiv + Präposition**, z. B.:

opportunity for	Gelegenheit
idea for	Idee
time for	Zeit
mistake for	Fehler

  Work experience is a good opportunity for you to find out which job suits you.
  Ein Praktikum ist eine gute Gelegenheit, herauszufinden, welcher Beruf zu dir passt.

- einem **Adjektiv**, das durch **too** oder **enough** näher bestimmt wird.

  The box is too heavy for me to carry.
  Die Kiste ist mir zu schwer zum Tragen.

  The weather is good enough for us to go for a walk.
  Das Wetter ist gut genug, dass wir spazieren gehen können.

3.2 Gerundium (-ing-Form) – *Gerund*

Bildung
Infinitiv + -ing

Beachte
- stummes -e entfällt
- nach kurzem betontem Vokal: Schlusskonsonant verdoppelt
- -ie wird zu -y

read → read<u>ing</u>

writ<u>e</u> → writ<u>ing</u>
sto<u>p</u> → sto<u>pp</u>ing

l<u>ie</u> → l<u>y</u>ing

Verwendung
Das *gerund* kann sowohl Subjekt als auch Objekt eines Satzes sein.

Subjekt: <u>Skiing</u> is fun.
Skifahren macht Spaß.
Objekt: He has given up <u>smoking</u>.
Er hat mit dem Rauchen aufgehört.

Manche Wörter ziehen die -ing-Form nach sich. Die -ing-Form steht z. B. nach:

- bestimmten **Verben**, wie z. B.:
to dislike	nicht mögen
to enjoy	genießen, gern tun
to finish	beenden
to give up	aufgeben
to keep	weitermachen
to consider	in Betracht ziehen

He <u>enjoys reading</u> comics.
Er liest gerne Comics.

My mother <u>keeps telling</u> me to study more.
Meine Mutter sagt mir ständig, dass ich mehr lernen soll.

- **Verb + Präposition**, wie z. B.:
to believe in	glauben an
to dream of	träumen von
to look forward to	sich freuen auf
to talk about	sprechen über

She <u>dreams of becoming</u> a lawyer.
Sie träumt davon, Anwältin zu werden.

- **Adjektiv + Präposition**, wie z. B.:
(be) afraid of	sich fürchten vor
famous for	berühmt für
good/bad at	gut/schlecht in
interested in	interessiert an

She is <u>good at playing</u> football.
Sie spielt gut Fußball.

- **einem Substantiv**, wie z. B.:
trouble	Schwierigkeiten
fun	Spaß

I have <u>trouble doing</u> my Maths homework.
Ich habe Schwierigkeiten, meine Mathehausaufgabe zu lösen.

- **Substantiv + Präposition**, wie z. B.:
chance of	Chance, Aussicht auf
in danger of	in Gefahr
reason for	Grund für

Do you have a <u>chance of getting</u> the job?
Hast du eine Chance, die Stelle zu bekommen?

- **bestimmten Präpositionen**, wie z. B.:
after	nachdem
before	bevor
by	indem; dadurch, dass
instead of	statt

Before leaving the room, he said goodbye.
Bevor er den Raum verließ, verabschiedete er sich.

3.3 Infinitiv oder Gerundium? – *Infinitive or Gerund?*

Einige Verben können sowohl **mit** dem **Infinitiv** als auch **mit der** *-ing*-**Form** stehen, **ohne** dass sich die **Bedeutung ändert**, z. B.
to love, to hate, to prefer, to start, to begin, to continue.

I hate getting up early.
I hate to get up early.
Ich hasse es, früh aufzustehen.

Bei manchen Verben **ändert sich** jedoch die **Bedeutung**, je nachdem, ob sie mit Infinitiv oder mit der *-ing*-Form verwendet werden, z. B.
to remember, to forget, to stop.

- *to remember* + Infinitiv:
  „daran denken, etwas zu tun"

  I must remember to post the invitations.
  Ich muss daran denken, die Einladungen einzuwerfen.

  to remember + *-ing*-Form:
  „sich erinnern, etwas getan zu haben"

  I remember posting the invitations.
  Ich erinnere mich daran, die Einladungen eingeworfen zu haben.

- *to forget* + Infinitiv:
  „vergessen, etwas zu tun"

  Don't forget to water the plants.
  Vergiss nicht, die Pflanzen zu gießen.

  to forget + *-ing*-Form:
  „vergessen, etwas getan zu haben"

  I'll never forget meeting the President.
  Ich werde nie vergessen, wie ich den Präsidenten traf.

- *to stop* + Infinitiv:
  „stehen bleiben, um etwas zu tun"

  I stopped to read the road sign.
  Ich hielt an, um das Verkehrsschild zu lesen.

  to stop + *-ing*-Form:
  „aufhören, etwas zu tun"

  He stopped laughing.
  Er hörte auf zu lachen.

3.4 Partizipien – *Participles*

Partizip Präsens – *Present Participle*

Bildung
Infinitiv + *-ing*

talk → tal<u>king</u>

Beachte
- stummes *-e* entfällt
- nach betontem Vokal: Schlusskonsonant verdoppelt
- *-ie* wird zu *-y*

writ<u>e</u> → writ<u>ing</u>

sto<u>p</u> → sto<u>pp</u>ing

l<u>ie</u> → l<u>y</u>ing

Verwendung
Das *present participle* verwendet man zur Bildung der Verlaufsformen, z. B.
- zur Bildung des *present progressive*,
- zur Bildung des *past progressive*,
- zur Bildung des *present perfect progressive*,
- zur Bildung des *future progressive**,

oder wie ein Adjektiv, wenn es vor einem Substantiv steht.

Peter is <u>reading</u>. *Peter liest (gerade).*

Peter was <u>reading</u> when I saw him.
Peter las (gerade), als ich ihn sah.

I have been <u>living</u> in Sydney for 5 years.
Ich lebe seit 5 Jahren in Sydney.

This time tomorrow I will be <u>working</u>.
Morgen um diese Zeit werde ich arbeiten.

The village hasn't got <u>running</u> water.
Das Dorf hat kein fließendes Wasser.

Partizip Perfekt – *Past Participle*

Bildung
Infinitiv + *-ed*

talk → tal<u>ked</u>

Beachte
- stummes *-e* entfällt
- nach betontem Vokal wird der Schlusskonsonant verdoppelt
- *-y* wird zu *-ie*
- Die *past participles* unregelmäßiger Verben muss man auswendig lernen. Einige wichtige Formen sind hier angegeben – weitere Beispiele sind z. B. in Wörterbüchern aufgeführt.

liv<u>e</u> → liv<u>ed</u>

sto<u>p</u> → sto<u>pp</u>ed

cr<u>y</u> → cr<u>ied</u>

be → been
have → had
give → given
go → gone
say → said

Verwendung
Das *past participle* verwendet man zur Bildung der Perfektformen, z. B.
- zur Bildung des *present perfect*,

He hasn't <u>talked</u> to Tom yet.
Er hat noch nicht mit Tom gesprochen.

Kurzgrammatik

- zur Bildung des *past perfect*,

  Before they went biking in France, they had <u>bought</u> new bikes.
  Bevor sie nach Frankreich zum Radfahren gingen, hatten sie neue Fahrräder gekauft.

- zur Bildung des *future perfect**,

  The letter will have <u>arrived</u> by then.
  Der Brief wird bis dann angekommen sein.

zur Bildung des Passivs

The fish was <u>eaten</u> by the cat.
Der Fisch wurde von der Katze gefressen.

oder wie ein Adjektiv, wenn es vor einem Substantiv steht.

Peter has got a well-<u>paid</u> job.
Peter hat eine gut bezahlte Stelle.

Verkürzung von Nebensätzen durch Partizipien – *Using Participles to Shorten Clauses*

Adverbiale Nebensätze (meist des Grundes oder der Zeit) und **Relativsätze** können durch ein Partizip verkürzt werden.

She watches the news, because she wants to stay informed.
→ <u>Wanting</u> to stay informed, she watches the news.
Sie sieht sich die Nachrichten an, weil sie informiert bleiben möchte.

Das Zeitverhältnis zwischen Haupt- und Nebensatz bestimmt die Form des Partizips:

- Das *present participle* verwendet man, um Gleichzeitigkeit mit der Haupthandlung auszudrücken.

  He did his homework <u>listening</u> to music.
  Er machte seine Hausaufgaben und hörte dabei Musik.

- *Having + past participle* verwendet man, um auszudrücken, dass die Nebenhandlung vor der Haupthandlung geschah.

  <u>Having done</u> his homework, he listened to music.
  Nachdem er seine Hausaufgaben gemacht hatte, hörte er Musik.

- Das *past participle* verwendet man auch, um einen Satz im Passiv zu verkürzen.

  Sally is a manager in a five-star hotel <u>which is called</u> Pacific View.
  → Sally is a manager in a five-star hotel <u>called</u> Pacific View.

Beachte

- Man kann einen Nebensatz der Zeit oder des Grundes verkürzen, wenn **Haupt- und Nebensatz dasselbe Subjekt** haben.

  When <u>he</u> was walking down the street, <u>he</u> saw Jo.
  → When <u>walking</u> / <u>Walking</u> down the street, <u>he</u> saw Jo.
  Als er die Straße entlangging, sah er Jo.

- Bei **Kausalsätzen** (Nebensätzen des Grundes) entfallen die Konjunktionen *as*, *because* und *since* im verkürzten Nebensatz.

  As <u>he</u> was hungry, <u>he</u> bought a sandwich.
  → <u>Being</u> hungry, <u>he</u> bought a sandwich.
  Da er hungrig war, kaufte er ein Sandwich.

- In einem **Temporalsatz** (Nebensatz der Zeit) bleibt die einleitende **Konjunktion** häufig erhalten, um dem Satz eine **eindeutige Bedeutung** zuzuweisen.

  When <u>he</u> left, <u>he</u> forgot to lock the door.
  → When <u>leaving</u>, <u>he</u> forgot to lock the door.
  Als er ging, vergaß er, die Tür abzuschließen.

  Tara got sick <u>eating</u> too much cake.
  Tara wurde schlecht, als/während/da sie zu viel Kuchen aß. [verschiedene Deutungen möglich]

- Bei **Relativsätzen** entfallen die Relativpronomen *who, which* und *that*.

I saw a six-year-old boy who played the piano.
I saw a six-year-old boy playing the piano.
Ich sah einen sechsjährigen Jungen, der gerade Klavier spielte. / ... Klavier spielen.

Verbindung von zwei Hauptsätzen durch ein Partizip – *Using Participles to Link Clauses*

Zwei Hauptsätze können durch ein Partizip verbunden werden, wenn sie **dasselbe Subjekt** haben.

Beachte
- Das Subjekt des zweiten Hauptsatzes und die Konjunktion *and* entfallen.
- Die Verbform des zweiten Hauptsatzes wird durch das Partizip ersetzt.

He did his homework and he listened to the radio.
He did his homework listening to the radio.
Er machte seine Hausaufgaben und hörte Radio.

4 Der Satz im Englischen

4.1 Wortstellung – *Word Order*

Im Aussagesatz gilt die Wortstellung
Subjekt – **P**rädikat – **O**bjekt
(*subject – verb – object*):
- Subjekt: Wer oder was tut etwas?
- Prädikat: Was wird getan?
- Objekt: Worauf / Auf wen bezieht sich die Tätigkeit?

Erklärungen und Beispiele zur **Bildung** des englischen **Fragesatzes** finden sich auch bei den verschiedenen Zeiten (vgl. Kap. 2.1) und bei den Modalverben (vgl. Kap. 1.6).

Beachte
- Orts- und Zeitangaben stehen oft am Satzende.
- Ortsangaben stehen vor Zeitangaben.

Cats catch mice.
Katzen fangen Mäuse.

We will buy a new car tomorrow.
Morgen werden wir ein neues Auto kaufen.
He moved to New York in June.
Er zog im Juni nach New York.

Kurzgrammatik

Conditional sentences

4.2 Bedingungssätze – *Conditional Sentences*

Ein Bedingungssatz (Konditionalsatz) besteht aus zwei Teilen: einem Nebensatz *(if-clause)* und einem Hauptsatz *(main clause)*. Im **if-Satz** steht die **Bedingung** *(condition)*, unter der die im **Hauptsatz** genannte **Folge** eintritt. Man unterscheidet drei Arten von Konditionalsätzen:

Bedingungssatz Typ I – *Conditional Sentence Type I*

Bildung

- *if*-Satz (Bedingung):
  simple present
- Hauptsatz (Folge):
  will-future

If you read this book,
Wenn du dieses Buch liest,

you will learn a lot about music.
erfährst du eine Menge über Musik.

Der *if*-Satz kann auch nach dem Hauptsatz stehen. In diesem Fall entfällt das Komma:

You will learn a lot about music if you read this book.
Du erfährst eine Menge über Musik, wenn du dieses Buch liest.

Im Hauptsatz kann auch

- ein modales Hilfsverb (z. B. *can, must, may*) + Infinitiv sowie

If you go to London, you must visit me.
Wenn du nach London fährst, musst du mich besuchen.

- die Befehlsform des Verbs (Imperativ) stehen.

If it rains, take an umbrella.
Wenn es regnet, nimm einen Schirm mit.

Verwendung

Bedingungssätze vom Typ I verwendet man, wenn die **Bedingung erfüllbar** ist. Man gibt an, was unter bestimmten Bedingungen **geschieht** oder **geschehen kann**.

Sonderform

Bedingungssätze vom Typ I verwendet man auch bei einer **generellen Regel**. Hierbei steht sowohl im Hauptsatz als auch im *if*-Satz das *simple present*.

If you mix blue and yellow, you get green.
Wenn du die Farbe Blau mit Gelb mischst, erhältst du Grün.

Bedingungssatz Typ II – *Conditional Sentence Type II*

Bildung
- *if*-Satz (Bedingung):
  simple past
- Hauptsatz (Folge):
  conditional I = would + Infinitiv

If I <u>went</u> to London,
Wenn ich nach London fahren würde,
I <u>would visit</u> the Tower.
würde ich mir den Tower ansehen.

Verwendung
Bedingungssätze vom Typ II verwendet man, wenn die **Bedingung nur theoretisch erfüllt** werden kann oder **nicht erfüllbar** ist.

Bedingungssatz Typ III – *Conditional Sentence Type III*

Bildung
- *if*-Satz (Bedingung):
  past perfect
- Hauptsatz (Folge):
  conditional II = would + have + past participle

If I <u>had gone</u> to London,
Wenn ich nach London gefahren wäre,
I <u>would have visited</u> the Tower.
hätte ich mir den Tower angesehen.

Verwendung
Bedingungssätze vom Typ III verwendet man, wenn sich die **Bedingung auf die Vergangenheit bezieht** und deshalb **nicht mehr erfüllbar** ist.

4.3 Relativsätze – *Relative Clauses*

Ein Relativsatz ist ein Nebensatz, der sich **auf eine Person oder Sache** des Hauptsatzes **bezieht** und diese **näher beschreibt**:
- Hauptsatz:
- Relativsatz:

The boy <u>who looks like Jane</u> is her brother.
Der Junge, der Jane ähnlich sieht, ist ihr Bruder.

The boy … is her brother.
… who looks like Jane …

Bildung
Haupt- und Nebensatz werden durch das Relativpronomen verbunden.
- Das Relativpronomen **who** bezieht sich auf Personen.

Peter, <u>who</u> lives in London, likes travelling.
Peter, der in London lebt, reist gerne.

- Das Relativpronomen **whose** bezieht sich ebenfalls auf Personen. Es gibt die Zugehörigkeit dieser Person zu einer anderen Person oder Sache an.

  Pari, whose parents are from India, is in my class.
  Pari, deren Eltern aus Indien stammen, ist in meiner Klasse.

  This is the boy whose mobile was stolen.
  Das ist der Junge, dessen Handy gestohlen wurde.

- Das Relativpronomen **which** bezieht sich auf **Sachen**.

  The film "Dark Moon", which we saw yesterday, was far too long.
  Der Film „Dark Moon", den wir gestern sahen, war viel zu lang.

- Das Relativpronomen **that** kann sich auf **Sachen** und auf **Personen** beziehen und wird nur verwendet, wenn die **Information** im Relativsatz **notwendig** ist, um den ganzen Satz zu verstehen.

  The film that we saw last week was much better.
  Der Film, den wir letzte Woche sahen, war viel besser.

Verwendung

Mithilfe von Relativpronomen kann man **zwei Sätze miteinander verbinden**.

London is England's biggest city. London is very popular with tourists.
London ist Englands größte Stadt. London ist bei Touristen sehr beliebt.

→ London, which is England's biggest city, is very popular with tourists.
London, die größte Stadt Englands, ist bei Touristen sehr beliebt.

Beachte

Man unterscheidet zwei Arten von Relativsätzen:

- **Notwendige Relativsätze** *(defining relative clauses)* enthalten Informationen, die **für das Verständnis** des Satzes **erforderlich** sind.

  The man who is wearing a red shirt is Mike.
  Der Mann, der ein rotes Hemd trägt, ist Mike.

  Hier kann das Relativpronomen entfallen, wenn es Objekt ist; man spricht dann auch von *contact clauses*.

  The book (that) I bought yesterday is thrilling.
  Das Buch, das ich gestern gekauft habe, ist spannend.

- **Nicht notwendige Relativsätze** *(non-defining relative clauses)* enthalten **zusätzliche Informationen** zum Bezugswort, die für das Verständnis des Satzes nicht unbedingt notwendig sind. Dieser Typ von Relativsatz wird **mit Komma** abgetrennt.

  Sally, who went to a party yesterday, is very tired.
  Sally, die gestern auf einer Party war, ist sehr müde.

4.4 Indirekte Rede – *Reported Speech*

Bildung und Verwendung

Die indirekte Rede verwendet man, um **wiederzugeben**, **was eine andere Person gesagt** oder **gefragt hat**.

Dazu benötigt man ein **Einleitungsverb**. Häufig verwendete Einleitungsverben sind: to say, to think, to add, to agree, to tell, to answer

In der indirekten Rede verändern sich die Pronomen, in bestimmten Fällen auch die **Zeiten** und die **Orts-** und **Zeitangaben**.

- Wie die Pronomen sich verändern, hängt von der **Situation** ab.

direkte Rede		indirekte Rede
I, you, we, you	→	he, she, they
my, your, our, your	→	his, her, their
this, these	→	that, those

direkte Rede	indirekte Rede
Bob says to Jenny: "I like you."	Bob says to Jenny that he likes her.
Bob sagt zu Jenny: „Ich mag dich."	*Bob sagt zu Jenny, dass er sie mag.*

- **Zeiten:**

Keine Veränderung, wenn das Einleitungsverb im *present tense*, im Futur oder im *present perfect* steht:

direkte Rede	indirekte Rede
Bob says, "I love dancing."	Bob says (that) he loves dancing.
Bob sagt: „Ich tanze sehr gerne."	*Bob sagt, er tanze sehr gerne.*

Die Zeit der direkten Rede wird in der indirekten Rede normalerweise **um eine Zeitstufe zurückversetzt**, wenn das **Einleitungsverb** im *past tense* oder *past perfect* steht:

direkte Rede	indirekte Rede
Bob said, "I love dancing."	Bob said (that) he loved dancing.
Bob sagte: „Ich tanze sehr gerne."	*Bob sagte, er tanze sehr gerne.*

simple present	→	simple past
simple past	→	past perfect
present perfect	→	past perfect
will-future	→	conditional I

Joe: "I like it."	Joe said he liked it.
Joe: "I liked it."	Joe said he had liked it.
Joe: "I've liked it."	Joe said he had liked it.
Joe: "I will like it."	Joe said he would like it.

- **Zeitangaben** verändern sich, wenn der Bericht zu einem späteren Zeitpunkt erfolgt, z. B.:

now	→	then, at that time
today	→	that day, yesterday
yesterday	→	the day before
tomorrow	→	the following day
next week	→	the following week

direkte Rede	indirekte Rede
Jack: "I'll call her tomorrow."	Jack says (that) he will call her tomorrow. [Der Bericht erfolgt noch am selben Tag.]
	Jack said (that) he would call her the following day. [Der Bericht erfolgt z. B. eine Woche später.]

▶ Reported speech

- Welche **Ortsangabe** verwendet wird, hängt davon ab, wo sich der Sprecher im Moment befindet, z. B.:

  here → there

Bildung der indirekten Frage
Häufige Einleitungsverben für die indirekte Frage sind:

- **Fragewörter** bleiben in der indirekten Rede **erhalten**. Die **Umschreibung** mit *do/does/did* **entfällt** in der indirekten Frage.
- Enthält die direkte Frage **kein Fragewort**, wird die indirekte Frage mit *whether* oder *if* eingeleitet:

Befehle/Aufforderungen in der indirekten Rede
Häufige Einleitungsverben sind:

In der indirekten Rede steht hier **Einleitungsverb + Objekt + (not) to + Infinitiv**

direkte Rede	indirekte Rede
Amy: "I was here when the accident happened."	Amy says (that) she was here when the accident happened. *[Der Bericht erfolgt noch an der Unfallstelle.]* Amy said (that) she had been there when the accident had happened. *[Der Bericht erfolgt z. B. am nächsten Tag an einem anderen Ort.]*
	to ask, to want to know, to wonder
Tom: "When did they arrive?" Tom: „Wann sind sie angekommen?"	Tom asked when they had arrived. Tom fragte, wann sie angekommen seien.
Tom: "Are they staying at the youth hostel?" Tom: „Übernachten sie in der Jugendherberge?"	Tom asked if/whether they were staying at the youth hostel. Tom fragte, ob sie in der Jugendherberge übernachteten.
	to tell, to order, to ask
Tom: "Leave the room." Tom: „Verlass den Raum."	Tom told me to leave the room. Tom forderte mich auf, den Raum zu verlassen.

▶ Hinweise, Tipps und Übungsaufgaben zu den Prüfungsbereichen

1 Listening

Hörverstehenstexte und die dazugehörigen Aufgabenstellungen können sehr unterschiedlich sein. Die Texte, die du im Rahmen deiner Abschlussprüfung, aber auch in Klassenarbeiten und Tests zu hören bekommst, spiegeln meist **reale Sprechsituationen** wider, d. h., man kann solche oder ähnliche Texte im „wirklichen Leben" hören. Die Inhalte der Texte können von der Begrüßungsansprache eines Piloten über die Lautsprecheransagen an einem Bahnhof bis hin zu Nachrichtenmeldungen, Radiointerviews oder Alltagsgesprächen reichen. Es kann sich auch einfach um kurze Berichte oder Podcasts zu den unterschiedlichsten Themen handeln. Genauso vielfältig wie die verschiedenen Arten von Hörtexten können auch die Aufgabenstellungen ausfallen. In diesem Kapitel werden dir die häufigsten Textarten und Aufgabenstellungen zum Kompetenzbereich „Listening" vorgestellt.

1.1 Strategien zum Bereich „Listening"

Vorgehen in der Prüfung

In Klassenarbeiten oder deiner Abschlussprüfung hörst du die **Hörverstehenstexte meist zweimal**.

Vor dem ersten Vorspielen eines Textes hast du in der Regel genügend Zeit, dir die **Aufgabenstellungen** auf dem Arbeitsblatt **anzusehen**. Lies sie dir sorgfältig durch und überlege genau, um welche Art von Aufgabe es sich handelt und was von dir verlangt wird. Überlege schon vor dem ersten Hören, auf welche Kerninformationen es in den Aufgaben ankommt. Darauf solltest du dich dann während des Hörens ganz besonders konzentrieren. | Arbeitsschritt **1**

Nun hörst du den Text zum ersten Mal. Zu den Aufgaben, die du während oder nach dem ersten Hören bereits beantworten kannst, kannst du gleich die **richtige Antwort aufschreiben oder abhaken**. Versuche, möglichst viele Aufgaben **während des Hörens** zu lösen, da die Pause nach dem ersten Hördurchgang oft recht kurz ist. Wenn du bei einer Aufgabe unsicher bist, grüble nicht darüber nach, wie die richtige Antwort lauten könnte, um nicht Gefahr zu laufen, die Lösungen zu den darauffolgenden Aufgaben zu verpassen. Lass einfach eine Lücke und versuche, die restlichen Aufgaben zu lösen. Du brauchst nicht nervös zu werden, wenn du nach dem ersten Hören noch nicht alle Lösungen notiert hast. Lass dich auch nicht verunsichern, wenn du nicht alles auf Anhieb verstehst. Die Texte enthalten absichtlich unbekannte Wörter, da du im Alltag auch in solche Situationen kommen wirst. | Arbeitsschritt **2**

Beim zweiten Hördurchgang kannst du zum einen deine **Antworten** noch einmal **überprüfen und** zum anderen **noch verbleibende Aufgaben beantworten**. Die Aufgabenstellungen folgen beim Hörverstehen der Textchronologie, d. h., wenn du z. B. die letzte Aufgabe zu einem Text nicht beantworten konntest, solltest du besonders am Ende des Textes aufpassen. | Arbeitsschritt **3**

Tipp

- Vor dem ersten Hören: Worum geht es? Lies die Aufgabenstellungen genau durch.
- Während des ersten Hörens (und ggf. in der kurzen Pause danach): Trage die Lösungen zu den Aufgaben ein, die du schon beantworten kannst. Welche Informationen fehlen dir noch?
- Während des zweiten Hörens (und ggf. in der kurzen Pause danach): Löse die restlichen Aufgaben. Überprüfe noch einmal die Aufgaben, die du bereits beim ersten Hördurchgang gelöst hast.

Vorgehen beim Üben

Zu Übungszwecken kannst du dir die Hörverstehenstexte ruhig so oft anhören, wie du möchtest. Lies sie aber nicht durch! Versuche, die Arbeitsaufträge nur durch Zuhören zu beantworten. Nur wenn du überhaupt nicht auf die richtige Lösung kommst, solltest du die Hörverstehenstexte im Lösungsheft lesen. Bei der Bearbeitung der Hörverstehensaufgaben in diesem Buch solltest du wie folgt vorgehen:

▶ Lies die Aufgabenstellungen genau durch. Hast du sie alle verstanden? Kläre unbekannte Wörter mithilfe eines Wörterbuches oder versuche, die Bedeutung zu erschließen.

▶ Höre dir den entsprechenden Text einmal an, sodass du weißt, worum es darin geht.

▶ Höre dir den Text noch einmal an, wenn du ihn noch nicht so gut verstanden hast. Diesen Schritt kannst du so oft wiederholen, wie es für dich hilfreich ist.

▶ Versuche, während des Hörens die Aufgaben zu lösen.

▶ Wenn du alle Aufgaben bearbeitet hast, solltest du die Richtigkeit deiner Lösungen überprüfen, indem du dir den Text ein weiteres Mal anhörst.

▶ Anschließend überprüfst du deine Antworten am besten anhand des Lösungsheftes. Wenn du viele Fehler gemacht hast, dann überlege genau, wie sie zustande gekommen sind. Hast du den Hörtext nicht genau verstanden? Hast du die Fragestellung falsch verstanden? Lies gegebenenfalls den Hörverstehenstext durch und wiederhole die gesamte Aufgabe ein paar Wochen später.

▶ Versuche, mit der Bearbeitung jeder weiteren Hörverstehensaufgabe in diesem Buch die Zahl der Hördurchgänge zu reduzieren, sodass du die Texte nur noch so oft anzuhören brauchst, wie es in der Aufgabenstellung vorgegeben ist.

▶ In der Abschlussprüfung werden die Texte in der Regel nur zweimal vorgespielt.

1.2 Häufige Aufgabenstellungen zum Bereich „Listening"

Dieses Kapitel enthält viele Aufgaben zum Hörverstehen. Hier kannst du dich mit den am häufigsten vorkommenden Aufgabenformaten vertraut machen und dein Hörverständnis intensiv trainieren, sodass du für Klassenarbeiten, Tests und deine Abschlussprüfung gut gerüstet bist.

Der Teil „Listening Comprehension" in deiner Abschlussprüfung besteht aus mehreren Teilen. Beachte, dass die Aufgabenformate variieren und auch von den hier vorgestellten Aufgabenformaten abweichen können. Im Folgenden werden dir die gängigsten Aufgabentypen für den Bereich „Listening Comprehension" vorgestellt.

Taking notes

Bei diesem Aufgabentyp sollst du bestimmte Informationen aus dem „listening text" heraushören und stichpunktartig notieren. Meist sollst du die Details aus dem Hörtext in eine **Tabelle**, ein **Cluster** oder ein Formular eintragen. Die Gestaltung kann ganz unterschiedlich ausfallen – lass dich dadurch nicht verunsichern. Da hier detailgenaues Verstehen gefordert ist, ist es besonders wichtig, dass du die Aufgabenstellung vor dem Hören des Textes aufmerksam durchliest, damit du weißt, worauf du beim Hören achten musst. Arbeite ganz konzentriert, damit du die geforderte Information beim Hören nicht verpasst. Wenn du einen Punkt nicht sofort verstehst, grüble nicht darüber nach, sondern versuche, die restlichen Aspekte zu ergänzen. Die noch fehlende Information kannst du beim zweiten Hördurchgang nachtragen. Oft kannst du Formulierungen wörtlich aus dem Text übernehmen – manchmal musst du aber auch Informationen zusammenfassen.

Beispiel

Archie: Hi, I'm Archie and I'm fifteen years old. I go to Park School in West Ham and I'd like to talk about our new canteen …

Task: Listen to text. Take notes to fill in the table.

Answer:

name	Archie
age	15
school	Park School

True or false

Auch diesen Aufgabentyp kennst du sicher schon lange aus dem Unterricht. Du sollst jeweils entscheiden, ob eine Aussage zum Hörtext richtig oder falsch ist. Auch hier wird die Formulierung in der Aufgabenstellung variiert.

Beispiel

Speaker: Katherine always went to school by bus. The bus ride was quite short, but it was thirty minutes to the bus station.

Task: Decide whether the statement is *true* or *false*. Tick (✓) the right box.

Answer: It was a long way to the bus station.   true ✓   false ☐

Matching

Eine weitere typische Aufgabenstellung ist „matching". Häufig hörst du hier kurze Äußerungen verschiedener Personen zu einem bestimmten Thema, denen du die entsprechenden Aussagen oder Gedankenblasen, die dir schriftlich vorliegen, zuordnen musst. Je nach Aufgabenstellung kannst du den Personen ein oder mehrere „statements" zuordnen. In der Regel bleibt mindestens eine Aussage übrig. Lies also die Aufgabenstellung genau.

Beispiel

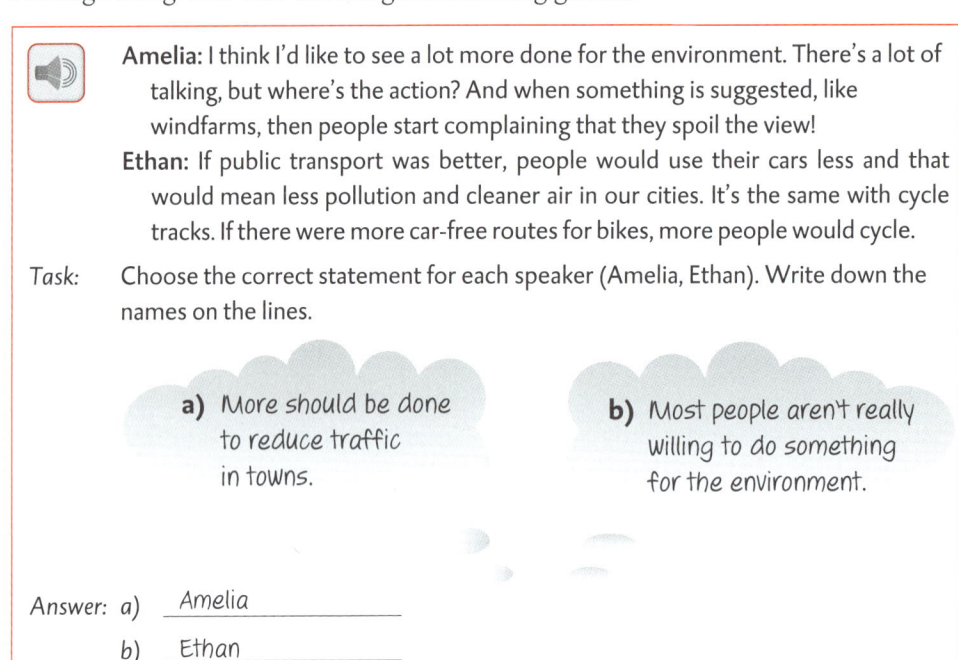

> **Amelia:** I think I'd like to see a lot more done for the environment. There's a lot of talking, but where's the action? And when something is suggested, like windfarms, then people start complaining that they spoil the view!
>
> **Ethan:** If public transport was better, people would use their cars less and that would mean less pollution and cleaner air in our cities. It's the same with cycle tracks. If there were more car-free routes for bikes, more people would cycle.
>
> *Task:* Choose the correct statement for each speaker (Amelia, Ethan). Write down the names on the lines.
>
> **a)** More should be done to reduce traffic in towns.
>
> **b)** Most people aren't really willing to do something for the environment.
>
> *Answer:* a) __Amelia__
> b) __Ethan__

Multiple choice

Dieser Aufgabentyp ist dir bestimmt auch schon sehr vertraut: Dir wird eine Frage mit mehreren Antwortmöglichkeiten oder ein Satzanfang mit mehreren möglichen Satzenden vorgegeben und du sollst entscheiden, welche Auswahlmöglichkeit am besten zum Inhalt des Textes passt. Meist weicht dabei die Formulierung der Aufgabenstellung etwas von der im Text ab, sodass du gut zuhören musst.

Beispiel

> **Reporter:** Today we're broadcasting live from Glastonbury Festival. Most people think it's just music and concerts, but there are lots more things to do and see – theatre performances, dance, even poetry. Let's take a look behind the scenes …
>
> *Task:* Listen to the radio report and tick (✓) the correct sentence ending.
> *Answer:* Glastonbury Festival is …
>
> ☐ for music lovers only.
> ☐ an important theatre and film event.
> ✓ an event with many different forms of art.

Listening

Answering questions

Manchmal werden dir in Klassenarbeiten oder der Abschlussprüfung auch Fragen zu einem Hörtext gestellt. Anhand der Arbeitsanweisung kannst du normalerweise erkennen, wie viele Aspekte du angeben sollst und ob Stichpunkte ausreichen oder ob du ganze Sätze formulieren sollst. Meist reicht es, wenn du in Stichworten antwortest – halte dich aber diesbezüglich unbedingt an die Arbeitsanweisung.

Beispiel

> **Speaker:** Have you ever wondered how some YouTube stars can make a living from their videos? Well, the most common way is to allow companies to place ads at the beginning of their videos. However, some YouTubers also go as far as promoting certain products or companies in the video itself.
>
> Task: There are different ways for YouTubers to earn money. Name **two**.
>
> Answer: ▶ _placing ads at the beginning of the video_
>
> ▶ _promoting products/companies in the video itself_

Completing sentences

Bei diesem Aufgabenformat sollst du Sätze vervollständigen. Oftmals musst du Satzanfänge beenden, manchmal aber auch Lücken mitten in einem Satz füllen. Auch hier ist detailgenaues Verstehen gefordert, sodass du ganz konzentriert arbeiten solltest.

Beispiel

> **Speaker:** The man's smartphone rang in the bus queue. He turned away to talk. When he turned around, the bus had gone without him.
>
> Task: Fill in the missing information.
>
> Answer: The man missed the bus because he had _turned away_ from it.

1.3 Übungsaufgaben zum Bereich „Listening"

Listening Test 1: Announcement on board

1. In this listening test, you will listen to an announcement on board a plane. Complete the mindmap with words that might come up in such a text. Add as many words as you can think of.

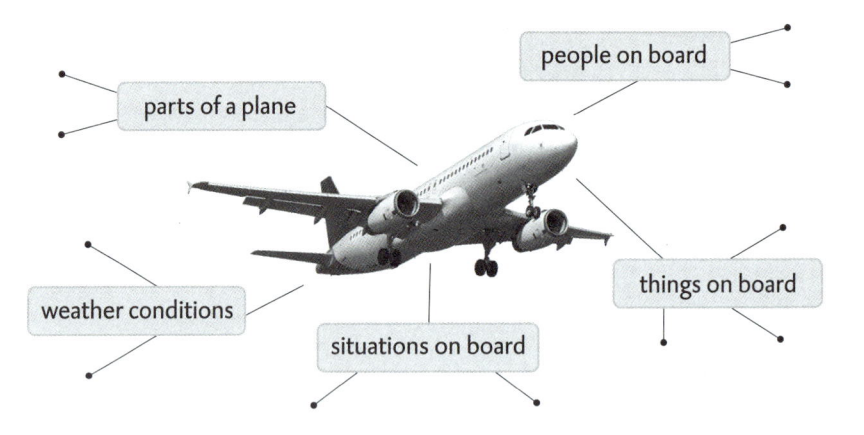

   - parts of a plane
   - people on board
   - things on board
   - situations on board
   - weather conditions

2. Before listening to the text read the following task carefully and mark all the keywords.

3. Now listen to the announcement twice and tick (✓) the right sentence endings.

   a) The announcement was made ...
      - [ ] on board Flight PA 7374.
      - [ ] on a flight to London Heathrow.
      - [ ] on board Flight BA 7374.

   b) The person speaking is ...
      - [ ] the purser.
      - [ ] the co-pilot.
      - [ ] the pilot.

   c) The plane will land in Singapore at about ...
      - [ ] 11.45 a.m.
      - [ ] 10.30 p.m.
      - [ ] 2.30 p.m.

   d) In Singapore, there will be ...
      - [ ] clear skies.
      - [ ] a lot of heavy rain.
      - [ ] sun and rain.

Listening Test 2: Booking a hotel room

1. Listen to two people talking on the phone.
   Listen to the dialogue twice.
   Decide whether the following statements are true or false.
   Tick (✓) the correct answer *true* or *false*.

		true	false
a)	The caller wants to book a hotel room near Waverley Station.	☐	☐
b)	Her parents know about the trip.	☐	☐
c)	Her parents married on 15th August.	☐	☐
d)	The Fringe Festival is in summer.	☐	☐
e)	You can see Edinburgh Castle from the hotel room.	☐	☐
f)	The room costs £165 per person per night.	☐	☐
g)	The hotel has usually got special offers in the low season.	☐	☐
h)	The hotel only offers breakfast.	☐	☐
i)	The hotel sends 12 newsletters a year.	☐	☐

2. Listen to the text one more time and imagine you are the hotel receptionist.
   While listening to the conversation, take notes.

   Old Waverley Hotel, Edinburgh

Receptionist in charge:	a)	Breckenridge
Customer's name:	b)	
Who wants to stay at the hotel?	c)	
Purpose of visit:	d)	
Duration of stay:	e)	
Can I put them on the mailing list?	f)	☐ yes ☐ no
E-mail address:	g)	

Listening

Listening Test 3: Dangerous Australians

1. You will hear a radio report about three of the most dangerous creatures in Australia. Listen to the report twice.
Take notes to fill in the table.
Write down one piece of information per box.

	Sydney Funnel-web spider	Blue-ringed octopus	Saltwater crocodile
How large are they?	a)	d)	g)
Where do they normally live?	b)	e)	h)
When was the last person killed?	c)	f)	i)

2. Listen to the text once more and complete the sentences.

   a) The poison of the funnel-web spider can _____

   b) The normal colour of the blue-ringed octopus is _____

   c) The blue rings appear when _____

   d) In crocodile areas, you should _____

   e) Some crocodiles weigh _____

Listening

Listening Test 4: Robben Island

1. Each week, *WorldRadio* takes a look at a different country to help holidaymakers decide where to go for their summer holidays – this week, the subject is South Africa. The presenter and her guest are talking about Robben Island, where Nelson Mandela spent many years in prison.

   Listen to the interview twice. While listening, take notes to fill in the table.

a)	today's function of the prison	
b)	who lives on Robben Island now	
c)	where the leaders had to stay	
d)	where or how messages could be passed on *(one item)*	
e)	number of years Nelson Mandela had to spend on Robben Island	
f)	reason why escaping from the island was nearly impossible *(one item)*	

Listening

2. Read the following tasks carefully. Then listen to the interview again.
   While you are listening, tick (✓) the correct box.

   a) To get to Robben Island visitors must make a …
      ☐ 13-minute boat journey.
      ☐ 30-minute boat journey.
      ☐ 17-kilometre boat journey.

   b) The maximum-security prison was …
      ☐ racially segregated.
      ☐ for political prisoners.
      ☐ for bank robbers and other criminals.

   c) The leaders and the "normal" prisoners …
      ☐ were not allowed to mix.
      ☐ tried to avoid each other.
      ☐ were often put in large 40-bed dormitories.

   d) In the evenings the prisoners …
      ☐ helped each other and talked a lot.
      ☐ wrote messages to pass on to their leaders.
      ☐ had long discussions with Nelson Mandela.

   e) Nelson Mandela never …
      ☐ argued with the prison guards.
      ☐ complained about the conditions in the prison.
      ☐ accepted anything the other prisoners wouldn't also get.

Listening Test 5: Things you didn't know about London

You will hear someone talking about London and some unusual facts about it.
Listen to the podcast twice and complete the sentences.

the Shard

1. London sees about _____ _____ a year.

2. Oslo's present for London is for _____.

3. The money from *Peter Pan* goes to a _____
   _____.

4. The Tube was the world's _____.

5. While a station was being made the builders found _____
   _____.

6. The Shard, a famous building in London, is _____ high.

7. Many tall buildings have _____.

Listening Test 6: The California Gold Rush

1. Listen to a radio report about the gold rush in California. Listen to the report twice and tick (✓) the correct ending to each sentence.

   a) The first person to find gold was ...
      ☐ a Native American.
      ☐ a settler.
      ☐ an Englishman.

   b) On the nugget there are ...
      ☐ teeth marks.
      ☐ many chips missing.
      ☐ three tests done.

   a gold nugget

   c) The news about the nugget ...
      ☐ went quickly across America.
      ☐ was stopped at first by the government.
      ☐ travelled slowly.

   d) People in New York first learnt about gold in California ...
      ☐ through a newspaper article.
      ☐ from stories about it.
      ☐ from a member of Congress.

e) People travelling west to seek gold …
   ☐ usually did not have a family.
   ☐ often had wrong expectations.
   ☐ knew they would have to work hard.

f) Van Valen's wife …
   ☐ moved to California to help her husband.
   ☐ only earned $ 500 in two years.
   ☐ had a very difficult life.

g) Most of the gold seekers …
   ☐ were successful enough to have comfortable lives.
   ☐ did not make a lot of money.
   ☐ returned home after a few years.

2. Listen to the report again. While listening, write short answers. Write one aspect per question.

   a) Where did the man find the gold nugget?

   b) Why was he sure that the metal was indeed gold?

   c) Who officially confirmed the rumours about gold?

   d) What did Benjamin Buckley do with his money?

   e) What happened in 1850?

Listening Test 7: The Stolen Generations

You will hear a radio interview between the presenter, Greg Masters, and his guest, Jenny Green, talking about Australia's "Stolen Generations". Listen to the interview twice and decide whether each sentence is true or false.

Put a tick (✓) in the correct box *true* or *false*.

		true	false
1.	The Aboriginal children were taken away from their families up until about 1970.	☐	☐
2.	The governments wanted to help Aboriginal people integrate.	☐	☐
3.	Most Aboriginal people thought their culture was better than the whites'.	☐	☐
4.	Most children were put into homes close to their families.	☐	☐
5.	The children had to take new names and speak English.	☐	☐
6.	In the homes, Aboriginal children received a good education.	☐	☐
7.	The government has never said sorry to the Aboriginal community.	☐	☐
8.	The problem has still not been completely solved.	☐	☐

Listening Test 8: Talking about the environment

You will hear a radio interview where two young people are talking to the presenter about the environment. Listen to the interview twice and decide whether each sentence is true or false.

Put a tick (✓) in the correct box *true* or *false*.

		true	false
1.	New energy sources are always welcomed.	☐	☐
2.	It's quicker for Lewis's mum to take the car than to walk.	☐	☐
3.	Public transport used to be better.	☐	☐
4.	People could be encouraged to leave their cars at home.	☐	☐
5.	Tourism can only make places better.	☐	☐
6.	There's a danger that the same mistakes will happen again.	☐	☐
7.	Cooperation is on the wish list.	☐	☐

Listening Test 9: Couchsurfing or wilderness?

1. Listen to four people talking about holidays.
   What kind of holiday does each of them like best?
   Write the correct names (John, Olivia, Hailey and Carter) on the lines next to the short descriptions (a–g). You can only use each name once. Be careful, there are three categories that do not match any statement. Put a cross (✗) on the lines of the statements that do not match.

   a) off the beaten tourist track   _____
   b) party and action, but at a low cost   _____
   c) a relaxing holiday for the whole family _____
   d) back to nature   _____
   e) peace and quiet in a luxurious atmosphere _____
   f) city trip with friends   _____
   g) community with other young travellers _____

2. Listen to the four people again. Fill in the grid with one piece of information per box.

	John	Olivia	Hailey	Carter
age:	a)	d)	g)	i)
kind of accommodation:	b)	e)	h)	j)
one activity:	c)	f)	✗	k)

Listening Test 10: Part-time jobs

You will hear a radio show in which three pupils are talking about part-time jobs. Who thinks what? Write the correct name (Lexi, Marc, Leo) next to the statement.
Listen to the interview twice.
Be careful: One statement does not fit. Mark this statement with a cross (✗).

1. ☐   I don't charge too much for my tutorials.

2. ☐   My job is exhausting, but I still like it.

3. ☐   I had to give up my job recently.

4. ☐   I regularly look after three children.

5. ☐   I need to prepare for my job.

Listening

Listening Test 11: What's on your plate?

Listen to the survey twice. Some people are talking about their eating habits. Who thinks what? Write the correct letters in the chart.
Be careful: There is one more statement than you need.

A I don't eat any animal products at all.

B I want to eat fewer sweets.

C Cooking for me means heating up what's in the freezer.

D Cooking is too much work for one person.

E I grow my own fruit and vegetables.

F I'm a meat-eater and I love barbecues.

G I always eat out at expensive restaurants.

H I'm not a strict vegetarian.

Henry	Liam	Clare	Finn	Colin	Hanna	Tessa

Listening Test 12: Integrated prom

1. You will hear an interview with two high school graduates in the USA. Listen to the interview twice and complete the sentences. .

   a) For Elijah it would have been unthinkable to go ...

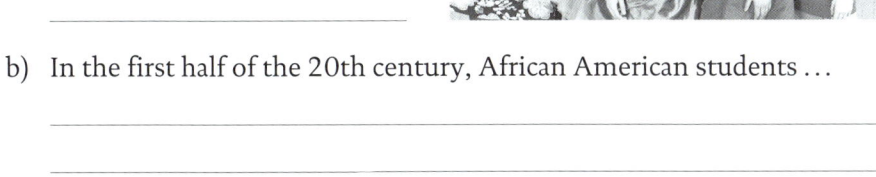

   b) In the first half of the 20th century, African American students ...

   c) In 2013 younger students couldn't go to the prom because ...

   d) Four students are the local high school heroes because ...

   e) Elijah thinks that in the 21st century ...

   f) A special moment for Emma was ...

   g) What makes Emma a little angry is that ...

Listening

2. Listen to the interview again two more times and complete the cluster about the history of proms in Rochelle, Georgia. Take notes and for each year or period of time write down …
   ❶ the number and kind of prom(s) and
   ❷ who they were or are organized by.

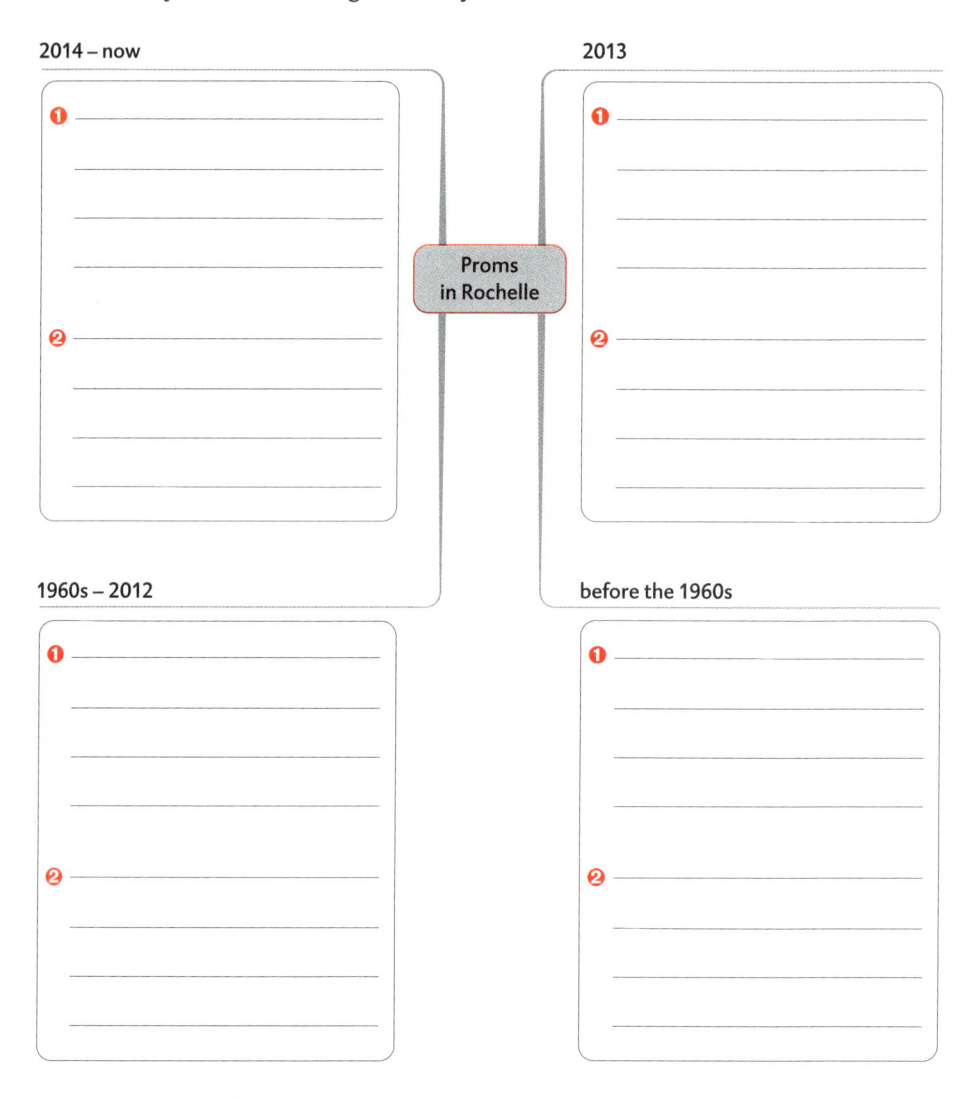

2014 – now
❶ _____
❷ _____

2013
❶ _____
❷ _____

1960s – 2012
❶ _____
❷ _____

before the 1960s
❶ _____
❷ _____

Proms in Rochelle

2 Reading – Text-based Tasks

Es gibt viele verschiedene Arten von Lesetexten. Ebenso vielfältig können die Aufgabenstellungen dazu sein. Die Textsorten und Aufgabenstellungen, die am häufigsten in Klassenarbeiten und in der Abschlussprüfung vorkommen, werden wir dir hier vorstellen.

2.1 Strategien zum Bereich „Reading"

Je nachdem, welche Art von Lesetext oder welche Art von Aufgabenstellung du bearbeiten musst, unterscheidet sich die Vorgehensweise. Manchmal musst du die Gesamtaussage des Textes erfassen *(reading for gist)* und manchmal sollst du Details aus dem Text herausfinden. Du musst dann den Text nach den geforderten Informationen durchforsten *(skimming* oder *scanning)*.

Arbeitsschritt 1
Zunächst einmal ist es sinnvoll, den Text an sich ganz genau zu betrachten. Manchmal kannst du bereits am **Layout**, d. h. an der Gestaltung des Textes, erkennen, um welche **Textsorte** es geht. Wenn du weißt, ob der dir vorliegende Text eine Werbeanzeige, ein literarischer Text oder ein Interview ist, dann bist du schon einen Schritt weiter. In der Abschlussprüfung kommt meist ein Sachtext, wie z. B. ein Zeitungsartikel, vor.

Arbeitsschritt 2
Als Nächstes solltest du den **Text** einmal **genau lesen**. Die meisten unbekannten Wörter kannst du ganz leicht aus dem **Sinnzusammenhang erschließen**. Lass dich also nicht aus der Ruhe bringen, wenn dir das eine oder andere Wort unbekannt ist. Ganz entscheidend ist, dass du dir bei diesem Arbeitsschritt einen guten **Überblick über den Inhalt** des Textes verschaffst.

Arbeitsschritt 3
Nun solltest du die **Aufgabenstellungen genau lesen**, damit du weißt, unter welchen Aspekten du den Text bearbeiten sollst. Wenn du jetzt den Lesetext im Hinblick auf die jeweiligen Aufgabenstellungen liest, kannst du dabei ganz gezielt wichtige **Schlüsselwörter** bzw. **Textpassagen markieren**, damit du sie bei der Bearbeitung der Aufgaben schnell wiederfindest.
So bist du für die Beantwortung der Aufgaben gut gerüstet!

Tipp
- Schau dir den Lesetext insgesamt an. Kannst du vom Layout auf die Textsorte schließen?
- Lies den Text genau durch und verschaffe dir einen guten Überblick über den Inhalt.
- Lies die Aufgabenstellungen sorgfältig. Markiere beim nochmaligen Lesen des Textes wichtige Textaussagen im Hinblick auf die Aufgabenstellungen.

2.2 Häufige Aufgabenstellungen zum Bereich „Reading"

Dieses Kapitel enthält viele verschiedene Aufgaben zum „Reading". Hier kannst du trainieren, wie man einen Text genau erschließt, und dich auf Aufgaben zum Leseverstehen in Klassenarbeiten und in der Abschlussprüfung gut vorbereiten. In deiner Abschlussprüfung kommen besonders häufig *matching, true/false or not in the text, finish the sentences, take notes* und *answer the questions* vor.

52 | Reading – Text-based Tasks

Match the headings with the parts of the text. / Match …

Es gibt viele verschiedene Arten von **Zuordnungsaufgaben**. Häufig sollst du einzelnen Textabschnitten *(parts of the text/paragraphs)* eine passende Überschrift *(heading)* zuordnen oder umgekehrt: Dir werden Überschriften vorgegeben, zu denen du passende Abschnitte im Text finden musst. Manchmal musst du auch verschiedenen Personen, Ländern, Organisationen etc. Informationen oder Aussagen zuordnen. Meistens ist es so, dass die Anzahl der Wahlmöglichkeiten nicht mit der Anzahl der Textabschnitte/Überschriften bzw. Personen/Länder etc. übereinstimmt. Daher ist es wichtig, dass du genau liest und am Ende noch einmal deine Lösung überprüfst. Zu zentralen Wörtern aus den Überschriften findest du häufig bedeutungsgleiche oder -ähnliche Wörter im Text. Halte danach Ausschau, wenn du Schwierigkeiten mit der Zuordnung hast.

Beispiel

Text:	Canada is the world's second-largest country after Russia. It consists of ten provinces and three territories. The country's smallest province is Prince Edward Island; the largest territory is Nunavut in the far north. There is the Pacific Ocean in the west, the Atlantic Ocean in the east and the Arctic Ocean in the north. In the south, Canada shares the world's longest land border with the USA.
Task:	Match the countries/provinces (❶–❸) with the correct information (**A**–**E**). Some of the information does not fit.

❶ Canada   **A** is the biggest country in the world.
❷ Russia   **B** is the biggest territory in Canada.
❸ Nunavut   **C** is the smallest country in the world.
                     D is one of the two countries which have the longest land border in the world.
                     E is the second-biggest province in Canada.

Answer:

❶	❷	❸
D	A	B

Decide whether the following statements are *true, false* or *not in the text.*

Hier sollst du entscheiden, ob **Aussagen** zum Text **richtig** oder **falsch** bzw. ob die Informationen gar **nicht im Text** enthalten sind. Es ist wichtig, dass du genau liest, denn ein einziges Wort kann ausschlaggebend sein, ob ein Satz korrekt ist oder nicht.

Beispiel

Text:	The first U.S. American boot camp for teenagers was created in the 1980s to reduce the number of young criminals.
Task:	Decide whether the following statement is true, false or not in the text. Boot camps have existed in the USA for about 25 years.
Answer:	*false*
Hinweis:	Da seit den 1980er-Jahren schon mehr als 30 Jahre vergangen sind, ist diese Aussage falsch.

Reading – Text-based Tasks

Finish the sentences using the information from the text.

Bei diesem Aufgabentyp sollst du vorgegebene Satzanfänge mithilfe von Informationen aus dem Text **vervollständigen**. Manchmal handelt es sich um eine **Multiple-Choice**-Aufgabe, in der du aus mehreren Satzenden das richtige auswählen kannst, gelegentlich sollst du aber eigenständig die **Lücken füllen**.

Bei Multiple-Choice-Aufgaben wird meist nicht genau dieselbe Formulierung wie im Text verwendet; du musst also nach Schlüsselwörtern mit ähnlicher Bedeutung suchen und den Text und die möglichen Antworten genau vergleichen. Oft unterscheiden sich die Antwortmöglichkeiten nur in einer Kleinigkeit.

Beispiel 1: Multiple Choice

Text:	In South Africa, young people born after 1994 – the year when Nelson Mandela was elected the first black president – are often referred to as "born frees". They are the first generation to grow up in a free and democratic society, the first who no longer experienced the system of racial segregation that had characterised South Africa for almost half a century.
Task and answer:	Finish the sentences using the information from the text. Tick (✓) the correct box. "Born frees" … ☐ are young people who were born in 1993 or earlier. ☐ never knew Nelson Mandela in their lifetime. ✓ were born when racial segregation had already been abolished.

Wenn du Sätze eigenständig vervollständigen sollst, ist es manchmal sogar möglich, Textstellen wörtlich aus dem Text zu übernehmen, meist musst du die Sätze aber an die Satzanfänge anpassen.

Beispiel 2: Sätze eigenständig vervollständigen

Text:	On Samhain, the Celtic version of our modern Halloween, the people lit bonfires.
Task:	Finish the sentence. On Samhain, bonfires …
Answer:	were lit by Celtic people / by the Celts.
Hinweis:	Hier musst du z. B. aus einem Aktivsatz einen Passivsatz machen.

Answer the questions.

Hier sollst du **Fragen zum Text beantworten**. Ab und zu kannst du Formulierungen aus dem Lesetext übernehmen, meist musst du deine Antworten aber selbst formulieren. Lies die einzelnen Fragen genau und suche die Antworten im Text. Achte bei der Beantwortung der Fragen darauf, ob ganze Sätze oder Stichpunkte verlangt sind. In deiner Abschlussprüfung wird bei diesem Aufgabentyp normalerweise von dir verlangt, dass du ganze Sätze schreibst.

Beispiel

Text:	Australia has long been one of the top gap-year destinations for young people from around the globe who have just finished school and want to travel for a year before starting a job or continuing their education.
Question:	When do many young people take a gap year?
Answer:	Many young people take a gap year after finishing school.

Find information in the text about … / Find reasons …

Manchmal werden dir verschiedene Themen oder Oberbegriffe vorgegeben, zu denen du **im Text Informationen finden** sollst. Lies die Aufgabenstellung wieder ganz genau. Normalerweise brauchst du hier keine vollständigen Sätze zu schreiben, sondern nur Stichpunkte. In diesem Fall lautet die Anweisung „**Take notes**". Wenn du eine passende Stelle findest, darfst du sie auch wörtlich aus dem Text übernehmen. Achte unbedingt darauf, wie viele Aspekte („items", „pieces of information", „reasons" etc.) du zu einem Thema nennen sollst.

Beispiel

Text:	At English schools pupils usually have to wear a school uniform. Although many pupils would prefer to be able to choose their clothes themselves, most of them also see the advantages of it. You never have to think about what to wear – which saves lots of time. And there aren't any arguments with your parents about whether or not a skirt is too short or the text on a T-shirt is suitable for school.
Task:	Find information in the text about the advantages of school uniforms. (two items)
Answer:	▶ wearing a school uniform saves time
	▶ no arguments with your parents about clothes

2.3 Übungsaufgaben zum Bereich „Reading"

Reading Test 1: "We may be 'born free', but …"

1 In South Africa, young people born after 1994 – the year when Nelson Rolihlahla Mandela was elected the first black president – are often referred to as "born frees". They are the first generation to grow up in a free and democratic society, the first who no longer experienced the system of racial segrega-
5 tion that had characterised South Africa for almost half a century.

During the so-called apartheid era, the population was divided into the following four racial groups: White, Bantu (black Africans), Coloured (of mixed ethnic origin)
10 and Asian. While people with British or Dutch roots enjoyed lots of privileges, the non-white groups (especially black people) were systematically oppressed. For example, they weren't allowed to vote and were
15 forced to live in particular areas called "homelands". Public facilities were usually segregated into white and non-white zones so that white people didn't have to share the same space with members of the other
20 groups.

For "born frees" like Mbali Legodi, a black teenager from Cape Town, this period seems far away. "Of course, my parents and grandparents have often told me about it, but I can't really imagine what it must have been like. I think for most of our generation, it's normal to move around freely or be allowed to
25 vote." Young South Africans nowadays take many of the hard-won privileges for granted, which has led some of the older generation to think of the "born frees" as spoiled or naive. Yet today's youngsters have to cope with problems of their own.

"Many of my friends are unemployed, there simply aren't enough jobs,"
30 Mbali says. According to recent statistics, about 50 per cent of South Africans between the ages of 15 and 24 are out of work. Black Africans seem to be particularly at risk of facing long-term joblessness. In addition, those who do find work also earn considerably less than the average white person. "I guess if you look at it from that perspective, not so much has changed. Even 20
35 years after the end of apartheid, the old inequalities are still in place."

Another problem is health: A large number of young people in South Africa are HIV-positive. Women are much more likely than men to be infected and suffer not only from insufficient medical treatment but also from social stigmatisation.

40 Like many of her generation, Mbali is frustrated with the government, who, she feels, is doing too little to fight HIV/AIDS, improve education or create new jobs. "If you ask me, our politicians are all corrupt. They only take our money to line their own pockets[1]."

Has she ever considered leaving South Africa and moving to another country? 45 "I knew you would ask that. But no, never. I mean, just look around you: I live in the most beautiful country in the world. There are so many creative people, people who want to change things. We may be 'born free', but there's still a lot for us to do in this society."

(501 words)

1 to line one's own pockets – to take money for yourself that does not belong to you

1. **Vorbereitung** – Bist du noch etwas unsicher beim Leseverstehen? Folgende Strategie hilft dir bei der Bearbeitung der Aufgaben.

    a) Lies zuerst einmal den Text aufmerksam durch, um dir einen Überblick zu verschaffen. Lies dann die Aufgabenstellung und alle Teilaufgaben von Aufgabe 2 aufmerksam durch und markiere in jeder Aussage Schlüsselwörter. Zusätzlich kannst du dir am Rand auf Deutsch oder Englisch notieren, nach welchen Inhalten du im Text Ausschau halten musst.

    b) Suche im Text gezielt nach den Themen und nach den Schlüsselwörtern, die du in den Aussagesätzen von Aufgabe 2a–f markiert hast. Denke dabei daran, dass im Text meist nicht genau dieselben Wörter verwendet werden wie in den Aussagen, sondern auch Begriffe mit ähnlicher Bedeutung vorkommen können.

Tipp

> Übe diese Strategie auch bei anderen Aufgaben und „Reading Tests". Auch wenn dir diese Vorgehensweise anfangs recht zeitaufwendig erscheint, schärft sie deinen Blick für Schlüsselwörter und hilft dir, den Überblick zu bewahren. Du wirst merken, dass du auf diese Weise beim Bearbeiten der Aufgaben zum Leseverstehen immer sicherer wirst.

2. Decide whether the following statements are true, false or not in the text. Tick (✓) the correct box.

		true	false	not in the text
a)	During the apartheid era black and white people couldn't live in the same neighbourhood.	☐	☐	☐
b)	Mbali's family have never suffered from oppression themselves.	☐	☐	☐
c)	Most young South Africans have a good chance of finding a job they like.	☐	☐	☐
d)	Nowadays a black person still does not have the same opportunities as a white person.	☐	☐	☐
e)	In South Africa, men have a higher risk of getting infected with HIV than women.	☐	☐	☐
f)	Mbali wants to go into politics.	☐	☐	☐

3. Match (❶–❹) to the information (A–G).
   Some of the information does not fit.

   ❶ Born frees
   ❷ South Africans with mixed ethnic background
   ❸ Mbali Legodi
   ❹ Political leaders in South Africa

   A … are suspected of being dishonest.
   B … have never had to fight for their rights.
   C … suffered from segregation and discrimination for many years.
   D … is thinking about emigrating.
   E … are doing their best to improve living conditions for black South Africans.
   F … heard stories about racial inequalities from her relatives.
   G … consider democratic values to be normal.

❶	❷	❸	❹

4. Find information about the different racial groups during the apartheid era.
   Write down two pieces of information.
   ▶ _____
   ▶ _____

5. Answer the question. Write in complete sentences.
   What could the South African government do to improve the situation for the born frees? (two items)
   _____
   _____

6. Finish the sentences using information from the text.
   a) For almost 50 years _____
   _____
   b) Long-term unemployment _____
   _____

7. Finish the sentences using the information from the text.
   Tick (✓) the correct statement. Only one option is correct.

   a) The term "born frees" refers to …
      ☐ white people.
      ☐ black people who were released from prison.
      ☐ Nelson Rolihlahla Mandela's children.
      ☐ young South Africans born after the end of apartheid.

   b) The policy of "homelands" meant that …
      ☐ white people returned to Britain and the Netherlands.
      ☐ black people had to move to separate areas.
      ☐ every citizen was given a plot of land by the state.
      ☐ South Africa became part of the British Empire.

   c) HIV/AIDS …
      ☐ has affected about 2.3 million South Africans.
      ☐ affects people not only physically, but also has social implications.
      ☐ is a top priority for South African politicians.
      ☐ affects all parts of the South African population in equal measure.

   d) The article shows that people like Mbali …
      ☐ love their country despite the many problems they face.
      ☐ are finally living in a country where everyone is treated equally.
      ☐ generally agree with South African politics after Mandela.
      ☐ are seeking their luck somewhere else.

Reading Test 2: Getting to know Canada

https://www.canadatravel.com

[About Canada] [Getting Here] [Destinations] [Activities] [Accommodation]

Canada – facts and figures

A Canada, whose name means "village" or "settlement", is the world's second-largest country after Russia. It consists of ten provinces and three territories. The country's smallest province is Prince Edward Island, named after Queen Victoria's father; the largest territory is Nunavut in the far north. There is the Pacific Ocean in the west, the Atlantic Ocean in the east and the Arctic Ocean in the north. In the south, Canada shares the world's longest land border with the USA. Four of the five Great Lakes are also part of the border between these two countries.

B Nunavut, which means "Our Land", is the coldest, largest and least populated territory. It is about the size of Western Europe, but only about 31,000 people live there, 85 % of whom are indigenous. It was created in 1999 and is therefore the youngest territory of Canada. Visitors can only fly into Nunavut as there are no roads that connect the 25 communities with each other or the rest of Canada. As rivers, lakes and the Arctic Ocean are frozen for three-quarters of the year, even very heavy vehicles can drive on the ice for more than six months. When the ice has melted, some communities can be visited by boat in July and August. In the summer months, the sun never sets, whereas in the winter, the sky is lit by the Northern Lights.

C There are two official languages in Canada – English and French – but that doesn't mean that every Canadian is bilingual. Quebec is the only Canadian province that uses French as its only official language. However, many people also speak English there, especially in Montreal and other popular tourist destinations.

D More than a century ago, in 1885, when people realised that it was necessary to protect plants and animals, the history of Canada's national parks started with the creation of Banff National Park in the province of Alberta in the Canadian Rockies. Today, Canada has got more than 40 national parks and park reserves, which vary from between 9 km² and 45,000 km² in size. Some of the most popular activities are wildlife viewing, hiking, mountain biking, horseback riding, climbing, kayaking or canoeing, cross-country skiing, ice skating, skiing and snowboarding.

E One of the most famous tourist attractions is the Niagara Falls, located in the Canadian province of Ontario and New York State. The term "Niagara Falls" comprises three waterfalls, namely the Horseshoe Falls, the American Falls and the Bridal Veil Falls. One way to experience the falls is to go on a breathtaking "Journey Behind the Falls", taking an elevator down to the bottom of the falls and watching the water fall down from behind. Thrill-seeking visitors, however, might want to go on a cruise that travels past the American and Bridal Veil Falls to get as close to the Horseshoe Falls as possible. Although a lot more visitors tend to look at the falls on the Canadian side of the border, the American side is also worth a visit.

About us | Contact us | Copyright | Press | En français

1. Find the correct headline (1–7) for each paragraph (A–E). Fill in the correct number in the grid below the box. There are more headlines than you need.

	Headlines
1	All the languages spoken in Canada
2	How to visit Niagara Falls
3	Geographical facts and background information
4	Life in the far North
5	Canada's official languages
6	Winter in Nunavut
7	National parks in Canada

A	B	C	D	E

2. Decide whether the following statements are true, false or not in the text. Tick (✓) the correct box.

	true	false	not in the text

   a) There are two countries that are larger than Canada. ☐ ☐ ☐
   b) Nunavut can easily be reached by a highway. ☐ ☐ ☐
   c) You will probably not have any language problems as a tourist in Quebec if you can only speak English. ☐ ☐ ☐
   d) Banff National Park is the biggest park in Canada. ☐ ☐ ☐
   e) Horseshoe Falls is the most powerful of the three waterfalls. ☐ ☐ ☐
   f) It is more popular to cross the border and visit the Niagara Falls from the U.S. side. ☐ ☐ ☐

3. Choose the right sentence endings. Tick (✓) the correct box. Only one sentence ending is correct.

   a) The text "Canada – facts and figures" is …
      ☐ a leaflet you might get on a tour to the Niagara Falls.
      ☐ an informative text that might be part of an online travel guide about Canada.
      ☐ an advertisement for a holiday in Canada.
      ☐ part of an online encyclopaedia about the history of Canada.

b) Canada is divided into …
- [ ] thirteen so-called "settlements".
- [ ] provinces and territories.
- [ ] ten provinces.
- [ ] three territories.

c) One part of Canada is named after …
- [ ] the English queen.
- [ ] a member of the British royal family.
- [ ] a nun.
- [ ] the first settler.

d) The majority of the population in Nunavut …
- [ ] are indigenous.
- [ ] are immigrants from Western Europe.
- [ ] were born there.
- [ ] like living in this remote territory.

e) A lot of people in Quebec speak …
- [ ] only English.
- [ ] an indigenous language.
- [ ] French.
- [ ] more than two languages.

f) If you want to spend an adventurous day at Niagara Falls, …
- [ ] you can climb down the rocks.
- [ ] you should go by boat.
- [ ] you should visit Bridal Veil Falls.
- [ ] it is best to visit the American side of the falls.

4. Finish the sentences using the information from the text.

a) The only way to get to Nunavut _____

b) In Nunavut in July and August you _____

c) Banff National Park _____

d) The Niagara Falls consist _____

5. Answer the questions in complete sentences.
   a) Why is Nunavut not a very populated region in Canada?

   b) What is special about the winter in Nunavut? (two items)

   c) What was the reason for the creation of the first national parks in Canada?

6. Note down three facts about Canada's national parks but do **not** write about Banff National Park. Use the information from the text.
   ▶
   ▶
   ▶

Reading Test 3: Cyberbullying

I was cyberbullied

The shocking story of how school bullies used a social networking site to target 15-year-old Christine, and how she learned to live with this horrible experience.

A A brave 15-year-old girl has revealed exclusively to *TeenLife* what happened to her when school bullies targeted her on one of the world's most used social networking sites.

B In a story that's shocked Gloucester, Christine Simmons became the subject of a hate campaign on a social networking site last November after she'd angered a girl in her class by chatting to a boy on the bus. The jealous girl, who we aren't naming, set up a chat group called "We Hate Christine". She then invited more than 200 people to join the group and post cruel messages. Horrified Christine, from Gloucester, found out from the bully herself. "I'd just come out of French class when she walked up and told me what she'd done. From the way she sounded, she was proud of it. I was shocked and upset and rang my mum in tears," she says.

C The offending group chat has now been deleted, but the bullying had a devastating effect on Christine. "I had a nervous breakdown and couldn't face going to school for a while. Finally my parents took me to see a psychologist, who has helped me a great deal."

D Although the school intervened immediately, it decided not to exclude the bully, meaning Christine has had to share classes with the girl. "It's definitely affected my schoolwork," she says. Christine wasn't sure if she should return to school after Christmas, until her family and friends persuaded her to do it. Christine's friends have rallied around her, trying to make things easier for her at school, but initially they were as shocked as she was. "I don't think my friends knew what to say at the time," she adds. "Some of them were angry about it, but they knew it had upset me a lot, so they tried to talk about other things to distract me." And she's relieved that things are getting back to normal. "At the moment I'm enjoying school," she admits. "I've tried to push what happened to me to the back of my mind, and I think I'm doing quite well."

E But it's not that easy when she has to see the girl who bullied her every day at school. "Recently she tried to apologise to me," explains Christine. As she walked past me in a corridor she said 'I'm sorry', but I just carried on walking. I thought she was probably just sorry for herself – she isn't very popular at school anymore."

F The headteacher of Christine's school said she couldn't comment on individual cases, but that she took reports of bullying seriously and that the school would "look at revising the cyberbullying policy". Brave Christine says: "I know I have to keep going to school. I want to become a lawyer and we start our GCSEs[1] soon, so I won't let anyone stop me from going."

G Unfortunately, Christine's case is not an exception: according to a recent survey by the British charity "Ditch the Label", about one in five young people between the ages of 12 and 20 in the UK were bullied in the past year – and cyberbullying is on the rise. Oftentimes, cyberbullying can easily be detected when online content (texts, tweets, posts, etc.) is mean or cruel. Sometimes, though, cyberbullying is not immediately obvious, for example when

64 Reading – Text-based Tasks

the bully creates a fake account on a social networking site in order to impersonate the victim and post personal information, embarrassing photos or video footage with the sole purpose to harm him or her. Cyberbullying is particularly hard on the victims because they usually don't know who the bully is and because they often don't know how many people have seen the messages or posts. What is more, online bullying can occur 24/7, so that the victims often feel as if they can't escape. Thomas Brown, a leading expert on cyberbullying, stresses that the most important thing a victim should do is talk to an adult and ask for help.

1 GCSE – General Certificate of Secondary Education (*erster Schulabschluss, vergleichbar dem Realschulabschluss*)

1. Match the headlines (1–8) to the paragraphs (A–G). One headline has already been matched correctly. There is one more headline than you need.

	Headlines
1	Apologising is not enough
2	Learning to live with it
3	How the horror started
4	Facts about cyberbullying
5	The immediate effect of the incident
6	Christine's future plans
7	Breaking the silence
8	Plans for the future

A	B	C	D	E	F	G
7						

2. Decide whether the following statements are true, false or not in the text. Tick (✓) the correct box

		true	false	not in the text
a)	Christine talked about the bullying in a blog.	☐	☐	☐
b)	One of the hate messages was from a girl Christine had thought was her friend.	☐	☐	☐
c)	Christine found out about the hate page because her friends told her about it.	☐	☐	☐
d)	Right after posting the first cruel messages, the bully felt sorry for what she had done.	☐	☐	☐
e)	Christine doesn't know yet whether she will return to school.	☐	☐	☐
f)	The headteacher told the bully to apologise to Christine.	☐	☐	☐
g)	The cases of cyberbullying are increasing.	☐	☐	☐

3. Finish the following sentences using information from the text.
   a) "We hate Christine" _____

   b) Christine's first reaction was _____

   c) Christine's performance at school _____

   d) When the bully tried to apologise, _____

   e) Christine dreams _____

4. Answer the following questions in complete sentences. Use the information from the text.
   a) What was the reason the bully posted hateful comments about Christine?

   b) Why was it particularly hard to come back to school after the bullying?

   c) What does Christine think about the bully's apology?

5. Why is cyberbullying often more hurtful than other types of bullying? Find three reasons in the text and write down your answers. You do not need to write full sentences.
   ▶ _____
   ▶ _____
   ▶ _____

6. Finish the sentences using the information from the text.
   Tick (✓) the correct statement. Only one option is correct.
   a) The girl who bullied Christine …
      ☐ obviously enjoyed what she was doing.
      ☐ told Christine about the hate page after their German class.
      ☐ talked to everyone in school about what she had done.
      ☐ is proud she has so many followers.

b) As a result of the incident …
- ☐ the bully had to leave school.
- ☐ the school hired a psychologist.
- ☐ Christine carried on as if nothing had happened.
- ☐ Christine had to get professional help.

c) Christine's friends …
- ☐ did their best to support her.
- ☐ said she shouldn't take the bullying so seriously.
- ☐ set up a hate page against the girl.
- ☐ urged her to inform the police.

d) Christine is enjoying school at the moment because she …
- ☐ doesn't have to see the bully anymore.
- ☐ is trying to forget what happened to her.
- ☐ has made some new friends.
- ☐ has managed to talk to the bully about what happened.

e) The headteacher said that …
- ☐ the school might change its rules about bullying.
- ☐ bullying wasn't such a big problem at her school.
- ☐ she was going to talk to experts about the incident.
- ☐ Christine was a very brave girl.

f) Christine thinks it is important for her to go to school now because …
- ☐ she is taking her final exams soon.
- ☐ she wants to show her parents that she will not give up.
- ☐ she does not want to be seen as a coward.
- ☐ this is the only way to go on seeing her friends.

g) The author of the article thinks that …
- ☐ the school should have expelled the bully.
- ☐ Christine is right to ignore the girl who was bullying her.
- ☐ Christine is very ambitious.
- ☐ life can become very difficult for the person who has been bullied.

Reading Test 4: Young refugees learn about U.S. on the soccer field

Young refugees in the United States are learning about each other and their new country on the soccer field. One player is teenage boy Win La Bar. His family is from Myanmar, also known as Burma. Win was born in Thailand after his family fled their Burmese homeland. Now he is one of about 200 refugee children who play at the North Phoenix Christian Soccer Club, founded in 1975, in the western state of Arizona, a leading state of resettlement. The players in the club's twelve teams are between six and eighteen years old and from over 30 different countries. Most of the refugee families are still early in their U.S. lives and are not yet financially stable. The club, however, would never decline a kid because of a lack of funds.

Win and his nine family members share two apartments. Win has his own bedroom, but his sister sleeps in a room with her three young children. Win's parents and three other children live in another apartment. He loves his new home because, as he says, "I've got a better chance to get a better education, and I get to play more soccer without worrying about gunshots." The soccer club has helped him make friends and learn about his new home. His coaches have taught his family about life in the United States. They have helped them to figure how to get food benefits and car insurance, for example. Win had never seen cars or planes before and comments how because of this it was "very different, very hard to adapt into this world. It's hard to understand." His mother doesn't speak English, or write in her own language, Karenni, so her children translate for her as needed. Win doesn't remember how he learned English, but one of the coaches tutored him and his younger siblings. Now he gets top grades.

Alondra Ruiz works for the soccer club. Officially, she is the club's administrator. In practice she is tutor, activities coordinator, chauffeur, and counsellor. She brings the players to games and drives them home. Sometimes she drives for hours a day, and hundreds of kilometers a week. If she did not do that, a lot of the players would not get to practices and games. But the club wants to make an effort.

During the rides the students ask Alondra Ruiz many questions about the United States. "I get the opportunity to teach the kids things that maybe their parents can't answer." Ruiz tells them, "you're not different. You're here. And you can become anything you want." She adds, "Being part of this club, and keeping kids busy is very rewarding to me because it's good for them, and it's good for the future." She goes on to say that what she hears often is that "they're being treated differently at school, that they're not being accepted."

The soccer field, however, doesn't discriminate based on how good your English is or what kind of house your family can afford. Ruiz stresses that she can relate to the kids' experiences one hundred percent. "I wasn't accepted coming from Mexico," she states. Whereas her husband has permission to work in the U.S., she is not here legally.

For Zara Doukoum, the cultural diversity of the club is the reason why she joined when she arrived from Gabon, where she was born after her family had fled from Chad. Her teammates and coaches give her a sense of community that goes beyond what she has in school and like Win, she finds comfort in fellow English learners. She knows from first-hand experience what the other refugee students have dealt with, including when people did not understand what they were saying when they were just learning to speak English. "Every refugee in America went through that," she says. This year she will graduate from Central High School, the public school attended by most of her teammates. After graduating, she wants to attend college, where she may play soccer or tennis. She says, "if that doesn't work for me, I see myself just helping around, giving back to the community the way people give to me."

Based on: Christopher Jones-Cruise, Anna Matteo, Voice of America Learning English, January 25, 2016. / Victoria Macchi, Voice of America: "Born to Play: A Refugee Soccer Team Grows in the American Desert"

1. Decide whether the following statements are true, false or not in the text. Tick (✓) the correct box.

		true	false	not in the text
a)	Win was born after his family had fled from their home country.	☐	☐	☐
b)	The La Bar family have little space in their new home as they have to share two bedrooms.	☐	☐	☐
c)	At the soccer club the refugee children can learn more than just soccer rules.	☐	☐	☐
d)	Alondra Ruiz loves spending a lot of time on the road for her job at the soccer club.	☐	☐	☐
e)	Alondra Ruiz and her husband are illegal immigrants.	☐	☐	☐
f)	Most of Zara Doukoum's teammates go to college in Phoenix.	☐	☐	☐

2. Finish the sentences using information from the text.
   a) 6- to 18-year-old refugee children _____
   _____

b) The majority of the refugee families whose kids play at the soccer club recently _____

c) Cars and planes _____
_____

d) Driving for hours _____
_____

3. Match the people and institutions from the text (a–d) to the statements (A–F) and write the correct letter in the boxes. Use each letter only once. Be careful, there are two statements that you do not need.
   a) Win La Bar ☐
   b) North Phoenix Christian Soccer Club ☐
   c) Alondra Ruiz ☐
   d) Zara Doukoum ☐

   A The most important thing for us is that the kids do well at school.

   B I'm really proud that I've made it this far. And believe me, school wasn't always easy, especially in the first few months.

   C I'm grateful for all the opportunities that are offered to me in the US.

   D I'd like to become a legal American citizen, too.

   E I know exactly what it feels like to start a new life in a new environment.

   F We offer an integration program for child refugees.

4. Answer the questions in complete sentences.
   a) What does Win like about his new life in America? (two items)
   _____
   _____

b) Why does it feel good for Alondra Ruiz to work for the soccer club?

_____
_____

c) What problems do child refugees have to cope with when they arrive in America? (two items)

_____
_____

5. Tick (✓) the correct statement. Only one option is correct.

a) Win La Bar was born in …
   ☐ Arizona.
   ☐ Burma.
   ☐ Thailand.
   ☐ Phoenix.

b) The La Bar family has benefitted from the soccer club because …
   ☐ the club paid for the family's car insurance.
   ☐ one of the coaches supported their children with their school work.
   ☐ the club will help Win to go to a top university.
   ☐ the club offers free food.

c) Alondra Ruiz …
   ☐ is a soccer coach.
   ☐ drives children to and from soccer training.
   ☐ works as a professional counselor.
   ☐ is an English teacher.

d) Zara Doukoum enjoys being at the soccer club because …
   ☐ teenagers from many different countries form a community there.
   ☐ she feels almost as accepted there as in her school.
   ☐ she can improve her soccer skills.
   ☐ she doesn't have to speak English there.

e) All in all, the North Phoenix Christian Soccer Club …
   ☐ is unique because no other American soccer club has members from so many different countries of origin.
   ☐ helps young refugees feel more self-confident and integrated.
   ☐ sends many of its players to top universities.
   ☐ is supported by the U.S. government as an example of integration.

Reading Test 5: A year in England

School life abroad

For this month's *Teens Abroad* magazine, our reporter Joe Thompson met Tanja Huber, an ordinary girl from Germany, who has been staying with a host family and going to an English school for the past few months.

When I met fifteen-year-old Tanja for the first time, I was very impressed by her English. "During the first month in which I did a language course in London and my four months here in Bristol I've learned a lot," Tanja says. "But when I first came here, I had a lot of problems." "My English was rubbish," she adds with a laugh and explains that this was one of the reasons why she decided to spend an entire school year in an English-speaking country. "I'm really happy that I've got another seven months to go."

Tanja says that she gets along with her host family really well and that she has become close friends with the two twin daughters. Tanja enjoys living with two "sisters", as her own brother, who is seven years older than she is, moved out three years ago. However, she sometimes misses her parents and her best friend Emma. "My parents and I talk on the phone regularly and Emma and I chat all the time," Tanja explains. During the last holidays, Emma even came to visit and they spent an exciting three days in London, where they went on the Harry Potter Studio Tour, for example. According to Tanja, the studio is well worth a visit.

Tanja goes to St Thomas College in Bristol. Although school is very different in England, Tanja has got used to it, and she says that she enjoys it a lot. Wearing a school uniform is one of the things she did not like at first, but that has changed. What she likes about it is that she does not have to think about what to wear to school every morning. "It saves a lot of time," she says. "I have to wear a dark red skirt and blazer or pullover with the school's coat of arms[1] and a white polo shirt. I especially like it that we are allowed to wear a polo shirt instead of a blouse, because it is much more comfortable." Registration is another thing that was new to her. As in all British schools, pupils at St Thomas College have to go to registration every morning and every afternoon after lunch to show that they are present. There is a quick registration in every lesson, too. "At first, I found it quite funny when teachers called out the pupils' names, and the pupils shouted out, 'Yes, sir' or 'Yes, ma'am', like in the military ... But actually, it's a good thing: if a pupil is not there, everyone knows immediately, so this makes it very hard to miss a class on purpose."

As school starts at 9 o'clock, Tanja is happy that she can sleep late even on school days (compared to Germany), because St Thomas College is just a five-minute bike ride away from home. So she sleeps until quarter past eight, has a quick shower and some fruit and cereal or a slice of toast and a cup of tea for breakfast before leaving the house with her "sisters" at quarter to nine. At the weekends, however, her host family sometimes prepare the traditional "full English breakfast" with bacon, sausages, baked beans, a fried egg and a grilled tomato. She says that she is glad that the full English breakfast is reserved for special occasions, though, because she prefers a healthier start to the day.

Although Tanja sometimes feels homesick, she has got so used to life in England that she wants to train with an English company after passing her GCSEs back in Germany and taking a gap year in Australia.

[1] coat of arms – Wappen

1. Decide whether the following statements are true, false or not in the text. Tick (✓) the correct answer.

	true	false	not in the text
a) Tanja has been at an English boarding school for the last few months.	☐	☐	☐
b) Tanja is glad that she doesn't have to go back to Germany soon.	☐	☐	☐
c) Tanja's brother is 22 years old.	☐	☐	☐
d) Tanja is a huge Harry Potter fan.	☐	☐	☐
e) Registration only takes place in the mornings.	☐	☐	☐
f) The full English breakfast includes sausages, egg, vegetables and cereal.	☐	☐	☐
g) After her GCSEs and some time abroad Tanja wants to go back to England.	☐	☐	☐

2. Match each paragraph of the text with one of the headings below and write down the lines ("lines … to …"). Be careful: there are more headings than you need. Cross out the ones you do not need or write down "no match".

   a) Plans for the future

   _____

   b) A healthy start to the day

   _____

   c) Spotting the difference

   _____

   d) Learning English abroad

   _____

   e) If it weren't for that uniform

   _____

   f) Tanja's daily routine

   _____

   g) Friends and family

   _____

3. Finish the sentences using information from the text.

   a) Tanja's English …

   ☐ has always been very impressive.

   ☐ has improved immensely since she came to England.

   ☐ helped her to solve a lot of problems.

   ☐ was still rubbish after she had done a language course.

b) Tanja's host sisters …
- [ ] are seven years older than she is.
- [ ] are three years older than she is.
- [ ] have become good friends of hers.
- [ ] have got an older brother too.

c) At St Thomas College, …
- [ ] all the female students have to wear blouses and skirts.
- [ ] the majority of the students enjoys wearing their school uniform.
- [ ] the colour of the school uniform is dark red.
- [ ] girls can wear trousers or skirts.

d) After a quick breakfast, Tanja …
- [ ] cycles to school on her own.
- [ ] and her "sisters" leave the house at 9 a.m.
- [ ] and her host sisters set off for school.
- [ ] takes a quick shower and then leaves for school.

4. Answer the questions in complete sentences.
   a) What was one reason Tanja wanted to spend a year at a school in an English-speaking country?

   _____

   _____

   b) What does Tanja enjoy about her stay in England? (two items)

   _____

   _____

   c) Why has Tanja changed her opinion about wearing a school uniform?

   _____

   _____

5. Compare English and German schools. Find three things that are different in Germany. You do not have to write in complete sentences.
   ▶ _____
   ▶ _____
   ▶ _____

Reading Test 6: The history of Halloween

1 What do you do on Halloween? Do you dress up in a scary costume and go trick or treating? Do you carve a Jack o'lantern and decorate your house with fake skeletons, spooky ghosts and spiderwebs? Or
5 are you one of the approximately 60,000 participants of the famous Village Halloween Parade in New York City? Whichever way you spend Halloween, are you also familiar with its history?

The origin of our modern holiday "Halloween" goes back to the old Gaelic
10 festival of "Samhain", which for the Celts marked the end of the harvest period and the beginning of the "dark season" of winter, and which was celebrated from sunset on October 31st to sunset on November 1st. It was the time when the cattle were brought back from their summer meadows and the preparation for the less fertile months began.

15 On Samhain, which was celebrated in what is now Ireland, the Isle of Man and parts of Scotland, the people lit bonfires and held special feasts and meals. There were also special offerings for the old gods and the "aos sí", which is a mystical and supernatural race comparable to fairies or elves, which the Celts commonly believed in. There was also the belief that on
20 Samhain – as well as on Midsummer's Eve – the borders between this world and the world of the spirits could be crossed more easily, which made it possible for the dead to visit our world once again. However, this was not only a frightening event. The Celts believed that their ancestors wanted to join them on this date to make sure that they were well and pro-
25 tected. That is why people put empty chairs next to their own, which were meant for the dead members of the family.

Of course, not only the good and gentle spirits came to visit our world. Therefore, the Celts often wore special clothes and costumes to hide from the unpleasant and dangerous spirits. In those costumes they sometimes
30 went from house to house and asked for blessings and small gifts. This tradition is still practised on Halloween by the many children that roam their neighbourhood playing "trick or treat". And just as the evil spirits that could do bad things to the people who did not welcome the dead, the children play tricks on people who do not open the door or give them sweets.

35 Between the 4th and the 10th centuries, the Roman Catholic Church took over many pagan and Jewish holidays and shifted their own special days to and around dates of existing festivals. The day of the birth of Christ, for example, became connected to the Roman "Festival of the Sun" and the "Passion" and "Resurrection of Christ" – now known as "Easter" – were linked
40 to the Jewish "Passover". Thus, the practice and celebration of "All Saints' Day", also called "All Hallows' Day", where Christians should think about their dead saints, was shifted to the main date of Samhain – November 1st – turning the night before into "All Hallows' Evening".

Over the years, decades and centuries, the phrase was shortened to become
45 the word "Halloween", which was still connected to the traditions and the
belief of the Gaelic Samhain, where the spirits of the dead came to visit the
living – just as the deeds of the Christian saints were commemorated on the
day of "All Saints".

Today, however, many people do not remember the origin of traditions like
50 going "trick or treating" or the carving of the pumpkins to look like evil spirits. They believe that it is just childish behaviour and has no purpose at all because the meaning behind those rites has been lost over the centuries.

1. Decide whether the following statements are true, false or not in the text. Tick (✓) the correct answer.

		true	false	not in the text
a)	There is a famous Halloween parade in a village near New York City.	☐	☐	☐
b)	The tradition of Halloween goes back to a Gaelic holiday.	☐	☐	☐
c)	The celebration of Samhain lasted for two days.	☐	☐	☐
d)	Samhain was celebrated in what is now the United Kingdom.	☐	☐	☐
e)	The "aos sí" are a kind of fairy.	☐	☐	☐
f)	Something similar to "trick or treating" already existed in Celtic times.	☐	☐	☐
g)	Christmas is linked to a Gaelic celebration.	☐	☐	☐
h)	The word "Halloween" was first used in the 10th century.	☐	☐	☐

2. Match each of these headings with a suitable paragraph from the text. Some paragraphs do not match. Write down the lines ("lines … to …").

   a) Links between religions

   _____

   b) The original tradition and its meaning

   _____

   c) Roots are forgotten

   _____

   d) Halloween today

   _____

   e) The history of Halloween – some basic facts

   _____

3. Finish the sentences using information from the text.
   a) After the harvest season _____

   b) Special feasts and meals _____

   c) The good and gentle spirits were not the only ones _____

   d) If you do not open your door on Halloween, _____

   e) The word "Halloween" _____

4. Answer the questions in complete sentences.
   a) What did the Celts look forward to on Samhain?

   b) How did the Celts try to protect themselves from evil spirits?

   c) What do the Jewish holiday of Passover and the Christian Easter have in common?

   d) Why do some people consider Halloween traditions to be childish behaviour?

5. Compare the Celtic festival of Samhain and Halloween today. Find two similarities and two differences. You do not need to write in complete sentences.

Similarities	Differences
▶ _____	▶ _____
▶ _____	▶ _____

Reading Test 7: Scientists say many "good" insects are disappearing

It is common to see many different kinds of insects while spending time outside in the summer. Some of these tiny creatures do not bother people and can even add beauty to the
5 natural environment. Examples of these are insects like ladybugs, butterflies and fireflies. Other insects can harm the environment or humans. Many are known to bite or sting. Some carry dangerous diseases. This group
10 includes insects like mosquitoes, ticks and cockroaches. The population of these insects seems to stay large and healthy. But scientists say this does not appear to be true for some flying insects that serve an important purpose. There is growing evidence that these insects are decreasing across the world. Many of these insects are very important to plant
15 growth and development. They also serve as a necessary link in the food chain and can help break down life when animals die.

One researcher looking into the current insect population is Doug Tallamy, a professor at the University of Delaware. He worries that a continual drop in the number of helpful insects could lead to disastrous results. If the insects
20 disappeared, Earth's important life forms would begin to go away too, Tallamy told the Associated Press. This could result in a total breakdown of the ecosystem. "How much worse can it get than that?" he asked.

Tallamy noted a statement by one of America's best-known biologists, E. O. Wilson of Harvard University. Wilson once called insects "the little things
25 that run the world." Wilson is now 89 years old. He told the AP that he remembers walking through Washington, D.C., in the past when it was "alive with insects, especially butterflies." Now, he said, "the flying insects are virtually gone."

Wilson said this point seemed to be confirmed during a drive he made last
30 year from Boston, Massachusetts, to the neighboring state of Vermont. He was surprised that, during his trip, he counted only one insect that had hit the car's front window. Several other scientists have carried out similar tests by checking how many insects hit their cars while traveling. An insect researcher from the University of Florida, Philip Koehler, reported that far few-
35 er insects hit his vehicle today than in the past.

Scientists say there are likely many reasons for the drop in flying insects. Most are related to the destruction of insect habitat caused by things like insecticides, other animals, pollution and climate change. More studies on insect populations covering large areas still have to be done, but international
40 research that has already been conducted suggests a downward turn. In 2006, a group of studies estimated there had been a 14-percent drop in ladybugs in the United States and Canada from 1987 to 2006. […] In Germany, a 2017 study found an 82-percent drop in the number of flying insects captured in

63 traps across the country, compared to levels recorded in 1990. Researchers say it is difficult to make similar comparisons in other areas. This is because similar insect counts were not done decades ago.

After the German study, other countries also started looking into the problem. Toke Thomas Hoye of Aarhus University in Denmark studied flies in a few areas of rural Greenland. He said he discovered an 80-percent drop in the insects since 1996. David Wagner of the University of Connecticut says other evidence leads him to believe the findings of the 2017 study are "clearly not a German thing." Wagner has measured drops in moth populations in the northeastern United States. "We just have to find out how widespread the phenomenon is," he said.

Adapted from: https://learningenglish.voanews.com/a/scientists-say-many-good-insects-are-disappearing/4589703.html
Bryan Lynn, "Scientists Say Many 'Good Insects' are Disappearing". VOA Learning English (based on reports by the Associated Press and online sources, edited by Ashley Thompson). 7th October 2018.

1. Decide whether the following statements are true, false or not in the text. Tick (✓) the correct box.

	true	false	not in the text
a) Cockroaches do not transmit diseases.	☐	☐	☐
b) Ticks are not in danger of dying out.	☐	☐	☐
c) The bee population is decreasing across the world.	☐	☐	☐
d) A lot of flying insects play an important part in the food chain.	☐	☐	☐
e) There used to be a lot of butterflies in Washington D.C.	☐	☐	☐
f) Finding out how many insects hit the windscreen of a driving vehicle is a new scientific method.	☐	☐	☐

2. What kinds of insects are decreasing according to the text? Give **two** examples.
   ▶ _____
   ▶ _____

3. Name **three** things that contribute to the disappearance of insects.
   ▶ _____
   ▶ _____
   ▶ _____

4. Match the people (a–e) to the statements (A–G) and write the correct letter in the boxes. Use each letter only once.
   Be careful, there are two statements that you do not need.
   a) Doug Tallamy ☐
   b) E. O. Wilson ☐
   c) Philip Koehler ☐
   d) Toke Thomas Hoye ☐
   e) David Wagner ☐

   A My windscreen test showed that the number of insects has decreased.

   B This worrying development is only true for Germany.

   C It would be a catastrophe if the number of beneficial insects steadily continued to drop.

   D In certain parts of USA, the number of moths has decreased.

   E The number of flies in Greenland has decreased significantly.

   F Butterflies have been studied for centuries.

   G I refer to insects as the little things that run the world.

5. Finish the sentences using information from the text.
   a) E. O. Wilson …
      ☐ is professor at the University of Florida.
      ☐ was the first researcher to conduct a "windscreen test".
      ☐ enjoys walking through Washington, D.C.
      ☐ is one of the best known biologists in the USA.

b) According to several studies, the number of ladybugs …
- [ ] decreased significantly in North America in the last decade.
- [ ] has recently dropped by 14 % worldwide.
- [ ] went down notably in the USA and Canada between 1987 and 2006.
- [ ] increased in the USA and Canada by 14 %.

6. Answer the following questions in complete sentences by using the information from the text.

   a) What drastic consequences might the disappearance of insects lead to?

   b) How did the number of insects develop in Germany between 1990 and 2017?

Reading Test 8: How will machines and AI change the future of work?

1 Several recent studies examined how machine automation and artificial intelligence (AI) will change the future of work. Some estimates[1] predict these technologies could displace[2] up to 30 percent of
5 workers worldwide by 2030.

One study was published by PricewaterhouseCoopers, an international company providing financial and tax services. It predicted about 38 percent of American jobs could be at high risk for automation by the early
10 2030s. In Germany, up to 35 percent of jobs could be at risk. The company said about 30 percent could be affected in Britain and 21 percent in Japan. The risk of being displaced will greatly increase for workers with less education, PricewaterhouseCoopers said. It estimated that in Britain, up to 46 percent of workers without a college degree could be at risk due to automation.
15 This would drop to about 12 percent for workers with undergraduate degrees or higher. "New smart machines have the potential to replace our minds and to move around freely in the world," the study said. It added that the greatest job displacement is expected to come in the areas of transportation, storage, manufacturing and retail[3].

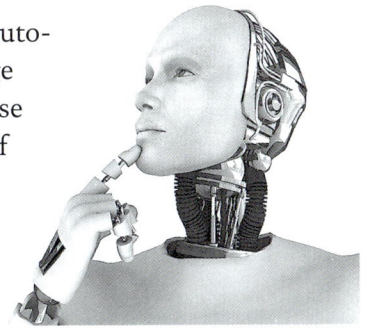

20 The RAND Corporation recently issued its own report on the future effects of automation and AI on jobs and the workplace. Osonde Osoba was a co-author of the report. He noted that fears over machines taking jobs from humans go back centuries. In 16th century England, for example, Queen Elizabeth famously refused an inventor's request for a patent for a device to make ma-
25 terial for clothing. The Queen explained that the device would lead to major job losses, forcing affected workers to become "beggars." Osoba agrees there will be major job disruptions[4] due to AI and automation, especially for lower skilled workers. But he told VOA he believes the future problems have been overestimated without historical evidence to back up the predictions. "It's
30 not so much that the jobs are getting displaced, it's more like tasks are getting displaced and jobs are reconfiguring[5] over time to account for that automation." He added that it will be very difficult for companies to completely automate most jobs, because they require a worker to perform many different duties and to react to unexpected situations.

35 The RAND report identifies three job types that will be very difficult to replace with a machine. These include jobs depending on human motor skills, positions requiring creative thinking and actions, and jobs dealing with intense social interaction.

There are recent examples of companies like Google and Facebook using AI to
40 limit certain kinds of content. Osoba says this can be problematic for machines, which do not understand cultural norms in the population. "So that understanding of cultural norms, or social norms or ethical norms, that's not something that's easy – at least so far we haven't found that easy to program into artificial intelligence."

45 The McKinsey Global Institute, a private think tank, has also studied the issue. Its research suggests that up to one-third of work activities across 46 nations could be displaced by 2030. "All workers will need to adapt, as their occupations evolve[6] alongside increasingly capable machines," the report said. McKinsey says this will require ongoing retraining of workers. In addition,
50 employees will be spending more time on activities difficult to automate. This includes tasks requiring emotional, creative and cognitive skills, the study said.

RAND Corporation's Osonde Osoba agrees. He says workers will increasingly have to be willing and prepared to regularly change jobs and roles to keep
55 up with technology. "If you are thinking about concrete things an individual might do to prepare themselves, I guess being more adaptable, being more flexible, being able to reeducate yourself to fit into a different job." He added that there will be a great need in the future for many more AI developers and researchers. For this reason, he suggests young people interested in these
60 areas start their career paths early to prepare for these high-paying, competitive jobs.

https://learningenglish.voanews.com/a/how-machines-and-artificial-intelligence-will-change-world-of-work/4165671.html

1 estimate – rough calculation
2 (to) displace – to replace, to take the place of
3 retail – selling
4 disruption – disturbance, complication
5 (to) reconfigure – (to) transform
6 (to) evolve – (to) develop

1. Decide whether the following statements are true, false or not in the text. Tick (✓) the correct box.

		true	false	not in the text
a)	Studies confirm that AI and automation will have a significant impact on the world of work.	☐	☐	☐
b)	It is likely that at least 54 percent of British workers with a university degree will be able to keep their jobs.	☐	☐	☐
c)	The fear that machines might take jobs from humans started in the 16th century in England.	☐	☐	☐
d)	Workers will still be needed in order to deal with unforeseen occurrences.	☐	☐	☐

	true	false	not in the text

e) Social networking sites and search engines are already using AI. ☐ ☐ ☐

f) AI developers and researchers will not be in high demand in the future. ☐ ☐ ☐

2. Finish the sentences using the information from the text.
   Tick (✓) the correct statement. Only one option is correct.

   a) According to current reports, …
      ☐ machines might replace about a third of all workers globally.
      ☐ automation particularly affects the finance sector.
      ☐ no one can predict the effects of AI and automation.
      ☐ technological innovation will create about 30 % more jobs.

   b) According to one study, …
      ☐ technological changes will affect Germany the most.
      ☐ fewer jobs are in danger in Japan than in the U.S.
      ☐ the potential for automation is lowest in Britain.
      ☐ Germany and the USA can expect a job boom.

   c) In future, lower-skilled workers will …
      ☐ have more or less the same job chances as college graduates.
      ☐ face a high risk of being unemployed.
      ☐ above all be needed in manufacturing and logistics.
      ☐ be forced to move to other countries to find work.

   d) Osonde Osoba thinks that …
      ☐ new technologies have always led to massive job losses.
      ☐ automation will create a new generation of beggars.
      ☐ more inventions and patents are needed.
      ☐ the effects of automation might not be as bad as we think.

   e) Automation will make …
      ☐ certain tasks unnecessary.
      ☐ whole branches of the economy disappear.
      ☐ more companies move to other countries.
      ☐ workers more satisfied than before.

f) According to Osoba, machines …
- [ ] allow people to do several tasks at the same time.
- [ ] won't replace jobs that require creativity and social skills.
- [ ] can react to unforeseen problems more easily than human workers.
- [ ] are absolutely vital for the car industry.

g) Osoba sees Google's and Facebook's use of AI to limit content …
- [ ] as an attempt to control the population.
- [ ] as proof that AI can beat human intelligence.
- [ ] as an example of the limits of artificial intelligence.
- [ ] as a violation of social norms.

h) In future, workers will have to …
- [ ] go back to university.
- [ ] become more and more productive.
- [ ] keep learning and deal with changing job requirements.
- [ ] look for jobs in the service sector.

3. What advice can young people extract from this article to be well-prepared for the changing world of work?
Refer to at least three aspects mentioned in the text.

▶ _____

▶ _____

▶ _____

4. Answer the following questions in complete sentences by using the information from the text.

a) In which way will the world of work have changed by the early 2030s?

_____
_____
_____

b) Which areas are most likely to be affected by automation?

_____
_____
_____

3 Use of Language

Der Bereich „Use of Language" bezieht sich auf die grundlegenden Fertigkeiten „**Wortschatz**" und „**Grammatik**". Ein reichhaltiger Wortschatz und sichere Grammatikkenntnisse sind nicht nur für Aufgaben in Tests und Prüfungen nötig, in denen gezielt nach diesen Bereichen gefragt wird. Sie sind auch die **Basis für** das **Lese- und Hörverstehen** und natürlich auch für die Aufgaben in den Bereichen **Schreiben**, **Sprachmittlung** und **Sprechen**. Ganz gleich, auf welchem Weg du dich in einer Sprache verständigen möchtest – ob du jemandem zuhörst oder etwas liest bzw. selbst sprichst oder etwas schreibst –, es ist immer wichtig, dass du die verwendeten Wörter und Satzkonstruktionen verstehst und selbst anwenden kannst. Wenn du beispielsweise die Zeitformen nicht beherrschst, wird es dir recht schwerfallen, einer Person begreiflich zu machen, ob das, was du ihr sagst, vergangen ist, jetzt stattfindet oder erst morgen oder übermorgen stattfinden wird. Beim Wortschatz ist es nicht nur wichtig, dass du viele Wörter kennst (z. B. zum Thema „Schule" oder „Freizeit"), es geht auch darum, dass du Verbindungen herstellen kannst und beispielsweise Wörter erkennst, die eine ähnliche Bedeutung haben („synonyms"). So funktionieren nämlich auch Prüfungsaufgaben zum Lese- oder Hörverstehen, denn in der Aufgabenstellung werden meist nicht genau dieselben Wörter wie im Text verwendet, sondern Synonyme oder Umschreibungen. Wenn du diese gleich erkennst, fällt es dir leichter, die passenden Textstellen – und die Antworten dazu – zu finden. In der Abschlussprüfung gibt es ebenfalls den Bereich „Use of Language", in dem du Aufgaben zum Wortschatz und zur Grammatik bearbeiten musst. Wie du dich darauf vorbereiten kannst und welche Aufgabenformen dich erwarten, wird auf den nächsten Seiten erklärt. Danach folgen einige Aufgaben zum Grundwissen (Kapitel 3.3) und schließlich kannst du dein Können in prüfungsähnlichen Aufgaben erproben (Kapitel 3.4).

3.1 Strategien zum Bereich „Use of Language"

Um in den Bereichen „Vocabulary" und „Grammar" fit für die Prüfung zu werden, gibt es verschiedene Tipps und Tricks.

Strategien zur Grammatik

Zu Beginn dieses Buches findest du eine **Kurzgrammatik** mit einer Übersicht über die wichtigsten Strukturen der englischen Grammatik. Zu einigen Themen, mit denen erfahrungsgemäß viele Lernende Schwierigkeiten haben, gibt es zusätzlich Lernvideos ▶.

Lernvideos

Mithilfe der Kurzgrammatik kannst du dir besonders die Bereiche noch einmal ins Gedächtnis rufen, die für Klassenarbeiten und die Abschlussprüfung relevant sind. Du kannst auf unterschiedliche Weise damit arbeiten:

Use of Language

Grammatik – Methode 1

Wenn du das Gefühl hast, dass du dich schon ganz gut in der englischen Grammatik auskennst, kannst du die Regeln und Beispiele erst einmal überspringen. Sollten dir dann beim Lösen der Aufgaben Fragen zur Grammatik einfallen, kannst du gezielt in der Kurzgrammatik Erklärungen und Beispiele zu einzelnen Strukturen nachschlagen. Damit du dich leicht zurechtfindest, sind die Bezeichnungen der grammatischen Strukturen in den Aufgabenstellungen **fett** gedruckt.

Grammatik – Methode 2

Vielleicht weißt du aber schon, dass du noch den einen oder anderen Schwachpunkt im Bereich Grammatik hast. Dann liest du dir am besten alle Erklärungen und Beispiele in der Kurzgrammatik sorgfältig durch. Überlege dir zu jedem Beispiel ein eigenes Beispiel. Präge dir auch das Beispiel zu den Regeln ein. Wenn du eine Regel mit einem bestimmten Beispiel verknüpfen kannst, fällt es dir vielleicht leichter, dir die Regel zu merken. Markiere gleich beim Lesen der Grammatik die Bereiche, die du noch intensiver üben möchtest. Unter Punkt 3.3 findest du Aufgaben, die sich auf die Kurzgrammatik beziehen.

Grammatik – Methode 3

Sieh dir Texte, die du in Klassenarbeiten oder als Hausaufgabe geschrieben hast und die deine Lehrerin oder dein Lehrer korrigiert hat, einmal nur im Hinblick auf Grammatik an. Oft sind Grammatikfehler z. B. mit der Abkürzung „Gr" markiert. Erkennst du Bereiche, in denen du noch Probleme hast? Frage nach, wenn du dir nicht sicher bist, bei welchen Strukturen du Fehler gemacht hast. Schlage diese Strukturen in der Kurzgrammatik nach und mache die passenden Übungen dazu.

Grammatik – Methode 4

Vielleicht findest du, dass Grammatik lernen und üben nicht sehr interessant ist. Hast du schon einmal ausprobiert, selbst eine Grammatikübung zu erstellen? Suche dir einen englischen Text zu einem Thema aus, das du besonders spannend oder interessant findest (z. B. aus dem Bereich Leseverstehen in diesem Buch oder einen Text, den ihr im Unterricht besprochen habt). Mache dir eine Kopie und lösche alle Verben. Zu den Lücken schreibst du nur die Grundform auf (z. B. „wrote" → „to write") und schon hast du eine Übung, mit der du Verbformen in allen Zeiten üben kannst. Und gleichzeitig beschäftigst du dich mit einem Thema, das dich interessiert. So kannst du Grammatik auch einmal ganz nebenbei üben.

Strategien zum Wortschatz

Lernvideo

Um im Bereich „Vocabulary" gut abzuschneiden, ist es wichtig, dass du langfristig und nachhaltig übst. Vokabeln zu lernen klingt nicht gerade spannend, für den Erwerb einer Fremdsprache ist es aber unerlässlich. Und es liegt an dir, kreativ zu sein und eine Methode zu finden, die zu dir passt und vielleicht sogar ein bisschen Spaß macht. Je größer dein aktiver Wortschatz ist, je mehr Wörter du also in der Fremdsprache kennst und selbst in Gesprächen oder beim Schreiben anwenden kannst, desto treffender und abwechslungsreicher kannst du dich in der Fremdsprache ausdrücken. Um den aktiven Wortschatz zu vergrößern, gibt es verschiedene Methoden. Sieh dir am besten das Lernvideo ▶ zum effektiven Vokabellernen an und lies dir die folgenden Seiten gut durch.

Natürlich ist zunächst einmal das **Vokabelheft** zu erwähnen. Du weißt, wie es funktioniert: Richte dir auf jeder Doppelseite **drei Spalten** ein: eine für den englischen Begriff, eine für die deutsche Bedeutung und eine, in der du den Ausdruck in einem Beispielsatz verwendest. Zum Lernen deckst du dann jeweils eine Spalte ab.

Wortschatz – Methode 1

Wesentlich effektiver ist es, die Vokabeln mit einem **Karteisystem** zu lernen. Falls du gerne am Computer oder mit dem Smartphone arbeitest, findest du viele Programme/Apps, die dich dabei unterstützen. Du kannst die Vokabeln aber natürlich auch auf Papierkärtchen notieren. Schreibe den englischen Begriff auf die Vorderseite der Karte. Notiere dazu auch einen englischen Satz, in dem die Vokabel vorkommt. So lernst du gleich die Verwendung des Wortes mit. Notiere auch sonst alles, was zu dem Begriff gehört. Bei Verben solltest du z. B. nicht nur den Infinitiv, sondern ggf. auch unregelmäßige Formen oder die Präposition, die das Verb nach sich zieht, ergänzen. Auf der Rückseite der Karteikarte schreibst du die deutsche Bedeutung der Vokabel auf.
Die Karteikartenmethode hat im Vergleich zum Vokabelheft **Vorteile**:

Wortschatz – Methode 2

▶ Du kannst die Karteikarten drei Stapeln zuordnen.
   Stapel 1: **Wörter, die neu für dich sind.** Diese Wörter solltest du mindestens jeden zweiten Tag durchgehen. Lies dabei auch immer den englischen Satz durch, den du auf der Karteikarte notiert hast. Manchmal ist es leichter, sich ein Wort im Satzzusammenhang zu merken als als einzelne Vokabel. Sobald du die neue Vokabel kennst, legst du sie auf Stapel 2 ab.
   Stapel 2: **Wörter, die du noch nicht so sicher im Kopf hast.** Diesen Stapel solltest du regelmäßig durchgehen und dabei die Vokabeln üben. Wenn du eine Vokabel sicher weißt, legst du sie auf Stapel 3 ab.
   Stapel 3: **Wörter, die du schon sehr gut beherrschst.** Diesen Stapel solltest du hin und wieder einmal durchblättern, um zu sehen, ob du alle Vokabeln noch richtig beherrschst.
   Eine App erkennt in der Regel selbst, welche Wörter du schon gut beherrschst und welche du noch üben musst. Sie unterstützt dich dabei, die schwierigen Wörter in regelmäßigen Abständen zu wiederholen.

▶ Bei einem System aus Papier bist du dafür etwas freier bei der Zusammenstellung der Wörter. Du kannst die Karteikarten je nach augenblicklicher Lernsituation nach **Wortfeldern** (z. B. *weather – wind, to rain, hot*) oder nach **Wortfamilien** (z. B. *business, businessman, businesswoman, busy*) ordnen. Dabei bist du sehr flexibel und kannst die Wortfelder bzw. Wortfamilien jederzeit erweitern bzw. umbauen.
   Egal ob mit dem Smartphone oder auf Papierkärtchen, ein paar Vokabeln kannst du bestimmt auch einfach zwischendurch – z. B. auf dem Weg zur Schule oder ins Kino – wiederholen.

Bei beiden Methoden, Vokabelheft oder Karteisystem, solltest du dir auch sinnvolle Ergänzungen zu den Vokabeln überlegen. Manchmal kann dir ein **Bild** dabei helfen, dir ein Wort oder eine Wendung besser zu merken. Füge also Zeichnungen oder Fotos hinzu. Denke auch an die **Aussprache** und sage die Wörter beim Lernen am besten laut vor dich hin. Wenn du dir unsicher bist, kannst du dir in einem Online-Wörterbuch (z. B. „LEO") die richtige Aussprache anhören.

| Use of Language

Wortschatz – Methode 3

Du kannst natürlich auch kreativ sein und dir deine **eigene Methode** zum Vokabellernen **ausdenken**. Das macht viel Spaß und bringt langfristig gesehen sicherlich den besten Lernerfolg.

Je intensiver du dich mit dem Wortschatz beschäftigst, desto besser kannst du ihn dir einprägen und desto schneller hast du auch die passenden Wendungen parat, wenn du etwas sagen oder schreiben möchtest.

▶ Zeichne dir **Mindmaps** zu gelernten Vokabeln. Du kannst sie – auch hier wieder abhängig von deiner augenblicklichen Lernsituation – nach Wortfeldern oder Wortfamilien zusammenstellen. Diese Mindmaps kannst du an zentralen Stellen in deinem Zimmer aufhängen. Jedes Mal, wenn du daran vorbeikommst, gehst du die entsprechenden Vokabeln im Kopf durch.

Beispiel

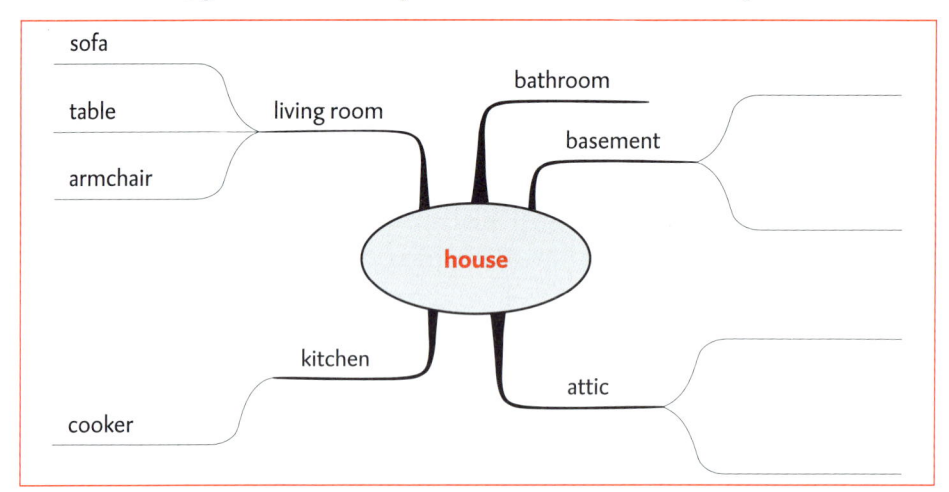

```
       sofa                                    bathroom
       table        living room
                                               basement
       armchair
                              ( house )
                    kitchen                    attic
       cooker
```

▶ Jedes Mal, wenn du eine neue Vokabel gelernt hast, schreibst du den **Begriff auf einen Zettel** und befestigst ihn am entsprechenden Gegenstand bei dir zu Hause. So klebst du beispielsweise einen Zettel mit dem Begriff „cupboard" an euren Küchenschrank. Das funktioniert zum Teil auch mit abstrakten Begriffen: Die Vokabel „proud" könntest du z. B. an das Regalfach heften, in dem deine Schulsachen sind. Denn sicherlich bist du „stolz" darauf, dass du in der Schule schon so weit gekommen bist, oder? Mit dieser „Zettelmethode" kannst du neue Vokabeln jedenfalls ganz einfach „im Vorbeigehen", trainieren.

▶ Du kannst auch deiner Fantasie freien Lauf lassen und dir eine Methode überlegen, die dir gefällt, selbst wenn sie ein bisschen verrückt ist – z. B. ein Video mit dem Smartphone zu Wörtern für „feelings" drehen oder eine Collage mit Ausschnitten aus Filmplakaten erstellen, zu denen du Verben schreibst, die die „Action" beschreiben ... Es liegt ganz bei dir.

Versuche grundsätzlich immer wieder, die neuen **Vokabeln anzuwenden**, am besten in vollständigen englischen Sätzen. Wenn du dich mit deinen Mitschülerinnen und Mitschülern unterhältst, könnt ihr daraus vielleicht ein richtiges Spiel machen.

Welche Methode du auch anwendest oder mit anderen Strategien kombinierst, lerne nie zu viele Vokabeln auf einmal! Am besten ist es, wenn du neue Vokabeln **in kleinen Gruppen** von sechs bis sieben Wörtern lernst. Lies sie dir zunächst ein paar Mal durch, wiederhole sie laut und lege sie dann für etwa 20 Minuten zur Seite. Dann fängst du von vorne an. Diese **Pausen** sind wichtig, damit sich das gerade Gelernte „setzen" kann. So wird es dir ein Leichtes sein, bald einen großen englischen Wortschatz anzusammeln.

> - Nutze Hilfsmittel wie eine Schulgrammatik oder die Kurzgrammatik in diesem Band. Schlage nach, wenn du Fragen zur Grammatik hast.
> - Beobachte deine Ergebnisse beim Schreiben kontinuierlich und übe Grammatikbereiche, die dir schwerfallen.
> - Lerne langfristig. In der Fremdsprache einen großen aktiven Wortschatz zu haben, ist sehr wichtig.
> - Lege ein Vokabelheft an oder arbeite mit einem Karteisystem. Lerne die Vokabeln im Satzzusammenhang.
> - Lerne deine Vokabeln immer in Sechser- oder Siebenergruppen. Mache zwischen deinen Lerneinheiten regelmäßig kleine Pausen, damit dein Gehirn das Gelernte verarbeiten kann.
> - Trainiere beim Lernen auch die Aussprache.
> - Sei kreativ beim Grammatik- und Vokabellernen: Zeichne Mindmaps, beschrifte Gegenstände in deinem Zimmer, mache deinen eigenen Lückentext …

Tipp

3.2 Häufige Aufgabenstellungen zum Bereich „Use of Language"

In den Übungsaufgaben in diesem Buch findest du im Kapitel 3.3 verschiedene **Aufgaben zum Grundwissen** – sowohl zur Grammatik als auch zum Wortschatz. Hier kannst du wichtige Bereiche der englischen Sprache noch einmal ganz **gezielt üben**, bevor du mit den prüfungsähnlichen Aufgaben zum Bereich „Use of Language" (Kapitel 3.4) weitermachst. Einige Aufgabenformen kennst du vielleicht schon aus dem Unterricht. Solltest du unsicher sein, was bei welcher Aufgabenform zu tun ist, liest du dir am besten die Erklärungen und Beispiele auf den folgenden Seiten aufmerksam durch.

In Prüfungen, Klassenarbeiten und Tests werden in der Regel keine einzelnen Grammatikformen mehr geprüft. Hier gibt es häufig gemischte Aufgaben mit verschiedenen Strukturen. Solche Übungen findest du auch am Ende der Grammatikübungen zum Grundwissen.

In Kapitel 3.4 kannst du dann anhand der prüfungsähnlichen Aufgaben für den „Ernstfall" trainieren.

Der Prüfungsteil „Use of Language" in deiner Abschlussprüfung beginnt mit Aufgaben, die sich auf den Lesetext beziehen und vor allem deine Wortschatzkenntnisse abprüfen. Auch in Tests und Klassenarbeiten werden dir diese und andere Aufgabentypen oft begegnen:

Find the synonyms.

Synonyme sind **Wörter, die** in etwa **das Gleiche bedeuten** wie das Ausgangswort. In der Prüfung lautet die Aufgabenstellung daher auch oft „Find words or expressions in the text that mean more or less the same". Normalerweise wird ein Textabschnitt angegeben, in dem du nach dem Synonym suchen sollst.

Beispiel

Text:	Many young people think that living in another culture for some time will give them the opportunity to learn something about themselves.
Task:	Find a word or expression in the text that means more or less the same: chance
Answer:	_opportunity_

Find the opposites.

Mit einer Aufgabenformulierung wie „Find the opposites" wirst du aufgefordert, die **Gegenbedeutung** zu mehreren vorgegebenen Wörtern zu finden. In der Prüfung wird dir meist die exakte Zeile angegeben, in der du das jeweilige Wort finden kannst. Lies dir immer den gesamten Satz durch und überlege, welche Bedeutung das Wort in diesem Zusammenhang hat. Genau zu dieser Bedeutung überlegst du dir dann das passende Gegenteil.

Beispiel

Text:	Many young people decide to spend a gap year abroad after finishing school …
Task:	Find an opposite in the text: **young** (Z. 1)
Answer:	_old_

Explain … / Give definitions.

Manchmal sollst du ein Wort oder mehrere **vorgegebene Wörter** in mindestens einem vollständigen Satz **erklären**, wobei dir dabei in der Regel eine Wahlmöglichkeit eingeräumt wird. Aus deiner Erklärung muss die Bedeutung des jeweiligen Wortes eindeutig hervorgehen. Verwende darin keine Wörter aus derselben Wortfamilie.

Beispiel

Text:	One environmental problem that particularly affects countries in northern Africa is desertification. Huge areas of land which were once used for farming or as pasture for cows or sheep are now deserts. For miles and miles all you can see are sand and stones.
Task:	Explain the following word in a complete sentence: **desert** (Z. 3)
Answer:	_A desert is a large area of land that has very little water and very few plants in it._

Auf die Aufgaben mit Bezug zum Lesetext folgen in der Prüfung noch ein **Lückentext** sowie weitere Aufgaben, die unabhängig vom Lesetext bearbeitet werden können. In diesem Abschnitt geht es um **Vokabeln und Grammatik**. Es werden nicht nur dein Wortschatz und deine Fähigkeit, mit dem Wortschatz umzugehen, geprüft, sondern auch deine Kenntnisse im Bereich der Grammatik.

Use of Language

Complete the text by using suitable forms of the words.

Oft musst du bei diesen Aufgabentypen **Wörter derselben Wortfamilie finden**. Ist eine Lücke mit einem Verb zu füllen, so sollst du entscheiden, in welcher Zeit das Verb steht und ob es sich um eine Aktiv- oder Passivform handelt. Darüber hinaus musst du andere **grammatische Formen** wie *if*-Sätze erkennen und die entsprechende Verbform bilden. Die Wörter, die du zu bearbeiten hast, stehen dabei in der Regel am Ende der Zeilen. Manchmal kann statt eines Wortes auch ein „?" stehen, für das du dann eigenständig ein geeignetes Wort finden und einsetzen sollst. Bei manchen Lücken sollst du aus zwei oder drei Möglichkeiten das passende Wort auswählen.

Beispiele

More than a century ago, in 1885, when people … that it was necessary to … plants and animals, the history of Canada's … parks started with the creation of Banff National Park. Today, Canada has got more … 40 national parks and park reserves, which vary from between 9 km² and 45,000 km² in size. Some … the … activities are watching wildlife, hiking, mountain biking, horseback riding, climbing, etc.	a) to realise b) protection c) nation d) ? e) of / off / from f) popularity

a) _realised_
b) _protect_
c) _national_
d) _than_
e) _of_
f) _most popular_

Natürlich können dir in Klassenarbeiten und Tests auch Lückentexte begegnen, in denen nur Wortschatz oder nur verschiedene grammatische Strukturen eingesetzt werden müssen.

Ask questions.

Lies dir bei dieser Aufgabe die Situationsbeschreibung ganz genau durch, denn sie gibt dir wichtige Informationen darüber, was du inhaltlich fragen könntest. Achte darauf, dass du die geforderte Zahl von Fragen formulierst. Die Anweisung „Use different question forms" bedeutet, dass sich die Fragen unterscheiden müssen, was die Zeitformen und die Art der Fragesätze betrifft. So solltest du sowohl Entscheidungsfragen (siehe Frage 1) als auch Fragen mit verschiedenen Fragewörtern stellen.

Beispiele

▶ Did you like it in the USA?
▶ Where did you start your journey?
▶ How have you been since you came back?

Hinweis: Auf eine Frage wie "Where did you travel?" würdest du keinen Punkt erhalten, da hier das gleiche Fragewort und die gleiche Zeitform wie in der zweiten Frage verwendet werden.

Use of Language

Paraphrasing

Bei dieser Aufgabe sollst du **Sätze** mithilfe eines vorgegebenen Schlüsselbegriffs **umformulieren**. Dabei werden dir jeweils zwei Sätze und ein „key word" in Klammern vorgegeben. Der zweite Satz enthält eine Lücke. Deine Aufgabe besteht darin, den zweiten Satz so zu vervollständigen, dass er dieselbe Bedeutung hat wie der vorgegebene erste Satz. Dabei musst du das „key word" verwenden, darfst es aber nicht verändern. Außerdem darf deine Lösung (inklusive „key word") in der Regel nicht kürzer als zwei und nicht länger als fünf Wörter sein.

Beispiel

Task:	Complete the second sentence so that it means the same as the first sentence. Use between two and five words including the word in brackets.
	As most young South Africans have grown up after the end of apartheid, they consider it normal to be living in a democratic society.
Solution:	(**Having**) _Having grown up_ after the end of apartheid, most young South Africans consider it normal to be living in a democratic society.

3.3 Übungsaufgaben zum Grundwissen

Grammatik

1. **Prepositions** – Look at the picture and choose the right prepositions to complete the sentences. You can use each preposition only once.

   inside – in front of – beside – between – at – under – outside – behind – on

   a) The family is sitting _____ their tent, _____ their car.

   b) Everybody is _____; there is no one _____ the tent.

   c) There is a tree _____ the car.

   d) The little girl is sitting _____ her sister and brother.

   e) There's lots of food _____ the table and a bowl of water _____ the table.

   f) The father is looking _____ the dog.

2. **Prepositions** – Fill in the prepositions in the following short texts.
   a) I got a letter _____ my brother today. He put the wrong stamps _____ the letter. As no one was _____ home when the postman came, he left a note _____ the front door. I had to go _____ the post office and pick _____ the letter myself. I had to pay 50 p _____ the extra postage.

   b) It happened _____ 31st October, _____ about nine o'clock _____ the evening. Amy had been waiting _____ her boyfriend _____ what seemed like hours. He had said he'd be there _____ six at the latest. She was just about to go back home, when he suddenly appeared right _____ her. Of course she was scared – but what else should you be _____ Halloween?

3. **Conjunctions/linking words** – Complete the following texts using the words from the box. There are two conjunctions you do not need.

   > after – although – and – as – as long as – as soon as – before (2×) – both … and – but – if – or – while

   a) _____ James McAlister has finished school, he is going to _____ apply for an internship with the American company Open Access Music Library _____ take a job with the Scottish firm UnlimitedAccess.co.uk. _____ he is in Scotland, he will be able to work with the American company online, _____ he will have to fly to the States to present himself _____ he can start to work for them.

   b) _____ Caroline's mother is a journalist, that is the last thing Caroline wants to become! _____ finishing school, Caroline is going to study medicine in London, _____ then she hopes she will be able to get some practical experience working in America _____ Canada. _____ still at school she has been doing some voluntary work at a hospital near her home. _____ she can study medicine, though, she really needs to study hard for her A-levels.

4. **Modal auxiliaries** – A school trip to London
   a) Mrs Smith is talking about a visit to London as a final trip before everyone leaves school.
   Complete what she says with a modal auxiliary from the box. You can use each item only once.

   > must – have to – can – can't – needn't

Use of Language

> We _____ fly or go by train, but we _____ go during your exams – that's clear – so we'll go on 26th July for a week. If you want to go to London, you _____ return the form to me by Monday. You _____ bring any money until next week – I'm not collecting it before then. But don't forget, I _____ _____ have the forms on Monday.

b) The class representative has sent Mrs Smith an e-mail about the London visit. Choose the correct modal auxiliary to complete the sentences.

I **1** find my form. **2** I have a new one, please? I think most people **3** come. Jenny **4** have a problem, though. Her parents say that she **5** pass her exams if she wants them to pay. She **6** afford the trip if her parents don't pay. Thomas says he **7** ask his parents' permission because he **8** go on every school trip. When we go to London, **9** we visit Madame Tussauds? Everyone **10** like to go there. Another suggestion is that we **11** have a party in Regent's Park on our last night. We **12** do that, won't we? I know that we **13** drink alcohol on a school trip, but we **14** have a barbecue and then we **15** have lots of fun together for the last time.

#			
1	☐ had to	☐ can't	☐ won't
2	☐ May	☐ Need	☐ Am allowed to
3	☐ needn't	☐ have to	☐ will be able to
4	☐ was allowed to	☐ must	☐ might
5	☐ has to	☐ will	☐ might
6	☐ shouldn't	☐ can't	☐ can
7	☐ mustn't	☐ needn't	☐ should
8	☐ is allowed to	☐ couldn't	☐ doesn't have to
9	☐ must	☐ could	☐ needn't
10	☐ will	☐ would	☐ has to
11	☐ may	☐ are able to	☐ should
12	☐ are able to	☐ will be allowed to	☐ could
13	☐ needn't	☐ shouldn't have	☐ mustn't
14	☐ could	☐ need	☐ mustn't
15	☐ may	☐ would	☐ have to

5. **Tenses** – Look at the photograph. Then complete the sentences using the "**present progressive**".

   a) The man in the van _____ (verkaufen) ice creams.

   b) The ice-cream man _____ (schauen) out of the side window.

   c) Another man _____ (stehen) behind the ice-cream van.

   d) The man behind the ice-cream van _____ (anrufen) a friend.

   e) No one _____ (kaufen) an ice cream.

   f) The ice-cream man _____ (warten) for customers.

6. **Tenses** – "**simple present**" or "**present progressive**"?
   First underline any signal words you can find in the sentences.
   Then fill in the correct verb form.

   a) Karen always _____ (zu Fuß gehen) to school.

   b) She _____ (tragen) her large school bag now.

   c) Karen and her family _____ (fliegen) to England this year.
   Normally, they _____ (fahren) there.

   d) Karen's dad _____ (arbeiten) on his computer at the moment. When he is busy he never _____ (sprechen) to anybody.

Use of Language

Present perfect or Simple past?

7. **Tenses (signal words)** – Below are signal words for the "**simple past**" and the "**present perfect**". Put the signal words with the correct tense.

already – ever – five years ago – for three weeks – in 2010 – how long – just – last month – last week – not … yet – since May – yesterday

simple past	present perfect

Since or For?

8. **Tenses (signal words)** – Which words or expressions take "since" and which ones take "for"?

   _____ 2012   _____ my birthday
   _____ six days   _____ Easter
   _____ last weekend   _____ a long time
   _____ three hours   _____ many years
   _____ last summer   _____ seven days

9. **Tenses** – "**simple past**" or "**past perfect**"?
   Put the verbs into the correct tenses.

   a) After Ellis Island _____ (serve) as a fort and execution site it _____ (become) an immigration center in 1892.

   b) It was there that doctors and officials _____ (decide) the futures of all those who _____ (leave) Europe in the hope of a new life in America.

   c) After they _____ (pass) through the baggage room, the newcomers _____ (climb) the long stairs up to the Great Hall.

   d) Once the doctors _____ (examine) everybody, officials _____ (come) and _____ (question) them.

   e) When they _____ (give) the right answers, they _____ (start) to explore the New World.

10. **Mixed tenses** – Ruby is keeping a blog about her first journey abroad. Fill in each gap with the correct tense – do not use the future.

Ruby's diary

July 3rd

We _____ (travel) all day and arrived in Dover just in time for the ferry. We _____ _____ (plan) to sleep on the ferry but it _____ (not be) really possible. We _____ _____ (get off) at Calais at about 3 o'clock this morning. Now we have to _____ (wait) here in the ferry terminal for a few hours. Our bus _____ (not leave) until 6 o'clock.

June 17th

Someone _____ (tell) me a few days ago to buy a rail card. I _____ (look) on the internet last night and I _____ (discover) it _____ (cost) £ 250 but it _____ (mean) we can _____ (travel) by train anywhere in Europe for a month – and _____ (sleep) on the trains overnight, too.

June 15th

Tina and I _____ (buy) lots of things for our trip; I hope we can carry everything. Tina _____ (not have) a lot of money so we're going to camp. We _____ _____ (borrow) a tent and two rucksacks last weekend from my parents. But I _____ (not know) which clothes to take with me.

June 1st

I _____ (live) in my student flat since September. I _____ (meet) a lot of people and I now _____ (have) many new friends. I _____ (ask) Tina yesterday if she wanted to come with me to the Continent in the summer holidays. She _____ (say) she'd love to come.

Hi, I'm Ruby. I ♥ animals, Thai food and yoga. I didn't travel a lot in the past, but I'm about to explore the world. Find out more.

email me!

find me on:
twitter
facebook

blog archive
May 2nd
April 25
April 3rd
March 19
March 15
February 14
older posts

12 comments

Use of Language

Talking about the Future

11. **Future tenses** – Use the "will-future", the "going-to-future", the "simple present" or the "present progressive" to complete the sentences.

    a) We _____ (go) to Hawaii next summer. We've already booked the tickets.

    b) Kimmy: "Oh no, look at the mess I've made in the kitchen!"
       Dani: "No problem. I _____ (help) you clean."

    c) The bus _____ (leave) at 9.21 a.m.

    d) Bailey _____ (turn) 18 next month.

    e) Look at the sky – there _____ (be) a thunderstorm!

    f) Noah and Sam _____ (meet) at the pub at 5 o'clock. Noah has booked a table at the King's Head.

    g) The film _____ (start) at 8.15 at the Royal Cinema and at 8.45 at the Rex. Where do you want to go?

    h) I'm looking forward to my birthday, because I _____ (have) a party. I haven't organised anything yet, though.

    i) At the moment, I don't earn much, but I hope I _____ (get) a promotion soon.

Active and Passive Voice

12. **Passive voice** – Choose the correct verb form for each gap.

    Ellie's flat __1__ sometime next week. Many things still __2__ before then. A lot of help __3__ to her by her friends already. The furniture __4__, but her pictures __5__ the walls later. The flat looks like it __6__ many years ago. It __7__ to Ellie last year by her parents, but until now she has never had enough money to paint the walls. The living room floor __8__ soon so that paint doesn't drip onto it. Once that __9__, Ellie's going to stay with her parents until the painting __10__.

1	☐ is decorated	☐ will be decorated	☐ has been decorated
2	☐ would be done	☐ have been done	☐ have to be done
3	☐ will be given	☐ is given	☐ has been given
4	☐ has been moved	☐ will be moved	☐ is moved
5	☐ was taken off	☐ are taken off	☐ will be taken off
6	☐ would be painted	☐ was last painted	☐ will be painted
7	☐ is given	☐ has been given	☐ was given
8	☐ will be covered up	☐ was covered up	☐ has been covered up
9	☐ has been done	☐ will be done	☐ had been done
10	☐ had been completed	☐ has been completed	☐ was completed

13. **Passive voice** – Put the verbs into the passive.
    a) English _____ (speak) all over the world.
    b) Last week a new crew _____ (send) up to the ISS.
    c) Up to now Atlantis _____ (not discover).
    d) The door should always _____ (lock).

14. **Infinitive or gerund?** – Read the information about three courses that are on offer at an activity centre. Fill in the gaps with either the "-ing-form" or the "to-infinitive". Add a preposition where necessary.

    1 _____ (climb) is a good sport, but you have _____ (be) fit. If you want to learn _____ (climb), it's probably best to start _____ (do) it on a climbing wall. There is no chance _____ (fall) very far because you'll have a rope _____ (stop) you from _____ (do) that. After _____ (learn, climb) on our wall we'll take you to a real mountain. We look forward _____ (see) you on our course.

    2 _____ (windsurf) is fun. On our courses we'll show you how to windsurf from the very beginning – you just shouldn't be afraid _____ (get) wet. Before _____ (go) onto the lake you'll learn how _____ (control) the windsurfer on the land. In this way, you'll avoid _____ (spend) many hours in the lake trying to pull yourself back onto the windsurfer.

    3 Have you ever been on a horse? _____ (ride – horse) is a very nice way _____ (see) the countryside. Our horses are friendly and there's very little danger _____ (have) an accident with one. You'll never forget _____ (get) onto a horse for the first time.

Use of Language

15. **Question words** – Read the advert and the answers to the questions carefully. Then write the questions.

    a) _____?
    The advert is for a party night.

    b) _____?
    There are three bands playing.

    c) _____?
    The party is in the Old Factory.

    d) _____?
    It starts at half past seven.

    e) _____?
    It costs £ 7.50.

    f) _____?
    Because the last bus leaves at 3.00 a.m.

PARTY NIGHT
Bands: Level Two, Big Feet, Loud 26

Area 1: HipHop – RnB
Area 2: Electro – House

**The Old Factory
Queen Street
Birmingham**

7.30 p.m. – 3.00 a.m.
Tickets: £ 7.50

Tel: 0876 /78465
e-mail: partynight@birmingham.co.uk
Buses to city centre every 30 mins.
Last bus 3.00 a.m.

16. **Conditional sentences** – Complete the gaps in the conditional sentences.

To...: amelia16@meyers.co.uk
Cc...:
Subject: theatre visit

Hi Amelia,
If I had more time, I _____ (write) a much longer e-mail to you. But I haven't, so this will be a short message. If you want a longer one, you _____ (have) to wait until next week!
I was in London last week, as you know. If you _____ (be) there, we could have gone to the theatre together. But that's why I'm writing. If you have time, _____ (you – want) to come to the theatre with me next weekend? I noticed two or three more shows that I would love to see. Would you be interested in going if I _____ (get) tickets? If you _____ (be), phone me tomorrow evening – I can book them online.
Oh, I almost forgot. Maxime _____ (come) with me last week if he hadn't had to fly to Paris to meet his mum ... but he wants to come with us next time if you _____ (not mind).
I _____ (send) you the theatre details if you would like to see what's on.
Love, Sam

Reported speech

17. **Reported speech** – Write the following sentences in reported speech.

    a) He says, "I want to listen to the radio because my favourite group are in concert today."

    He says that ...

    b) She told us, "I think the book was better than the film."

    c) He said, "Yesterday we lost the football match. We played badly."

    d) The man explained, "I was here when the accident happened. It was no one's fault."

18. **Reported speech** – Two people tell you about one of their favourite objects. Write what they say in reported speech. In the first part of the exercise the words you need to change are underlined to help you.
    Underline the words in the second part that need changing before you start.

    a) George said, "<u>This</u> <u>is</u> the only trophy <u>I</u> <u>have</u> ever won.
    <u>I</u> <u>don't</u> need another reason to keep it, <u>do</u> <u>I</u>?
    It <u>sits</u> on a shelf and sometimes <u>I</u> <u>show</u> people <u>my</u> greatest sporting award."

    George said that ...

    b) Katy wondered, "Why do I keep the teddy bear?" She answered, "I don't really know. I bought it during our holiday last year because it looks so happy. It sits here above my sofa, smiles across the room and makes me think of the nice holiday we had in Sweden. There is no other reason for keeping it. It's just a souvenir."

Use of Language

19. **Mixed grammar** – Write down the suitable form of the words or find a word or expression yourself where there is a "?".

A Little Boy's Dream – Disneyland

Walt Disney … first theme park, Disneyland, opened in 1955. … park became a huge success. Hundreds of thousands … people visit it every year.

Walt Disney … in 1901 as the fourth son of Elias and Flora Disney. His childhood was poor and bitter. There was only one period in … he was happy: When he was five years old, his father tried to run a farm near the small town of Marceline in Missouri. After five years he … give up the farm for financial reasons. The boy liked a lot of things about life on the farm; he particularly enjoyed … for the animals. But what he liked … was the quiet, uncomplicated atmosphere of nearby Marceline. He was fascinated … the romantic charm of this small town in the Midwest. To him it was simply the … town he knew.

a) ?
b) A / The / –
c) ?
d) bear
e) who / that / which
f) must
g) care   h) much
i) in / by / with
j) beautiful

a) _____
b) _____
c) _____
d) _____
e) _____
f) _____
g) _____
h) _____
i) _____
j) _____

20. **Mixed grammar** – Write down the suitable form of the words or find a word or expression yourself where there is a "?".

Just another day

Henry ... began to move. His bed was the long corner bench of the old bus station just off Toddington's main street. He stood up, stretched his cold and aching body and began his ... routine of packing up his belongings into a few plastic bags. He usually went to the market place, ... somewhere comfortable to sit and played a few tunes on his tin whistle. Once he had earned enough money, he would buy his breakfast.
Henry shuffled towards the High Street ... all he owned. He didn't like people that much. They scared ... So he walked looking down at the pavement. After years of living on the streets Henry knew ... to find things that he ... use.
As he turned into the main street he saw a folded piece of paper on the ground. He put his plastic bags down and bent stiffly to pick it up. Money – ... ten-pound note. This was enough ... Henry with a week of breakfasts, but of course it wouldn't.
Henry woke up slowly on his usual bench in the bus station. Around him lay the bottles ... he had emptied yesterday.
He was ... He got up, collected his things together and packed them into his bags for just another day on the streets.

a) slow
b) day
c) find
d) carry
e) him / himself / his
f) ?
g) can

h) the / a / –
i) provide

j) who / whose / that
k) hunger

a) _____
b) _____
c) _____
d) _____
e) _____
f) _____
g) _____
h) _____
i) _____
j) _____
k) _____

Wortschatz

21. **Word fields** – Complete the mind maps below.

a) Use the words from the box to complete the three mind maps. You can use each word only once.

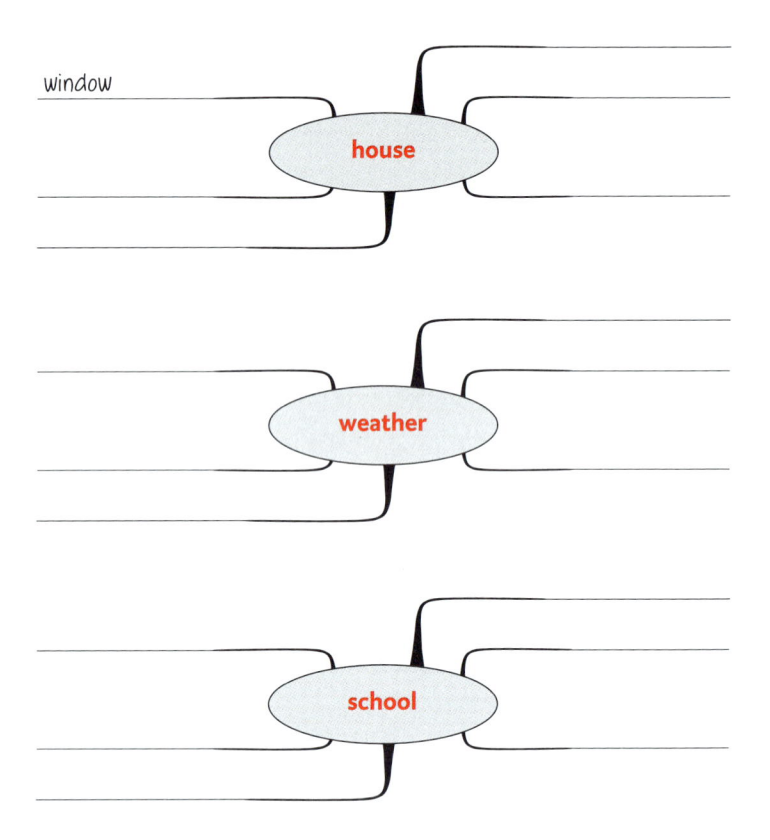

> pencil – pupil – rain – storm – teacher – door – computer – cold – wall – bedroom – hot – book – sun – floor – lesson – snow – kitchen

window → **house**

weather

school

b) Make a mind map for "furniture". This time you do not have any help.

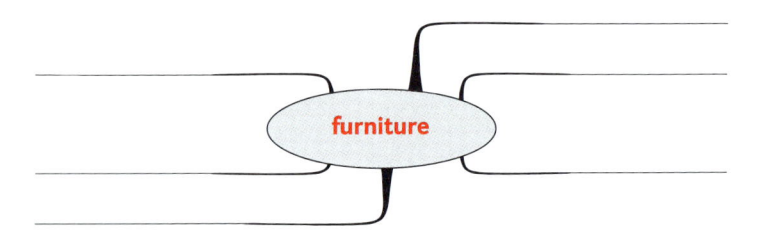

furniture

22. **Word fields** – Find the missing nationalities, countries and languages. Complete the table.

the people	the country	the language
(the) Australians	Australia	English
	England	
(the) French		
(the) Spanish		
		Italian
(the) Americans		
	Germany	
		Dutch
(the) Turkish		
(the) Canadians		

23. **Word fields** – Fill in the missing words.

Peter moved to Poland two months ago. As he doesn't speak any Polish yet, he started a language course last week. The other students in his course are from lots of different countries. Jenny, for example, is from Bournemouth in the South of _____. She's _____. Jan comes from Amsterdam in _____. He's _____. Ismael is _____. He's from Istanbul. Istanbul is in _____. Then there's Pietro. He comes from Rome, the capital of _____. Pietro only speaks _____. Louise used to live in Paris. She's _____. Some people in _____ only speak _____, but Louise speaks Portuguese and English, too. José is from Madrid, the capital of _____. He isn't _____, because he was born in Mexico, where people also speak _____. The girl Peter likes the most is called Sophia. She's _____. She was born in Quebec. That is why her native language isn't English, but _____.

106 / Use of Language

24. **Word fields** – Each job has something to do with an object, people or animals. Join them together.

❶	doctor	A	restaurant
❷	vet	B	boat
❸	pilot	C	children
❹	builder	D	plants
❺	mechanic	E	plane
❻	teacher	F	house
❼	sailor	G	cars
❽	gardener	H	hospital
❾	chef	I	animals

❶	❷	❸	❹	❺	❻	❼	❽	❾

25. **Words in context** – Read the following story carefully and fill in the missing words. You are only given the first letter.

London is the c_____ of England. It's a very l_____ city with m_____ interesting b_____. It's also a city with a great nightlife. There are lots of c_____, theatres, and, of course, clubs, r_____ and pubs. There is a_____ lots to do and see. You can v_____ Buckingham Palace or see Downing Street where the prime minister l_____. There is also a big wheel called the "London Eye". From the t_____ of it there is a f_____ view over London, but it is very h_____! The b_____ way to see London, though, is on f_____ or by a city tour on a r_____ double-decker b_____. London is a w_____ city – everyone should visit it s_____.

26. **Words in context** – Fill in the missing words and phrases. Add the preposition "of" where necessary.

On _____ (date: 5/8) last year I went to Paris for the day. The flight was only 75 minutes long. In Paris, I bought a lot of things. They had lovely biscuits, so I got six _____ (Packungen) very nice ones. Paris was very hot, so I had to carry a _____ (Flasche) water around with me. I drank so many _____ (Flaschen) water I didn't count them all. I bought my mum a _____ (Glas) French marmalade and my dad a _____ (Liter) French wine. I had a great time!

27. **Crossword puzzle** – Find out the name of this famous American singer by solving the crossword puzzle.
    1. A bison is a very large American animal, but many people call it a ???.
    2. Columbus ??? America.
    3. When you look back at things that have happened to you, you ??? them.
    4. A lot of ??? in New York City are skyscrapers.
    5. When you start a list you sometimes begin by saying ???, secondly, …
    6. Many people ??? eating chocolate.
    7. If you find something very interesting, you are often ??? by it.
    8. A guitar and a piano are ???.

    The famous American singer who won the Nobel Prize in Literature in 2016 is _____.

28. **Opposites** – Make the opposite of each sentence. The word that you have to change is underlined.
    a) The train is <u>late</u>.

    b) I have just <u>missed</u> the last bus home.

    c) I've <u>lost</u> my watch.

    d) He's <u>sold</u> a car.

    e) Julie's water bottle is <u>full</u>.

Use of Language

29. Synonyms – Find words or expressions which mean more or less the same.

a) The <u>frontier</u> between the USA and Mexico is 1,954 miles long.

b) The <u>entire</u> world was shocked when the popular actor died so young.

c) Last year he <u>at last</u> got the academy award he had been hoping for for so long.

d) <u>Huge</u> skyscrapers shape the skyline of Manhattan.

e) Do you have any plans to spend some time <u>abroad</u> after your GCSEs?

f) If you live in an English-speaking country for a few months, your English will <u>improve</u> significantly.

g) Just a few more miles. We're <u>almost</u> there!

h) When I saw her face, I knew <u>at once</u> what had happened.

30. Definitions – Write in complete sentences to explain the meanings of the following words.

a) century

b) to shake hands

c) a first aid kit

d) rubbish

e) school subject

f) immigrant

g) to explore

31. **Word families** – Complete the following table.

verb	noun(s)	adjective(s)	noun(s)
to fascinate	fascination		fame
to know		strong	
to live			science
	invitation	active	
to translate		influential	
to mean			origin
to succeed		significant	
to differ			nature
to vary		possible	
	work		use
to enter			pride
	decision	educational	
to weaken			hunger
	connection	tragic	

32. **Word forms** – Read the text. Write down the suitable form of the words or find a word or expression yourself where there is a "?".

I really like music. I have never played a _____ (music) instrument in my life but I have always found _____ (sing) fascinating. For me they are _____ (interest) in two ways. First, I find that as time goes _____ (?) they remind me of things that have happened in my _____ (live). I remember my first girlfriend, for example, by a piece of music that was always _____ (?) the radio at that time. Secondly, I'm fascinated with what the lyrics really _____ (meaning). It was only _____ (recent), for example, that I discovered what Bob Marley was singing about in his song "Buffalo Soldier". Buffalo soldiers were _____ (Africa) who fought for the Americans against the Native Americans. June is also a _____ (create) but maybe not very _____ (fame) singer-songwriter. Although I _____ (probable) won't remember many of her songs in the future, I can relate to the _____

(express) of _____ _(feel)_ in her lyrics and enjoy her live _____ _(perform)_. If you ever find the time, listen to a song carefully and try to find _____ _(?)_ what it is about and why it was written – you'll probably find it interesting too.

33. **Word forms** – Write down the suitable form of the words or find a word or expression yourself where there is a "?".

The Guinness Book of Records

You can easily find the … to any kind of questions in *The Guinness Book of Records*. This book lists interesting, funny and sometimes … records achieved by people, animals and plants. It also contains records set up by …, entertainment and hi-tech.
… the book first appeared in 1955, it immediately became a bestseller in Britain. Since 1955 people have not only taken an interest … the records listed in the book, they have also tried to break records or to set new records because they want to get into the book with their own … You can even find facts in the book about the most stupid dinosaur, the Stegosaurus. This dinosaur must have been … stupid, since he was about nine metres long, … his brain was only as big as a walnut.

a) to answer
b) not – to believe
c) busy
d) When / While / Although
e) ?
f) to achieve
g) extreme
h) as / because / but

a) _____
b) _____
c) _____
d) _____
e) _____
f) _____
g) _____
h) _____

34. **Word forms** – Write down the suitable form of the words or find a word or expression yourself where there is a "?".

St. Valentine's Day

According to one Christian legend, the ... Emperor Claudius II ordered his soldiers not to ... He believed that married men would want to stay at home rather than fight in wars. A ... priest by the name of Valentine, however, married ... couples ... He was arrested and put to death on ... for disobeying the Emperor's orders.

Today ... celebrate that day by sending Valentines to chosen partners. Valentines are ... cards with lyrics and symbols expressing affection.

The cards are often sent anonymously. Instead of the sender's name there are symbols of love such as ..., roses, rings or doves. In Britain and ..., a lot of people ... that getting married on Valentine's Day is a guarantee of long-lasting love.

No wonder that register offices and churches are booked out for marriage ceremonies months in ...

a) Rome
b) marriage
c) Christ
d) youth   e) secret
f) 14/02
g) love
h) greet
i) ?
j) American
k) belief
l) advanced

a) ___
b) ___
c) ___
d) ___
e) ___
f) ___
g) ___
h) ___
i) ___
j) ___
k) ___
l) ___

35. **Word forms** – Write down the suitable form of the words or find a word or expression yourself where there is a "?".

Ireland's Patron Saint

St. Patrick, the … patron saint, was probably born in Wales. As a boy he was kidnapped and taken to Ireland as a … He managed to escape and flee to the continent, where he became a priest and later a bishop. The Pope sent him back to the British Isles to bring Christianity to the Celts. … his mission he is said to have driven all the snakes out of Ireland into the sea, and indeed, there have been no snakes in Ireland to the … day.

Irish people … St Patrick's Day on 17th March. In Ireland this day is a … holiday. People attend mass and most businesses are closed, with the important … of restaurants and bars.

All over the world, people of Irish … celebrate this day. They dress in green, because Ireland is known as the "Green Isle".

Here's an … world record that was set up on St Patrick's Day in 2012: In Bradon, Ireland 1,263 people dressed up as leprechauns, … people!!

a) Ireland
b) slavery
c) While/During/Despite
d) presence
e) celebration
f) nation
g) except
h) original
i) amaze
j) 1,263 (in words)

a) _____
b) _____
c) _____
d) _____
e) _____
f) _____
g) _____
h) _____
i) _____
j) _____

3.4 Prüfungsähnliche Aufgaben zum Bereich „Use of Language"

Use of Language – Test 1

Volunteering in Australia

1 Australia has long been one of the top gap year destinations for young people from around the globe who have just finished school and want to travel for a year before starting a job or continuing their education. Many of them feel they want to do "something useful" during this time and decide to do volun-
5 tary work for a few weeks.

There are all sorts of projects in Australia in need of volunteers who are willing to get their hands dirty for a while. Most of those projects focus on the protection of wildlife, such as looking after endangered animals like the tree kangaroo, the flatback sea turtle or the southern hairy-nosed wombat. By col-
10 lecting rubbish, planting trees or removing plants that do not naturally belong to the Australian landscapes, volunteers can help to restore the typical living space of these species[1]. Constructing and maintaining walking trails or building fences in national parks are also very common activities. Sometimes volunteers also get the chance to assist on research programmes, setting up
15 cameras to monitor endangered species, for example.

Some of these volunteers are international travellers, but Australia is also known as a nation of volunteers with 38 % of women and 34 % of Australian men volunteering regularly. Apart from spending an adventurous time and making new friends, many volunteers also cherish the feeling of learning
20 something about the environment and contributing to its protection. Amber, from Arizona, says, "This program has taught me a great deal about conservation and what it takes to keep parts of a country safe for animals and plants. Life is too precious not to help the world and give something back." It is especially young people who set out on a gap year who feel that volunteering
25 also makes a difference to themselves. "I've grown as a person and conquered so many fears," says Maggie from Canada.

[1] species – group of very similar plants or animals

1. Find words or expressions in the text that mean more or less the same.
   a) world (lines 1–5): _____
   b) opportunity (lines 6–15): _____
   c) (to) overcome (lines 16–26): _____

2. Find the opposites.
   a) finished (line 2): _____
   b) dirty (line 7): _____
   c) protection (line 20): _____

Use of Language

3. Explain **two** of the following words in complete sentences.

   a) volunteer (line 6): _____

   b) common (line 13): _____

   c) (to) assist (line 14): _____

4. Vocabulary – Grammar
   Read the text. Find the suitable forms of the words and write them down. Find words of your own to replace the question marks.

   ### Whale deaths on the rise

   Scientists have reported a sharp increase in the number of _____ whales found on Pacific beaches in Mexico, the US and Canada. However, only 10 % of whales strand, _____ 90 % sink onto the ocean floor.
   Marine mammal¹ scientists want to find out why so many whales _____ this year. There are several theories that try to give an _____.
   Recent research shows _____ there may be a _____ between the animals' deaths and warming sea waters. The Arctic is getting warmer _____ than any other place on the planet. The rise in water temperature is killing some important food sources of whales and allows toxic algae _____ _____.
   Besides climate change and the lack of food, _____ and ship strikes are probably _____ for the deaths of many animals. Collisions with ships _____ happen near big harbours with a lot of shipping traffic.
   Scientiests agree that _____ the cause is the first step to understanding how _____ the problem.

   a) death
   b) while/although /however
   c) (to) die
   d) (to) explain
   e) ?
   f) connect
   g) fast
   h) growth
   i) to pollute
   j) responsibility
   k) typical
   l) know
   m) solution

   1 mammal – *Säugetier*

5. Ask questions.
   You meet Zachary Smith after he has worked as a volunteer in New Zealand. Ask him **three** questions about his experiences. Use different question forms or different tenses.
   ▶ _____
   ▶ _____
   ▶ _____

6. Complete the second sentence so that it has a similar meaning to the first sentence. You must use between two and five words including the word in brackets.

   > **Example**
   > The volunteers cleaned up 156 tonnes of rubbish.
   >
   > **(by)** 156 tonnes of rubbish ___were cleaned up by___ the volunteers.

   a) When planning your gap year, you probably feel overwhelmed.
      (might) _____ when planning your gap year.

   b) You need to have a working holiday visa in order to be able to earn some money during your gap year.
      (if) _____ some money during your gap year, you need to a have a working holiday visa.

   c) The organisation "Conservation Volunteers Australia" requires international volunteers to be over the age of 18.
      (which) "Conservation Volunteers Australia" _____ _____ requires international volunteers to be over the age of 18.

   d) Most volunteers have a blast, and learn a lot about themselves and the country where they work.
      (but) Most volunteers not _____ they also learn a lot about themselves and the country where they work.

Use of Language – Test 2

Hearing loss among clubbers

1 Research among clubbers in the UK has come to some surprising results – nine out of ten young people show signs of hearing loss after a night out. The first symptoms of hearing damage include fuzzy or dull hearing, tinnitus (a constant ringing in the ear), or oversensitivity to certain sounds, and these
5 symptoms were found in 90 % of the people studied.

One way to stop this is to use earplugs. But, as fashion goes, earplugs aren't all that popular. Young clubbers are worried about the way they look, and also worry that they would block out the sound. Less than 3 % of clubbers actually protect their hearing with earplugs.

10 A British charity for deaf people is now trying to change the situation by starting a campaign to find cool new designs to make earplugs more popular. Art and design students are being asked to invent new styles and designs for earplugs to make them more attractive to clubbers. The charity is also offering the winner of the competition the chance to gain work experience in different
15 British design firms.

The problem of hearing loss among party goers is not as unimportant as it may seem – the World Health Organisation claims that loud noise is the number one cause of hearing loss worldwide.

1. Find the opposites in the text.
   a) loser (lines 10–15): _____
   b) quiet (lines 16–18): _____

2. Find words or expressions in the text that mean more or less the same.
   a) astonishing (lines 1–5): _____
   b) specific (lines 1–5): _____
   c) to think of (lines 10–15): _____
   d) reason (lines 16–18): _____

3. Choose **two** of the following words and give a definition.
   a) popular (line 7): _____
   _____
   b) to protect (line 9): _____
   _____
   c) competition (line 14): _____
   _____

4. Vocabulary – Grammar
Complete the text by using suitable forms of the words. Find a word of your own where there is a question mark.

Infrasound

Infrasound is sound that is too low to be detected by the human ear. It is _____ believed that the first observation of naturally occurring infrasound was after the volcanic eruption of Krakatoa in 1883. One of the _____ pioneers of modern infrasonic research was the French _____ Vladimir Gavreau, born in Russia as Vladimir Gavronsky. He became _____ in infrasonic waves during an experiment in his lab in the 1960s, when he and his assistant experienced pain in the ear although no audible sound _____ be detected by his microphones. However, some animals are able to recognise infrasonic waves that _____ disasters can cause, and elephants have been known _____ infrasound from two and a half miles away. In 2003 people at a concert _____ to rate their responses to a variety of pieces of music, some of which were accompanied by infrasonic parts. 22 % of the _____ reported feelings of anxiety, uneasiness, extreme sorrow, fear and chills down the spine, _____ correlated with the infrasonic events.

a) general
b) important
c) science
d) interesting
e) can
f) nature
g) hear
h) ask
i) participate
j) ?

5. Ask questions.
Imagine you are at a music festival. You are talking to Ben, a huge fan of the band that is about to go on stage. Ask him three questions in relation to the festival and the band. Use different question forms or different tenses.

▶ _____
▶ _____
▶ _____

Use of Language

6. Complete the second sentence so that it has a similar meaning to the first sentence. You must use between two and five words including the word in brackets.

   Example
   Recently researchers discovered that nine out of ten young clubbers show symptoms of hearing loss.

   (**by**) Recently it __was discovered by researchers__ that nine out of ten young clubbers show symptoms of hearing loss.

   a) If you don't wear earplugs during a night at a noisy club, it is likely that you will suffer from hearing loss in the future.
   (**unless**) _____ during a night at a noisy club you will probably suffer from hearing loss in the future.

   b) Most young people never wear earplugs.
   (**used**) Most young people are _____ earplugs.

   c) People with earplugs could be the new fashion stars.
   (**wear**) People _____ could be the new fashion stars.

   d) The campaign required young designers to create fashionable earplugs.
   (**aim**) _____ was to make young designers think about cool new earplugs.

   e) Some young designers are looking forward to competing.
   (**wait**) Some young designers can't _____ part in the competition.

Use of Language – Test 3

Climb ban in force at Australia's famous desert rock

1 The world-famous climb to the top of Uluru, the sacred red rock in central Australia, has closed permanently. Indigenous people have long asked tourists not to walk on the ancient sandstone monolith because of its spiritual significance. But the closure of the climb is not universally popular. Thousands
5 of visitors poured into the Uluru National Park in 2019 for the chance to reach the summit of the namesake monolith one last time.

It closed in October 2019 at the request of Indigenous leaders, who believe the rock is of immense cultural importance. They believe it is sacred and has a power and a spirituality like nowhere else. Donald Fraser, an Aboriginal elder,
10 is relieved. "The burden will be lifted as of today, as I am speaking. I can feel it. Now is the time for the climb to have a good rest and heal up," he said on the day the climb was closed.

Aboriginal groups had long asked visitors to the site in the central Australian desert not to scale Uluru for cultural reasons. The rock is 348 metres high and
15 is taller than the Eiffel Tower in Paris. But some of the last tourists to reach the summit were happy to disregard the wishes of the local Indigenous community. "I understand it is a sensitive topic. My view is that Australia should be for all Australians. So I have got no problem at all with people climbing the rock and I think it is a natural human instinct to see something like that and
20 want to climb it," one climber said.

In 1985, control of the rock had been handed back to Aboriginal people by the Australian government. Authorities believe that closing the climb will not damage the local tourism industry, which is vital to this remote part of the country. The number of people climbing the rock had fallen in previous
25 years, according to Mike Misso, the manager of the Uluru-Kata Tjuta National Park. "Over many years, the number of people wanting to climb had actually been declining. And before the climb closure was announced, it was less than 10% who actually climbed Uluru," he said. It is not universally popular, but closing the climb will bring to an end years of distress for Aboriginal people.

Adapted from: Phil Mercer, Voice of America Learning English, October 27, 2019.

1. Find words and expressions in the text that mean more or less the same.

   a) top (lines 1–6): _____

   b) enormous (lines 7–12): _____

   c) isolated (lines 21–29): _____

Use of Language

2. Find the opposites.
   a) disregard (line 16): _____
   b) previous (line 24): _____
   c) closure (line 27): _____

3. Explain **two** of the following words in complete sentences.
   a) ancient (line 3): _____
   _____
   b) (to) scale (line 14): _____
   _____
   c) (to) decline (line 27): _____
   _____

4. Vocabulary – Grammar
   Complete the text by using suitable forms of the words. Find words of your own to replace the question marks.

   ### Australia's Aboriginal people
   The word "aborigine" _____ "the people who were here from the beginning". In fact, Aboriginal people have been living in Australia _____ at least 40,000 years. Until Europeans arrived in Australia, they _____ there very _____. They usually lived in family groups _____ as tribes.
   Land is very important to the Aboriginal people. They believe that it _____ for them by their ancestors and, therefore, much of it is sacred, such as Uluru, for example, _____ white people used to call "Ayers Rock". In the past, Aboriginal people lived off the land of their ancestors. They were hunters, fishermen and gatherers. A gatherer was a collector – a person who collected food such as eggs, berries and insects. Every day the _____ went hunting or fishing and the women and children did the gathering. This meant their food was always fresh but they _____ understand nature very _____.

   a) mean
   b) ?
   c) live d) happy
   e) know
   f) make
   g) ?
   h) man
   i) must
   j) good

5. Ask questions.
   Imagine you are spending six months in Australia. Your host dad climbed Uluru before it was closed to the public in 2019. Ask him three questions about this experience.

   ▶ _____
   ▶ _____
   ▶ _____

6. Complete the second sentence so that it has a similar meaning to the first sentence. You must use between two and five words including the word in brackets.

   > **Example**
   > The management of the Uluru-Kata Tjuta National Park closed the climb to the top of Uluru.
   >
   > **(by)** The climb to the top of Uluru ___was closed by___ the management of the Uluru-Kata Tjuta National Park.

   a) Park management closed the climb with the aim of giving the sacred mountain some rest.

   (order) Park management closed the climb _____ the sacred mountain some rest.

   b) Large signs at the bottom of Uluru show tourists that they mustn't climb the mountain.

   (prohibited) Large signs at the bottom of Uluru show tourists that _____.

   c) In October 2019, the climb to Uluru was closed permanently.

   (since) The climb to Uluru _____ 2019.

   d) "You should definitely watch the film "Rabbit-Proof Fence" about three Aboriginal girls who walk for nine weeks through the Outback to return to their families.

   (worth) The film "Rabbit-Proof Fence", which is about three Aboriginal girls who walk for nine weeks through the Outback to return to their families, _____.

4 Writing

Viele Schüler*innen sind der Meinung, dass sie sich auf den Bereich „Writing" nicht vorbereiten können, da die Aufgabenformen sehr stark variieren und die Note – wie im Deutschunterricht – ohnehin stark von der individuellen Einschätzung der Lehrkraft abhänge. Erschwerend kommt im Fach Englisch noch die Fremdsprache und die damit verbundene Fehleranfälligkeit hinzu. Aus diesen Gründen beschäftigen sich manche Lernende erst gar nicht mit dem Kompetenzbereich „Writing", obwohl man in diesem Bereich die meisten Punkte in der Abschlussprüfung erreichen kann.

Mache nicht den gleichen Fehler! Lies die folgenden Seiten gut durch. Du wirst sehen: Eine sinnvolle und erfolgreiche Vorbereitung auf das Schreiben englischer Texte ist möglich.

4.1 Strategien zum Bereich „Writing"

Langfristige Vorbereitung

Genau wie auf den Bereich „Use of Language" kannst du dich auf die „Writing"-Aufgaben in Klassenarbeiten und Prüfungen nur langfristig gut vorbereiten. Wenn du dir erst zwei Tage vor der Prüfung überlegst, dass du in diesem Bereich noch Schwächen hast, dann ist das für eine sinnvolle Beschäftigung mit diesem Thema definitiv zu spät.

Schaue bzw. höre dir englischsprachige Interviews mit deinen Lieblingsstars im Internet (z. B. bei YouTube) oder im Fernsehen an. Sieh dir Kinofilme im Original an, entweder im Kino – falls sie in deiner Stadt im Original vorgeführt werden – oder auf DVD bzw. über einen Streaming-Dienst im Internet (z. B. Netflix). Als Hilfe kannst du dir – falls möglich – auch die englischen Untertitel einblenden lassen und die Dialoge mitlesen. *(Methode 1)*

Versuche, möglichst viel in englischer Sprache zu lesen; auch hier wirst du im Internet fündig. Du kannst dich z. B. über Themen, die dich interessieren, im Online-Lexikon Wikipedia informieren. Hier gibt es übrigens auch den Bereich „Simple English", falls dir die Texte zu schwierig sind. Oder probiere, Romane und Geschichten auf Englisch zu lesen. Deine Lehrerin oder dein Lehrer kann dir sicher Tipps für geeignete Bücher geben. Du wirst sehen: Mit der Zeit verstehst du mehr und mehr und Ausdrücke und Redewendungen kommen dir immer vertrauter vor, sodass du sie für deine eigenen Texte verwenden kannst. *(Methode 2)*

Eine gute Übung ist es auch, dich viel in der Fremdsprache zu unterhalten. Sprich doch hin und wieder mit deinen Freundinnen, Freunden oder deinen Geschwistern Englisch. So wird dir das eigenständige Formulieren immer leichterfallen. *(Methode 3)*

Wichtig ist also, dass du dich mit der englischen Sprache auch in deiner Freizeit beschäftigst. Dabei geht es nicht nur darum, das Schreiben englischer Texte zu üben, sondern ganz generell sollst du möglichst viel mit dem Englischen in

Kontakt kommen. So kannst du deinen Wortschatz erweitern und Sicherheit im Gebrauch der Fremdsprache erwerben, die du zum Verfassen eigener Texte brauchst.

Das Schreiben eines Textes

Es gibt viele verschiedene Arten von Texten, wie z. B. Briefe oder E-Mails, Artikel und Fantasiegeschichten. Ganz gleich, welche Art von Texten du schreiben musst, die Vorgehensweise ist dabei immer ähnlich.

Arbeitsschritt **1** **Lies die Aufgabenstellung gut durch** und überlege genau, was darin von dir verlangt wird. Erhältst du mit der Aufgabenstellung bestimmte Vorgaben (z. B. Stichworte oder Anfang/Ende einer Geschichte), die du in deinen Text einbringen musst? Oder sollst du einen „freien" Text schreiben?

Arbeitsschritt **2** Wenn du mehrere Themen zur **Auswahl** hast, dann suche dir dasjenige aus, in dem du dich am besten auskennst. Es hat keinen Sinn, einem Freund in einem Brief von den Abenteuern beim Skifahren zu erzählen, wenn du noch nie Wintersport betrieben hast. Vermeide nach Möglichkeit also Themen, zu denen du nichts zu sagen hast.

Arbeitsschritt **3** Hast du dich für ein Thema entschieden, dann solltest du dir genau überlegen, was du dazu schreiben könntest; mache dir im Vorfeld einige **Stichpunkte**. Beachte dabei genau die Vorgaben aus der Aufgabenstellung (z. B. in Form von Bildern oder Stichworten) und überlege dann, was du noch hinzufügen musst. Nimm dazu ein Notizblatt und lass deiner Fantasie freien Lauf.
Eine gute Möglichkeit, deine Ideen zu sammeln und zu ordnen, bietet eine **Mindmap**. Bei dieser Methode stellst du den zentralen Begriff, um den es bei deinem Text geht, in das Zentrum und notierst sternförmig alle weiteren Begriffe, die dir zum Thema einfallen.

Arbeitsschritt **4** Nachdem du einige Notizen zum Thema angefertigt hast, schaust du noch einmal genau auf die Aufgabenstellung und achtest darauf, dass **alle geforderten Aspekte** in deiner Aufstellung berücksichtigt sind.

Arbeitsschritt **5** Nun musst du den **Text formulieren**. Gehe dabei Schritt für Schritt die Aufgabenstellung durch und formuliere die einzelnen Sätze aus. Gute inhaltliche Ideen sind dabei genauso wichtig wie ein **klarer Aufbau** deines Textes. Achte auch darauf, dass du Abhängigkeiten, Folgen etc. durch entsprechende Konjunktionen, also durch Bindewörter wie z. B. „because" oder „although", deutlich machst. Versuche also, den Satzbau zu variieren, und greife auf Redewendungen zurück, die du gelernt hast. Schreibe jedoch kurze, überschaubare Sätze, falls du unsicher bist; so kannst du Grammatikfehler leichter vermeiden. Wenn du etwas nicht ausdrücken kannst oder dir der Wortschatz fehlt, dann versuche, einen anderen Aspekt zu finden.
In Kapitel 4.3 findest du eine Zusammenstellung vieler nützlicher Formulierungen, die dir beim Aufsatzschreiben helfen werden. Lerne sie auswendig. Du wirst sie immer wieder einsetzen können.

Achte auch darauf, dass du die geforderte **Wortzahl** nicht zu sehr über- oder unterschreitest, denn in beiden Fällen werden dir Punkte abgezogen.

Nimm dir auf jeden Fall die Zeit, **deinen Text** abschließend noch einmal in Ruhe **durchzulesen**. Achte dabei auf die inhaltliche Geschlossenheit deines Textes. Ist alles logisch aufgebaut? Gibt es keine Gedankensprünge? Hast du die einzelnen Aspekte *(prompts)* in der Aufgabenstellung bearbeitet? Hast du die geforderte Anzahl von Aspekten beachtet (z. B. „Write about two aspects.")? Wichtig ist aber auch, dass du noch einmal gezielt nach Rechtschreib- und Grammatikfehlern suchst und diese entsprechend verbesserst.

Arbeitsschritt 6

Dieses Verfahren kommt dir vielleicht ein bisschen zeitaufwendig und umständlich vor. Versuche aber dennoch, genau danach vorzugehen: Du wirst bemerken, dass es dir bei den Hausaufgaben, in den Klassenarbeiten und natürlich erst recht in der Prüfung wertvolle Zeit spart. So wird es kaum passieren, dass du die falsche Aufgabe auswählst und das erst merkst, wenn du schon mitten im Schreiben bist. Klar sollte dir allerdings auch sein, dass du dieses Verfahren üben musst.

Tipp

- Lies die Aufgabenstellung genau und analysiere sie.
- Wähle die für dich geeignete Aufgabe aus.
- Mache dir einige Stichpunkte.
- Überprüfe, ob du alle Aspekte der Aufgabenstellung berücksichtigt hast.
- Formuliere den Text anhand der Aufgabenstellung und der vorgegebenen *prompts* Schritt für Schritt aus.
- Lies deinen Text abschließend noch einmal genau durch und überprüfe dabei, ob alles logisch aufgebaut und verständlich geschrieben ist.
- Verbessere Rechtschreib- und Grammatikfehler.

4.2 Häufige Aufgabenstellungen zum Bereich „Writing"

In deiner Abschlussprüfung ist der „Writing"-Teil sehr wichtig. Es gibt immer zwei Aufgaben, wobei du bei der ersten rund 100 Wörter schreiben musst und bei der zweiten ungefähr 160 Wörter. Halte dich in etwa an die Vorgabe, um Punktabzug zu vermeiden.
Der Inhalt deiner Texte zählt ein Drittel, Sprache und Rechtschreibung werden ebenfalls mit je einem Drittel bewertet. Wenn du allerdings das Thema inhaltlich nicht triffst, gibt es für die ganze Aufgabe 0 Punkte.
Die folgenden Aufgabenformate sind typische Arbeitsaufträge, die häufig in Klassenarbeiten und deiner Abschlussprüfung vorkommen können.

Give your opinion.

In dieser Aufgabe sollst du zu Aussagen, die oft provozierend sind, **deine eigene Meinung** kundtun. Dabei musst du beachten, dass du zunächst entweder der Aussage zustimmst oder ausdrückst, dass du nicht damit einverstanden bist. Hilfreiche Wendungen dazu findest du in Kapitel 4.3.

Danach folgt deine begründete Meinung. Es ist wichtig, dass du hier wirklich gute Argumente für deine Meinung findest und sie auch in Worten ausdrücken kannst. Vorsicht, manchmal wird von dir verlangt, dass du auf zwei Aussagen eingehst. Lies also die Aufgabenstellung genau.

Beispiel

Aussage:	Smoking should be forbidden.
Zustimmung:	I think that is quite right because it is not healthy. It can cause lung cancer, not only for the person who smokes but also for other people who do not smoke but inhale the smoke. It is especially dangerous for small children or unborn babies. Other drugs are prohibited too, so why should smoking be allowed?
Ablehnung:	I do not think that is right. Adults know what is good for them. They should have the right to decide what they want to do. Eating too much fat or sugar is unhealthy too, but no one would think of banning those. The state cannot regulate everything; there are some decisions people should be able to make themselves.

Write a comment.

In einem „comment" sollst du zu einer Aussage, die oft ein kontroverses Thema anspricht, **Stellung nehmen**. Die Arbeitsanweisung enthält häufig den Zusatz: „Discuss the pros and cons and give your own opinion." Wichtig ist dann, dass du **Argumente** nennst, die **für und gegen die Aussage** sprechen, bevor du Position beziehst.

Beginne immer mit einem einleitenden Satz und drücke nach dem Hauptteil, in dem du die Argumente abwägst, deine **eigene Meinung** aus. Insgesamt sollst du bei diesem Aufgabenformat in deiner Abschlussprüfung rund **100 Wörter** schreiben.

Beispiel

Aussage:	Smoking should be forbidden.
Antwort:	That smoking is unhealthy is a well-known fact. The question, however, is whether smoking should be generally prohibited. We live in a free country, so people should have the right to decide what they want to do, even if their actions are harmful to themselves. Eating too much fat or sugar is unhealthy too, but no one would think of banning those. However, tobacco is addictive and smoking can cause lung cancer, not only for the person who smokes but also for other people who only inhale the smoke. It is especially dangerous for small children or unborn babies. All in all, as other drugs are forbidden, I strongly believe that smoking should be prohibited as well.

Write a letter / a report / a story / a blog entry ...

Dies ist der zentrale Teil einer Abschlussprüfung und eine typische kreative Aufgabenstellung in Klassenarbeiten. Wichtig ist, dass du dir ganz genau die Aufgabenstellung durchliest. Darin bekommst du in der Regel viele Hinweise, wie und für welchen Zweck du einen Text formulieren sollst.

In der Prüfung sollte dein Text rund 160 Wörter umfassen. Besonders häufige Aufgabenstellungen sind z. B.:

- **Brief** oder **E-Mail:** Hier musst du entweder einen persönlichen Brief an einen Freund/eine Freundin bzw. an Verwandte oder ein offizielles Schreiben verfassen. Sieh dir die Aufgabenstellung genau an und analysiere im ersten Schritt, welche Art von Brief/E-Mail von dir verlangt wird. Achte auf ein angemessenes Layout und die typischen Wendungen für Anfang und Ende. Manchmal wird dir eine E-Mail vorgegeben, auf die du antworten sollst, oder du erhältst eine Stellenanzeige, zu der du ein Bewerbungsschreiben verfasst. Auch Beschwerdebriefe sind typische Aufgaben in diesem Bereich.

- **Geschichte:** Du sollst dir eine Geschichte zu einem bestimmten Thema ausdenken. Als Hilfe wird dir meist der erste und/oder der letzte Satz vorgegeben. Achte darauf, dass deine Geschichte zu den Vorgaben passt.

- **Tagebuch- oder Blogeintrag:** Ähnlich wie bei einer Geschichte werden dir ein Thema für deinen Eintrag und manchmal auch der erste/letzte Satz des Textes vorgegeben.

- **Texte zu Bildern:** Statt eines Themas kann dir für deinen kreativen Text auch ein Foto vorgegeben werden, zu dem du dir eine Geschichte überlegen sollst. Nimm dir Zeit, das Foto genau anzusehen, und mache Stichpunkte auf einem Notizzettel, was auf dem Foto zu sehen ist. So fällt es dir leichter, einen Text zu schreiben, der auch wirklich zu diesem Bild passt.

4.3 Hilfreiche Wendungen zum Bereich „Writing"

Die folgenden Wörter und Ausdrücke helfen dir beim Schreiben von Texten. Du solltest sie auswendig lernen. Die Wendungen sind übrigens auch als digitale „MindCards" verfügbar, mit denen du am Smartphone oder Tablet üben kannst.

Writing

**Formulierungshilfen zur Strukturierung von Texten
(z. B. für eine persönliche Stellungnahme)**

einen Text einleiten	To begin with, ... First of all, ...
einen Text abschließen	To sum up, ... / In summary, ... / All in all, ... To conclude, ... / In conclusion, ...
Argumente aufzählen	Firstly, ... Secondly, ... Thirdly, ... Finally, ...
Argumente gegeneinander abwägen	On the one hand ... On the other hand ...

auf Widersprüche hinweisen / etwas einräumen	but however yet although despite / in spite of in contrast to otherwise nevertheless
zusätzliche Aspekte anführen	In addition, … Moreover, … Furthermore, … Not only that, but … Another important point is … Another aspect to mention is …
Beispiele geben	for example / e.g. for instance like such as
Gründe anführen	Due to … Thanks to … The reason for this is that … because (of) as since therefore
auf die Folgen von etwas hinweisen	As a result, … Consequently, …
die eigene Meinung ausdrücken	In my opinion / view, … Personally, I think / believe that … To my mind, … As far as I am concerned, … As for me, …
Zweifel / Sorge ausdrücken	I am not quite sure whether … I doubt that … I am concerned / worried that …
Zustimmung ausdrücken	(Yes,) I think so, too. I agree with this statement. That is right / correct. I am of the same opinion.
Ablehnung ausdrücken	(No,) I do not think so. I do not agree. / I disagree. That is wrong / not correct. I am not of the same opinion.

Formulierungshilfen für E-Mails und Briefe

Anrede und Schlussformeln in formellen E-Mails und Briefen (z. B. Geschäftsbrief / Anfrage)

wenn du den <u>Namen</u> des Ansprechpartners <u>nicht kennst</u>:

Sehr geehrte Damen und Herren,	Dear Sir / Madam,
	Dear Sir or Madam,
Mit freundlichen Grüßen	Yours faithfully,

wenn du den <u>Namen</u> des Ansprechpartners <u>kennst</u>:

Sehr geehrte Frau Roberts,	Dear Mrs Roberts,
Sehr geehrter Herr James,	Dear Mr James,
wenn du nicht weißt, ob die Frau verheiratet ist oder nicht	Dear Ms Bell,
Mit freundlichen Grüßen	Yours sincerely,

Layout eines Geschäftsbriefes

```
                                    24 Castle Street      ⎫
                                    Blackburn             ⎬ Absender
                                    Lancashire            ⎪ (ohne Namen)[1]
                                    LK6 5TQ               ⎭

                                    6th March 20…           Datum[2]

   Mrs J. Fox                                             ⎫
   Dane Cleaners                                          ⎪ Name + Adresse
   3 Arthur Road                                          ⎬ des Empfängers
   Doddington                                             ⎪ (bei Geschäfts-
   NE3 6LD                                                ⎭ briefen)


   Dear Mrs Fox,                                            Anrede

   Thank you for your letter …




   Yours sincerely,                                         Schlussformel
   *Adam Smith*                                             Unterschrift
   Adam Smith                                               Name
```

1 Die Adresse des Absenders kann auch auf der linken Seite stehen.
2 Das Datum kann auch links stehen. Die Schreibung 6 March 20… / March 6 / March 6th ist alternativ möglich.

Tipp

In formellen E-Mails und Briefen musst du die Langformen der Verben verwenden (z. B. „I am" anstelle von „I'm").

Anrede und Schlussformeln in persönlichen E-Mails und Briefen

Liebe Jane,	Dear Jane,
Viele Grüße / Liebe Grüße	Best wishes,
	Love, *(nur bei sehr guten Freunden; von Frauen häufiger verwendet als von Männern)*

Mögliche Einleitungs- und Schlusssätze

Danke für …	Thank you for …
Ich habe … erhalten.	I received …
Ich hoffe, dass …	I hope that …
Wie geht es dir?	How are you?
Im letzten Brief hast du mir von … erzählt.	In your last letter you told me about …
Im letzten Brief hast du mir erzählt, dass …	In your last letter you told me that …
Entschuldige, dass ich … vergessen habe, aber …	Sorry that I forgot to …, but …
Sage bitte … / Richte … bitte aus …	Please tell …
Es wäre schön, wenn wir uns treffen könnten.	It would be nice if we could meet.
Bitte richte … (schöne) Grüße aus.	Best wishes to … / Please give my (best) regards to … / Please say hi/hello to … from me.
Bitte schreibe mir bald zurück.	Please write soon.
Ich freue mich darauf, bald von dir zu hören.	I'm looking forward to hearing from you soon. / I hope to hear from you soon.
Ich freue mich auf deinen Brief.	I'm looking forward to your letter.
Ich werde dich anrufen.	I'll call / ring you.

Weitere häufig vorkommende Redewendungen / Ausdrücke

sich entschuldigen	I'm sorry …
etwas bedauern / Enttäuschung ausdrücken	It's a pity that … / I'm disappointed that … / I was deeply disappointed by …
an etwas erinnern	Please remember to …
eine Bitte äußern	Could / Would you …, please?
einen Wunsch äußern	I'd like to … / I'd love to …
einen Entschluss mitteilen	I've decided to … / I'm going to … / I've made up my mind to …
eine Absicht mitteilen	I intend to … / I will … / I want to … / I'm planning to …

Interesse ausdrücken	I'm interested in …
Freude ausdrücken	I'm happy/glad about …
Überzeugung ausdrücken	I'm convinced that …/I'm sure that …
nach dem Preis fragen	How much is it?/… does it cost?
Ich hoffe, dir hat … gefallen.	I hope you liked/enjoyed …
Ich muss jetzt …	I have to … now.
Ich denke, es ist besser …	I think it's better to …
sich beschweren	I am sorry but …/I am afraid I have to complain about …
eine Leistung (z. B. die Rückerstattung der Kosten) einfordern	I would like to ask you for (a refund).

Auskunft geben über sich selbst

Ich wohne in …	I live in …
Ich wurde am … in … geboren.	I was born in … on (17th May, 2004).
Ich interessiere mich für …	I'm interested in …
Ich war schon in …	I've (already) been in …/to …
Ich möchte gerne … werden.	I'd like to be a/an …
Mir geht es gut.	I'm fine.
Mir geht es nicht gut.	I'm not/I don't feel well.
Ich mag …	I like …/I enjoy …
Ich mag … lieber (als …)	I prefer … to …/I like … better (than …)
Ich weiß … noch nicht genau.	I still don't know exactly …
Ich plane, … zu tun.	I plan to …
Ich freue mich (sehr) auf …	I'm (very much) looking forward to … I'm (very) excited about …
Ich konnte nicht …	I wasn't able to …/I couldn't …
In meiner Freizeit …	In my free time/spare time …
Ich nehme regelmäßig an … teil.	I take part in … regularly.

Verben des Sagens (z. B. für Fantasiegeschichten)

sagen	to say sth/to tell sb sth
fragen	to ask/to enquire
sich fragen	to ask oneself/to wonder
antworten	to answer/to reply/to respond
flüstern	to whisper
schreien	to call (out)/yell/scream/shout
erwähnen	to mention

4.4 Übungsaufgaben zum Bereich „Writing"

1. Improve the sentences below. Choose the best word from the box for each gap.

   > dark – horror – long – loud – narrow – old – sandy –
   > seafood – small – so – summer – terrible – quickly – young

   a) The _____ house was at the end of the _____ street.

   b) Jane likes listening to _____ music in her _____ bedroom.

   c) The _____ boy ran away _____.

   d) We had a _____ meal in the _____ restaurant.

   e) I didn't like the _____ film because it was _____ boring.

   f) My _____ holiday was great.

   g) There was a _____, _____ beach with no one on it.

   h) The sky was very _____ before the storm.

2. Look at the photograph. What can you say about it? Take some notes.

   _____
   _____
   _____
   _____

3. Look at the photo again. Answer the following questions in complete sentences.

   a) Where does the scene take place?
      It takes place in front of a building.

   b) Describe who you can see …
      ▶ in the foreground: _____

      ▶ in the background: _____

   c) Describe …
      ▶ the boy's face: _____
      ▶ what he is holding: _____
      ▶ where he is in relation to the others: _____

   d) Describe …
      ▶ the other people's clothes: _____

      ▶ what they are doing: _____

4. Look at your answers to task 3. Improve each answer by adding more information – an adjective, an adverb or an additional phrase.

   a) Where does the scene take place?
      It takes place in front of a **big white/grey** building – **probably outside**
      a school building.

   b) Describe who you can see …
      ▶ in the foreground: _____

      ▶ in the background: _____

   c) Describe …
      ▶ the boy's face: _____
      ▶ what he is holding: _____
      ▶ where he is in relation to the others: _____

d) Describe…

- the other people's clothes: _____

- what they are doing: _____

5. What is the story behind the picture? Think of four questions you could ask about the picture.

   ▸ _____

   ▸ _____

   ▸ _____

   ▸ _____

6. Imagine what is going on between the boy in the foreground and the other teenagers. Think of answers to the questions you asked in task 5 and write a short story in about 160 words.

7. What is the story behind the picture?

Write a story in about 160 words and include at least four of the following aspects:
- Who took the photo?
- Where was the photographer travelling to?
- When was the photo taken?
- Why was the photographer allowed into the cockpit?
- What did the pilot explain?

Writing

8. Read the following statements and imagine they are from your contacts on a social networking site. Do you like them or not? Collect ideas for possible answers and fill in this grid:

Statements	Arguments for 👍	Arguments against 👎
❶ Action films are only for boys.		
❷ In times of climate change, flying should be at least twice as expensive as it is today.		
❸ People who eat meat are killers.		

9. Choose **two** of the topics in task 8 and give your opinion in about 100 words.

Topic	

___
___
___
___
___
___
___
___

Topic	

___
___
___
___

10. What would you do in the following situations? Write about 100 words.

   a) A friend has invited you to his birthday party. You go, but when he opens the door, you realise that you have forgotten his present.

   b) You come home from school. You notice that the school bag is not yours.

   c) You see somebody beating his dog in the street.

Writing

11. Write a comment in about 100 words. Discuss the pros and cons and give your own opinion on the following topic:
    Living in a small village is better than living in a city.

    _____

12. Write a comment in about 100 words. Discuss the pros and cons and give your own opinion on the following topic:
    Pupils should be allowed to choose whatever subjects they want.

    _____

13. Choose the correct address for each situation.
    a) In a letter to Carlos Fernandez, your pen friend from South America:
        ☐ Dear Mr Fernandez,
        ☐ Sir,
        ☐ Hi Carlos,

b) In an e-mail to Diana Watson, the manager of a hotel you stayed at (you only know her name and have never met her in person):
- [ ] Dear Ms Watson,
- [ ] Dear Mrs Watson,
- [ ] Dear Sir/Madam,

c) In a letter of application to the personnel manager of a company:
- [ ] Dear lady or gentleman,
- [ ] Dear Sir or Madam,
- [ ] Dear everyone,

d) In an e-mail to Linda Evans, your grandmother:
- [ ] Dear Granny,
- [ ] Hi Evans,
- [ ] Dear Mrs Evans,

14. Choose the correct ending for each situation.

a) In a letter to Carlos Fernandez, Mike's new pen friend from South America:
- [ ] Love, Mike
- [ ] Best wishes, Mike
- [ ] Yours sincerely, Mike

b) In an e-mail to Diana Watson, the manager of a hotel you stayed at (you only know her name and have never met her in person):
- [ ] Yours sincerely,
- [ ] Love,
- [ ] Best wishes,

c) In a letter of application to the personnel manager of a company:
- [ ] Regards,
- [ ] Yours faithfully,
- [ ] All the best,

d) In an e-mail to Linda Evans, your grandmother:
- [ ] Yours sincerely,
- [ ] Yours faithfully,
- [ ] Love,

15. Put the information below into a good letter layout. Think of the right punctuation and remember that some words have to be written with a capital letter.

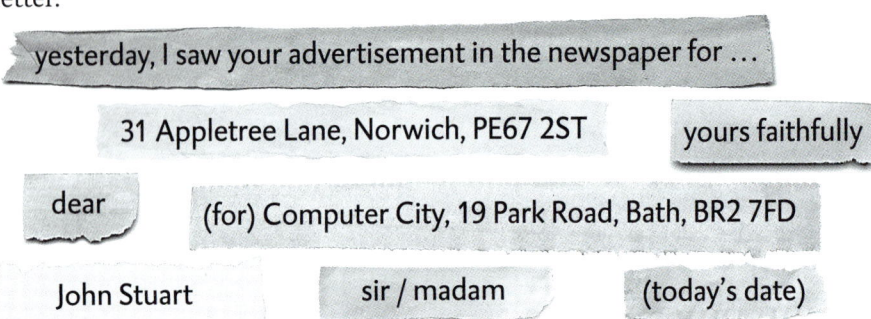

- yesterday, I saw your advertisement in the newspaper for …
- 31 Appletree Lane, Norwich, PE67 2ST
- yours faithfully
- dear
- (for) Computer City, 19 Park Road, Bath, BR2 7FD
- John Stuart
- sir / madam
- (today's date)

16. Imagine you have spent a fantastic holiday with other young people in an English-speaking country. After returning home you write a message to your American friend about your holiday.

a) To collect some ideas, make a mind map before you start to write your message. Some questions have been included to help you.

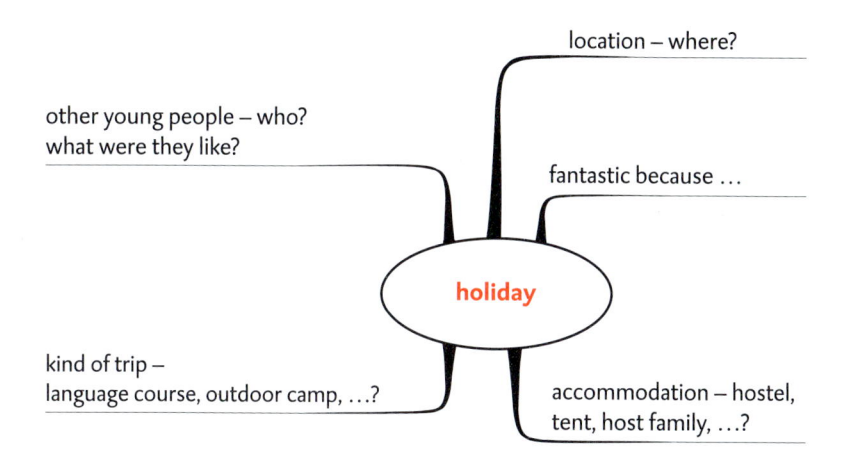

- location – where?
- other young people – who? what were they like?
- fantastic because …
- kind of trip – language course, outdoor camp, …?
- accommodation – hostel, tent, host family, …?

holiday

b) Choose your best ideas and write a chat message to your friend in about 160 words.

Writing

17. You are back from another holiday, which was a real nightmare. Write an e-mail and complain to the English travel agency. Use at least two of the ideas in the pictures and write about 160 words.

First impression of our hotel room

Sea view? Construction site

Cockroaches as roommates

An...: Susan.Philips@DreamTours.Brighton.co.uk
Cc...:
Betreff:

18. You see an advertisement for a holiday in Britain online and you want some more information.

Treat yourself to a city break!

London – Birmingham – Liverpool – Edinburgh – Glasgow – Cardiff

From £ 50 per night
- 3-star or 4-star hotels
- breakfast included
- a place for everyone: single, double or family rooms
- optional: sightseeing tour package
- airport shuttle possible
- ticket service

Any questions? Just get in touch –
Write an email to info@citybreak.co.uk **or use our** contact form

Use the contact form below to write a formal message in about 160 words. Ask for more information about the city and hotel you are interested in. Say when you would like to come and what type of room you need.

Ask about at least two of the following aspects:
- price
- hotel location
- facilities (e. g. gym, spa, Wi-Fi)
- sightseeing tour package
- airport shuttle
- interesting events during your stay

Contact us

First Name	
Last Name	
Email	
Subject	
Your message	

Send

19. Read the following job advertisement on a company's website.
Before you write a letter of application, look at the following list of ideas. Choose ten ideas you could use in your letter.

HOLIDAY JOBS AT ICSD LIMITED –
FANTASTIC OPPORTUNITY FOR STUDENTS

Have you done some work experience and would now like to gain more practical knowledge as well as make some good money during your holidays?
Apply to ICSD.

What we are looking for:
upbeat[1] and organised 16 plus students to add to our successful customer service team for a period of at least four weeks

What you have to do:
record phone or postal orders from German- or English-speaking customers, and update the database

What you need:
- excellent phone manner
- knowledge of Word and Excel
- good standard of German and English, both written and oral

You will be given two days' training before you start work.

Please send in a letter of application and your CV to:
Julia Weston, Personnel Manager (ICSD Ltd.), Coopers Row, London, W1A 2JQ, United Kingdom.

---

[1] upbeat – fröhlich, optimistisch

- [ ] I found the advertisement on your company's website.
- [ ] My teacher told me to apply for a job to improve my language skills.
- [ ] I could start work in July and stay for six weeks.
- [ ] I have good computer skills and like working with people.
- [ ] I like sports and working with small children.
- [ ] I am a very creative and outgoing person and would like to work in education.
- [ ] I am good at organising things.
- [ ] I am fluent in English and German.
- [ ] I would like to gain some work experience abroad.
- [ ] I am very good at languages, but have never worked with Excel.
- [ ] How many days off would I have if I worked for the company for six weeks?
- [ ] Enclosed: CV and certificates
- [ ] Enclosed: school reports and sports diploma
- [ ] Please give me the job – I'll do my best.
- [ ] I did work experience with a German company last year.

☐ I would like to be a member of your team.
☐ Please call me as soon as possible.
☐ I'm sure the job will be fun.
☐ I look forward to hearing from you.
☐ I'll do the job, but only if you can arrange a place for me to stay.

20. Now write a formal letter of application in answer to the advertisement from task 19. Write about 160 words.

21. You get the holiday job at ICSD Limited (tasks 19/20). Two weeks before you start work, you get an e-mail from Julia Weston.
Answer it in about 160 words.

From: jweston@icsd.co.uk
To:
Cc:
Subject: last questions

Hi ...,

We're very happy that you'll be starting work at ICSD soon. I'm sure you'll be a great help to our customer service team. My colleagues can't wait to get to know you.
I have a few last questions so that we can get everything settled for your stay with us:
I've found a nice host family for you. The Johnsons have a son your age, so there will be someone to show you around and give you some inside tips for your free time. They also have a cat and a dog. Is that OK or do you have any allergies?
Please tell me whether or not you're vegan or vegetarian or if there's anything else the family needs to know.
Do you already know when you'll arrive in London? Please let me know, then I'll make sure there's someone to pick you up at the airport or train station.

Kind regards,
Julia

Writing

22. Write a story.

    a) Look at the beginning of a story. Then collect ideas for the rest of the story. The following questions are there to help you.

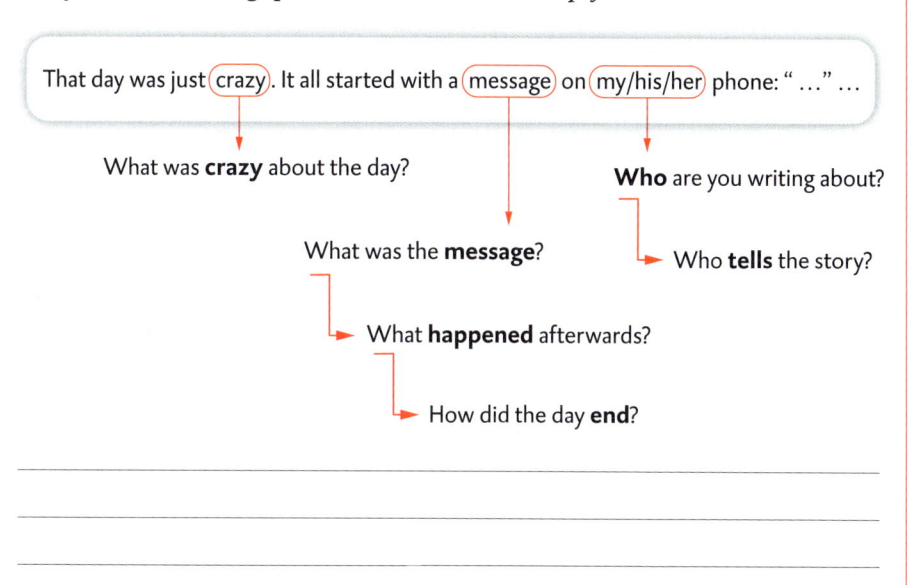

    > That day was just (crazy). It all started with a (message) on (my/his/her) phone: " … " …

    - What was **crazy** about the day?
    - What was the **message**?
    - What **happened** afterwards?
    - How did the day **end**?
    - **Who** are you writing about?
    - Who **tells** the story?

    b) Finish the story in about 160 words.

23. Finish the following story. Write about 160 words.

   Hi, I'm X23 and it's my first day on planet Earth. ...

24. Write a diary entry with the following ending. Write about 160 words.

   ... And those red lights were the last I ever saw of him/her.

25. For a school project you and your classmates have decided to live without social networks for one week.
Write an article for your English school magazine about your experiences during this week. Write about 160 words.

5 Interpreting

In diesem Teil sollst du in **zweisprachigen Kommunikationssituationen** deine Fähigkeiten und Fertigkeiten im Umgang mit der englischen und deutschen Sprache beweisen. Verstehst du schriftliche und mündliche Texte und kannst Informationen **adressatengerecht** wiederholen bzw. weitergeben? Hier geht es darum, dass du Inhalte vom Englischen ins Deutsche oder umgekehrt – Informationen vom Deutschen ins Englische – überträgst. Du sollst hier jedoch **keine wortwörtliche Übersetzung** anfertigen, sondern Informationen **sinngemäß** weitergeben. Das bedeutet, dass es oftmals viele sprachliche Möglichkeiten gibt, wie du etwas in die andere Sprache übertragen kannst.
Teil E deiner Abschlussprüfung enthält normalerweise zwei Aufgaben.

5.1 Häufige Aufgabenstellungen zum Bereich „Interpreting"

Answer the questions in German/in English.

Die Basis für dieses Aufgabenformat ist ein englischer oder deutscher Text, den du zunächst einmal lesen und verstehen musst. Zu diesem Text beantwortest du dann Fragen in der jeweils anderen Sprache. Diese Aufgabe ähnelt den Aufgaben zum Leseverstehen. Der Unterschied besteht darin, dass du **Fragen zu einem englischen Text auf Deutsch, Fragen zu einem deutschen Text auf Englisch beantwortest**. Auch hier ist keine Übersetzung verlangt; du sollst lediglich die passenden Informationen aus dem Text heraussuchen und diese in der anderen Sprache notieren. Stichpunkte sind meist ausreichend – halte dich jedoch an die Aufgabenstellung.

> *Text:* Based on the 1994 Disney animated film, the musical *The Lion King* tells the moving story of Simba, a lion cub, whose father is killed by his mean uncle. After living in exile, Simba returns to the kingdom now ruled by his uncle, avenges his father's death and becomes the new king. *The Lion King* is a worldwide success.
>
> *Frage:* Warum rächt sich Simba an seinem Onkel?
>
> *Antwort:* Simba tötet seinen Onkel, weil dieser Simbas Vater getötet hat.

Beispiel

Dolmetschaufgaben

Hier wird dir eine Situation vorgegeben, in der es notwendig ist, **Sachverhalte sinngemäß** ins Deutsche und/oder ins Englische zu **übertragen**. Manchmal handelt es sich um ein richtiges Gespräch, in dem eine englischsprachige und eine deutschsprachige Person miteinander kommunizieren möchten, aber die Sprache des jeweils anderen nicht (gut genug) beherrschen. Deine Aufgabe ist es dann, vom Deutschen ins Englische und vom Englischen ins Deutsche zu dolmetschen. Manchmal sollst du aber auch nur Informationen in eine Richtung/Sprache übertragen. Lies also die Aufgabenstellung genau und halte dich exakt an die Vorgaben. Achte darauf, dass du die Informationen so formulierst, dass sie adressatengerecht formuliert sind. Das bedeutet, dass du mit einem fremden Erwachsenen anders sprichst als mit einem guten Freund oder einer guten Freundin.

Beispiel

> *Task:* Heute können Fans von Miley live mit ihrem Star chatten. Deine kleine Schwester Leonie möchte mit ihr sprechen, kann aber noch nicht so gut Englisch. Du hilfst ihr:
>
> **Leonie:** Frag mal, wann sie zum ersten Mal auf der Bühne stand.
> **Du:** _Miley, when did you first appear on stage?_
> **Miley:** As an actress or as a singer?
> **Du:** _Als Schauspielerin oder als Sängerin?_

5.2 Übungsaufgaben zum Bereich „Interpreting"

1. At the restaurant – Look at these German sentences. What would you say to the waiter in English?

    a) Frage den Kellner, ob es noch freie Plätze im Restaurant gibt.

    b) Wenn du Platz genommen hast, bitte um die Speisekarte.

    c) Frage, ob der Kellner ein Gericht empfehlen kann.

    d) Bestelle etwas zu essen (Vorspeise, Hauptgang und Dessert).

    e) Äußere den Wunsch nach einer Tasse Kaffee.

    f) Sage, dass das Eis sehr gut geschmeckt hat.

    g) Teile dem Kellner mit, dass du zahlen möchtest.

2. Internet habits – Read the German sentences. Then you can start putting the questions in English to your e-pal from New Zealand.

    Frage deine Gesprächspartnerin,

    a) ob sie in der Freizeit regelmäßig das Internet nutzt.

    b) wie viele Stunden wöchentlich sie online ist.

c) welche Seiten oder Apps ihr am besten gefallen.

d) was für sie das Schlimmste am Internet ist.

e) welche Art von Webseiten bzw. Online-Diensten die meisten Jugendlichen in Neuseeland nutzen.

f) ob sie das Internet auch dazu nutzt, Nachrichten anzusehen.

g) ob es irgendwelche deutschen Seiten gibt, die ihr besser gefallen als englischsprachige.

3. You are on an exchange in Britain. Your German friend Samuel wants to buy two tickets for the pop group "Dance" as a birthday present for his exchange partner. You help him because his English is not so good.

   Verkäufer: Hello, how can I help you?

   Du: Hello.

   Samuel: *Sagst du ihm, dass ich gerne zwei Karten für das Dance-Konzert hätte?*

   a) **Du:** _____

   Verkäufer: They have two concerts. One on Friday and one on Saturday. Which concert does your friend want to go to?

   b) **Du:** _____

   Samuel: *Nimm besser das Freitagskonzert, da bin ich sicher, dass mein Austauschpartner Zeit hat. Und frag bitte, wie viel die Karten kosten.*

   c) **Du:** _____

   Verkäufer: The tickets for Friday are £ 15 or £ 24.

   d) **Du:** _____

   Samuel: *Frag doch bitte noch, was da der Unterschied ist.*

   e) **Du:** _____

   Verkäufer: The £ 24 tickets are near the front but you can still see a lot with the cheaper ones.

   f) **Du:** _____

Samuel: *Gut, dann nehme ich zwei Karten zu 15 £ für das Freitagskonzert.*

g) **Du:** _____

Verkäufer: All right. Two for £15. That's £30, please.

Du: £30. There you are.

Verkäufer: Thank you. And here are your tickets. Bye-bye.

4. The school year has just started and Cameron is new at your school. He is an Australian exchange student who only speaks a little bit of German.
Your teacher, Mr Waas, has lots of information for him and asks you to explain the most important things to him in English.

a) Kannst du Cameron bitte sagen, dass er am Montag als Erstes Chemie bei Frau Müller hat.

b) Der Chemieraum ist recht schwer zu finden. Vielleicht kannst du dich ja vor dem Lehrerzimmer mit ihm treffen und dann könnt ihr gemeinsam hingehen?

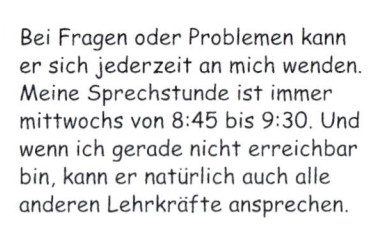

c) Bei Fragen oder Problemen kann er sich jederzeit an mich wenden. Meine Sprechstunde ist immer mittwochs von 8:45 bis 9:30. Und wenn ich gerade nicht erreichbar bin, kann er natürlich auch alle anderen Lehrkräfte ansprechen.

d) Cameron ist nicht der einzige Austauschschüler. Es gibt noch zwei Mädchen aus den USA und einen Jungen aus Kanada, die das Schuljahr an unserer Schule verbringen werden. Um sie alle willkommen zu heißen, veranstalten wir kommenden Donnerstag um 16 Uhr ein kurzes Treffen mit der Schulleitung. Es wird auch eine Schulführung geben, bei der Cameron dann sämtliche Fragen zur Schule und zum Unterricht stellen kann, die sich bis dahin ergeben.

e) Smartphones sind an unserer Schule grundsätzlich verboten. Da Cameron aber noch fast kein Deutsch spricht, darf er die ersten Wochen das Wörterbuch auf seinem Telefon benutzen. Diese Sonderregelung wurde bereits von der Schulleitung genehmigt. Er soll aber bitte den Kolleginnen und Kollegen selbstständig Bescheid geben.

Interpreting

- a.
- b.
- c.
- d.
- e.

5. At the station – You are at the ticket office at the station. The English traveller in front of you hardly speaks any German. Help him to buy the right ticket.

   Traveller: I need a ticket to Stuttgart on Monday morning. I think the best train for me would be at 9 o'clock.

   a) **You:** _____

   Clerk: *Soll es ein einfaches Ticket sein, oder möchte er die Rückfahrt gleich mitbuchen?*

   b) **You:** _____

   Traveller: I need a return ticket. I'd like to be back here at 7 pm.

   c) **You:** _____

   Clerk: *Okay. Das kostet 40 €. Bei einer Platzreservierung würden noch 4 € pro Strecke dazu kommen.*

   d) **You:** _____

   Traveller: Oh, the ticket is very expensive. Is there a discount for senior citizens?

   e) **You:** _____

   Clerk: *Nein, leider nicht. Kannst du den Herrn bitte fragen, ob er das Ticket trotzdem möchte und wie er bezahlen will?*

   f) **You:** _____

   Traveller: I'd like to pay cash. When do I have to be at the station on Monday and which platform is it?

   g) **You:** _____

   Clerk: *Es wäre gut, wenn er eine Viertelstunde vor der Abfahrtszeit an Gleis zwei ist.*

   h) **You:** _____

   Traveller: No problem. Thank you.

Interpreting | 157

6. Your exchange partner from England has just arrived. Your parents would like to talk to her, too, but her German and their English are not very good. You must act as the mediator and explain things to Chloe in English and to your parents in German. Complete the conversation.

Vater: *Hallo, Chloe. Hattest du eine gute Reise?*

a) **Du:** _____

Chloe: Yes, it was fine but very long. I'm quite tired now.

b) **Du:** _____

Mutter: *Vielleicht will sie duschen. Ich habe schon Handtücher in ihr Zimmer gebracht. Kannst du ihr das sagen?*

c) **Du:** _____

Chloe: That would be nice. We travelled overnight and we couldn't shower this morning.

d) **Du:** _____

Vater: *Ich erinnere mich auch an solche Reisen. Sag Chloe, dass du ihr nach dem Duschen zeigen wirst, wo alles ist. Wenn sie fertig ist, können wir zu Mittag essen.*

Chloe: What did your father say?

e) **Du:** _____

Mutter: *Isst Chloe alles? Gibt es irgendetwas, das sie nicht mag?*

f) **Du:** _____

Chloe: The only thing I really hate is spinach.

g) **Du:** _____

Vater: *Ich esse auch keinen Spinat. Spinat ist wirklich fürchterlich.*

h) **Du:** _____

7. Dein Vater hat einen Freund aus England zu Besuch. Dieser möchte ein paar Tage mit seiner kleinen Tochter nach München fahren. Ihr schaut euch gemeinsam einen Hotelprospekt an. Da dein Vater gerade nicht zu Hause ist, beantwortest du die Fragen des Gastes auf Englisch.

   a) Where is the hotel?
   _____

   b) Where can I park my car?
   _____

   c) I'd like to visit some sights in Munich. How can I get to the sights?
   _____

   d) Does the hotel allow children as well?
   _____

   e) In the brochure they mention a "Fitnessraum". That's a gym, isn't it? What are the opening hours?
   _____

   f) And what about meals?
   _____

   g) How can I book a couple of nights in the hotel? *(2 items)*
   _____

   h) Can I pay by credit card or do I need cash?
   _____

   i) Do I need to pay any advance charges before I arrive there?
   _____

The English visitors

Hotel Bavaria München ☆☆☆
Ankommen und rundum wohlfühlen

Verbringen Sie entspannte Urlaubstage in unserem idyllischen Landhotel, welches dank seiner naturnahen Lage am Stadtrand Münchens viel Ruhe und Erholung bietet.

Dennoch können Sie aufgrund der ausgezeichneten Verkehrsanbindung alle Sehenswürdigkeiten Münchens mit dem Bus oder der S-Bahn bequem und schnell erreichen. Ihr Auto können Sie währenddessen sicher in unserer hoteleigenen Garage lassen.

Kinder dürfen sich auf dem neu errichteten Spielplatz an der frischen Luft austoben und der bestens ausgestattete Fitnessraum kann von unseren erwachsenen Gästen rund um die Uhr genutzt werden.

Unser hauseigenes Restaurant serviert neben internationaler und bayerischer Küche auch vegetarische Gerichte sowie Diätkost. Teilen Sie uns am besten vorab telefonisch Ihre Wünsche mit.

Weitere Informationen und Buchung:
www.hotel-bavaria-munich.de
Tel.: **089/723489**

Bezahlen können Sie selbstverständlich bar oder mit Kreditkarte.

Interpreting

8. Read the following text and answer the questions in English.

   a) How hot does it have to be so that the pupils can go home earlier?

   b) Who decides this?

   c) Will there be a bus to take the pupils home if they have "Hitzefrei"?

   d) Does "Hitzefrei" always mean that the last lessons are cancelled?

   e) What about the younger pupils? Can they be sent home, even though their parents might not be at home?

   f) Do the pupils have to go to soccer practice when it is very hot?

Liebe Eltern, liebe Schülerinnen und Schüler,

die erste Hitzewelle des Jahres steht an, daher hier zur Erinnerung die Hitzefrei-Regelungen an unserer Schule:

- 😊 Nur wenn die Temperaturen in den Klassenräumen bereits um 10 Uhr morgens die 25°-Marke überschreiten, können Unterrichtsstunden ausfallen. Die Temperaturmessung erfolgt an verschiedenen Standorten im Schulgebäude durch den Hausmeister.

- 😊 Über den Ausfall von Stunden bestimmen die Schulleitungen aller Schulen der Region gemeinsam. Die Abfahrtszeiten der Schulbusse werden koordiniert und entsprechend vorverlegt.

- 😊 Liegen die Temperaturen mehrere Tage lang bereits am Vormittag über 25 °C, so werden alle Stunden des Schultages auf 35 Minuten verkürzt. Eine solche Regelung wird ggf. bis spätestens 12 Uhr des Vortages bekannt gegeben.

- 😊 Sollten Sie auch im Falle von „Hitzefrei" eine Betreuung Ihres Kindes wünschen, so geben Sie bitte beiliegendes Formular unterschrieben an uns zurück. Eine Betreuung bis 14 Uhr wird auf Wunsch gewährleistet.

- 😊 Bei extremen Temperaturen und erhöhten Ozonwerten findet kein Sportunterricht im Freien statt. Die Neigungsgruppen Fußball und Leichtathletik müssen dann entfallen, der reguläre Sportunterricht wird in die Sport- bzw. Schwimmhalle verlegt.

- 😊 Während der Hitzewelle ist Trinken im Unterricht selbstverständlich erlaubt. Bitte geben Sie Ihren Kindern ausreichend Getränke bzw. Kleingeld für den Getränkeautomaten mit.

gez. Die Schulleitung

9. Du bist gerade mit Freunden auf einer Europareise und findest im Internet ein Angebot für günstige Flüge von Paris nach London. Lies dir die Buchungsbedingungen der Fluggesellschaft durch und beantworte die Fragen auf Deutsch.

FastFly – Booking information and conditions

FastFly does not issue **tickets**. Bookings and the check-in are an online service only. However, in London and Paris we have an airport counter for emergencies, forgotten details or for extra baggage. Using this service costs an extra £ 30 – additional baggage costs £ 50 more per bag.

Booking: fill in all details in the online booking form including payment details. Please note that you cannot reserve seats on this flight. We offer an express service for an extra £ 10 each way. Using the express service means that you are in the first group of people on and off the plane.

Once you have completed the booking form, no **changes** or **refunds** are possible.

You may carry one bag with you as **hand luggage**. Hand luggage must be no larger than 50 cm x 40 cm x 25 cm and weigh no more than 12 kg. Handbags and laptops cannot be carried separately.

Sharp objects such as knives or scissors may not be carried in hand luggage. Liquids must be put into a clear plastic bag available at both airports. You are not allowed to take more than 250 ml in liquids with you.

Once you have completed your **booking**, you will be given a check-in number. We will also send this to you by e-mail. You can check in online or via our mobile app 24 hours before your flight leaves. Once you have checked in, you can either print out our boarding card or use the mobile boarding pass on your smartphone. You will need this document at the airport.

When you book your flight, don't miss out on the **great offers** that FastFly provide: 50 % off airport parking; 30 % off car rental; 15 % off many hotels in Paris and London.

a) Wie kann man einen Flug bei „FastFly" buchen?

b) Was kann man tun, wenn man in Paris mit dem Personal der Fluggesellschaft sprechen muss? Was muss man dabei beachten?

c) Was bedeutet „express service"?

d) Wie viel kostet dieser Service für den Hin- und Rückflug?

e) Welche Regelungen gelten für den Fall, dass man den Flug absagen muss?

f) Wie viele Gepäckstücke darf man mitnehmen?

g) Wann und wie kann man einchecken?

h) Welche Vorteile hat es, wenn man mit „FastFly" fliegt? *(2 Aspekte)*
   ▶
   ▶

10. Für ein Projekt zu Städten in Kanada musst du Informationen über Vancouver recherchieren. Du findest diesen Text und notierst dir die wichtigsten Informationen zu folgenden Aspekten auf Deutsch:
    a) Lage von Vancouver *(2 Fakten)*
       ▶
       ▶
    b) Wetter und Klima *(2 Fakten)*
       ▶
       ▶
    c) zwei Attraktionen der Stadt und was man dort machen kann
       (ein Aspekt für jede der beiden Attraktionen)
       ▶
       ▶

d) möglicher Grund, warum Vancouver eine so saubere Stadt ist

_____

e) Ziele der Stadtverwaltung für die Zukunft *(2 Ziele)*
- _____
- _____

Vancouver B.C.

Vancouver is a beautiful city with more than 630,000 inhabitants on the west coast of Canada, about 50 kilometres away from the border to the United States, but about 3,500 kilometres away from Ottawa, the capital of Canada. And it is definitely a rainy city. To be precise, it is the 9th rainiest place in Canada, and people say that if it rains in Canada, it rains in Vancouver. Vancouver is surrounded by water on three sides and is close to the Rocky Mountains. Its climate is one of the mildest in Canada. It is situated in the province of British Columbia, which is the third-largest province after Quebec and Ontario. The capital city of this province is not Vancouver but Victoria.

Vancouver is a popular tourist destination. Some of the must-sees are Christ Church Cathedral, Chinatown, Vancouver Art Gallery and the Capilano Suspension Bridge. Stanley Park, which is located on a peninsula in the heart of Vancouver, is one of the largest innercity parks in North America and definitely worth a visit, with many attractions for the entire family on offer. Kitsilano, or "Kits", as the neighbourhood is usually called, is also popular among tourists. It is a fantastic destination if you want to do sports at Kits beach, eat out or go shopping.

Many tourists also visit Gastown, the city's original settlement, to see the Gastown Steam Clock and to take a walk around the cobblestone[1] streets.

Vancouver is a very clean city, much cleaner than most European or US cities, maybe because city authorities issue tickets for smoking, spitting or peeing in public places. What is more, Vancouver wants to become the greenest city in the world. That is why city authorities devised an action plan to reach this goal. One of the aims, for example, is to make sure that every inhabitant lives within a five-minute walk of a park. They also want to plant 150,000 more trees and want to convince the inhabitants of Vancouver to walk and cycle more or use public transport.

1 cobblestone – *Kopfsteinpflaster*

11. Read the following text and answer the questions in **German**.

Thanksgiving: An American Tradition

The American holiday of Thanksgiving is celebrated every year on the fourth Thursday in November. The holiday is during fall – the main season for harvesting crops. Thanksgiving is an autumn harvest festival like those found in many cultures around the world. On this day, most Americans gather with friends and family. Many take time to think about what they are thankful for, cook up a storm, and eat. A lot. The star of most Thanksgiving dinners is a roasted turkey but there are many side dishes too, such as mashed potatoes, sweet potatoes and vegetable casseroles, for example. For some people, the best part of the meal is dessert. The quintessential Thanksgiving dessert is pie. Pumpkin, cherry, apple or pecan pie are all great ways to finish off a Thanksgiving meal … if you are not too full of food by that point!

Thanksgiving Travel

Some Americans must travel long distances to be with their families. In fact, the Sunday after Thanksgiving is the busiest travel day of the entire year. This is usually when people return home from family gatherings.

Not everyone can make the return home each Thanksgiving, so young people living in cities away from their hometowns sometimes celebrate "Friendsgiving" – a Thanksgiving meal with their friends instead of their family. They gather at someone's apartment or house and have a "potluck". This is a meal where everyone who is invited brings food to share with others.

Beyond the Table

Thanksgiving is a big day for television, games and other entertainment. One tradition is the television broadcast of Macy's Thanksgiving Day Parade. It takes place each year in New York City. Workers of the Macy's store on Herald Square organized the first parade in 1924. Many of the workers were immigrants and wanted to hold a big parade like the ones in Europe, so they dressed in costumes and borrowed some animals from the zoo, such as elephants, camels and donkeys. They also carried small balloons that floated just overhead.

Many professional football games are also played on Thanksgiving. Fans of the sport enjoy relaxing and watching a game or two after eating a big Thanksgiving meal. Some start Thanksgiving Day early – and in a healthy way. So-called "Turkey Trot" races take place in many towns and cities. These events involve runners dressing up in a Thanksgiving-related costume and running a short distance – usually five kilometers.

Serving Those Less Fortunate

Certainly, not everyone in America has an easy Thanksgiving. The United States is home to many poor and homeless people. Some cannot afford a Thanksgiving dinner. Others are without friends or families. Many religious and service organizations around the country try to fill these needs. Some provide community dinners at churches and other centers. Some groups also deliver Thanksgiving meals to people too sick or old to leave their homes.

Adapted from: Caty Weaver, Ashley Thompson, Voice of America Learning English, November 22, 2017

a) Wann wird in den USA Thanksgiving gefeiert?

b) Was versteht man unter „Friendsgiving" und „potluck"?
   ▸ _____
   ▸ _____

c) Wie lief die erste „Macy's Thanksgiving Day Parade" ab? *(2 Aspekte)*
   ▸ _____
   ▸ _____

d) Welche Distanz müssen Teilnehmer*innen an einem „Turkey Trot"-Rennen normalerweise laufen?

e) Auf welche Weise versuchen religiöse oder gemeinnützige Organisationen, bedürftige, einsame oder alte Menschen an Thanksgiving zu unterstützen? *(2 Aspekte)*
   ▸ _____
   ▸ _____

12. Lies den Text über Mount Rushmore und mache dir Notizen zu folgenden Aspekten.

    a) Warum wurde das Denkmal gebaut?

    b) Welche Probleme traten bei der Fertigstellung auf? *(2 Probleme)*
       ▸ _____
       ▸ _____

    c) Aus welchen Gründen wurden George Washington und Abraham Lincoln für Mount Rushmore ausgewählt? *(je ein Aspekt)*
       ▸ George Washington: _____
       ▸ Abraham Lincoln: _____

    d) Welche Kosten fallen für einen Besuch an?

Welcome to Mount Rushmore

Four presidents – **George Washington**, **Thomas Jefferson**, **Theodore Roosevelt** and **Abraham Lincoln** – await your visit to Mount Rushmore, South Dakota.

History
The story started in 1920 when a man called Doane Robinson had the idea for a project to encourage people from all over the country to visit South Dakota. However, it was many years before enough money was raised to begin the work. The faces then took 14 years to carve out of the mountain and they were not completed until late 1941. During this time many problems occurred, one of which involved the face of Thomas Jefferson that started life on George Washington's right-hand side, but after 18 months it was decided that the face would be better on his left, so it was blown up and the work had to be started again.

Why these four presidents?
The presidents chosen were very important figures in American history. As you look at them, they are:
1. George Washington (1732 – 1799), who was the first president of the USA and seen as the founder of the country after independence from Britain.
2. Thomas Jefferson (1743 – 1826), who wrote the Declaration of Independence and increased the size of the USA by adding 15 states to it. He was America's third president.
3. Theodore Roosevelt (1858 – 1919), who was the 26th president and very important for America's economy and for workers' rights. He was also responsible for getting the Panama Canal built.
4. Abraham Lincoln (1809 – 1865), who played a major role in the American Civil War and kept the Union together during this difficult time. He was the 16th president and spoke out for the abolition of slavery, too.

Visits
We recommend you allow two hours for your visit. There is no entrance fee but parking costs $11. There is no camping allowed at Mount Rushmore National Memorial and there are no hotels.

Directions
Follow Highway 16 to Keystone and then take Highway 244 – this leads you directly to the monument.

Illumination
The faces are illuminated during the following periods:
May – July: 9.00 p.m. (until midnight)
August – September: 8.00 p.m. (for three hours)
October – April: every night for one hour after dark

South Dakota
GREAT FACES. GREAT PLACES.

6 Speaking – Kommunikationsprüfung

Immer wieder wird im Unterricht auch deine mündliche Kommunikationsfähigkeit überprüft. Die baden-württembergischen Realschüler*innen müssen im Rahmen der Realschulabschlussprüfung auch eine mündliche Prüfung ablegen. Die sogenannte **Kommunikationsprüfung** findet im Frühjahr – und somit vor den schriftlichen Prüfungen – statt. Die Note der Kommunikationsprüfung zählt zweifach zur Prüfungsnote, die schriftliche Prüfung dreifach.

6.1 Strategien zum Bereich „Speaking"

Langfristige Vorbereitung

Sich in einer Fremdsprache mündlich auszudrücken, erfordert Übung. Man kann sich nicht kurzfristig – quasi über Nacht – auf diesen Prüfungsbereich vorbereiten. Will man in einer mündlichen Prüfung gut abschneiden, dann sollte man **langfristig** und **nachhaltig** an der Sprechfertigkeit arbeiten.

Es ist deshalb sinnvoll, wenn du möglichst frühzeitig damit beginnst, dich auch in deiner Freizeit mit Englisch zu beschäftigen. Du kannst z. B. englische Filme oder Serien anschauen, da du dadurch nicht nur deinen Wortschatz erweiterst, sondern sich auch dein Sprachgefühl verbessert. Schau dir doch einfach einmal deinen Lieblingsfilm oder deine Lieblingsserie auf Englisch an. Wenn du schon weißt, was passiert, ist es oft gar nicht so schwer, der Handlung zu folgen. Wenn es am Anfang noch sehr anstrengend sein sollte, kannst du auch Untertitel benutzen; die Hauptsache ist, du bleibst dran. Auch englischsprachige Clips und Hörspiele sind eine gute Vorbereitung. Vielleicht verabredest du dich auch zu englischen Gesprächsrunden oder ihr spielt englische Spiele zusammen. Das Wichtigste ist, deinen aktiven und passiven Wortschatz zu erweitern und die Scheu vor der fremdsprachlichen Kommunikation zu verlieren.

Übungsmöglichkeiten bietet dir natürlich auch dein Englischunterricht. Nimm aktiv am Unterrichtsgeschehen teil, d. h., melde dich so oft wie möglich und sprich Englisch. So gewinnst du Routine und wirst nach und nach gelassener. Wenn du dabei künftig auch noch die folgenden grundsätzlichen Tipps und Hinweise berücksichtigst, klappt das mit der Zeit sicherlich recht gut.

> **Tipp**
> - Sprich deutlich und nicht zu schnell.
> - Frage nach, wenn du etwas nicht verstanden hast.
> - Vermeide es, mit *yes* oder *no* zu antworten. Mit solchen Antworten kannst du keine Gespräche in Gang halten und auch deine Sprechfertigkeit nicht unter Beweis stellen.
> - Lerne, Sachverhalte auf unterschiedliche Weise auszudrücken, damit du nicht ständig dieselben Formulierungen wiederholst.
> - Versuche, die Unterhaltung selbst zu bestimmen, vor allem in Gruppendiskussionen. Auf diese Weise sprichst du über **deine** Themen. So hast du mehr zu sagen und bist selbstbewusster bei dem, was du sagst.

6.2 Die Kommunikationsprüfung

Ablauf der Prüfung

Die Kommunikationsprüfung kann entweder als Einzel- oder als Tandemprüfung durchgeführt werden.

▶ Es sind immer zwei Lehrkräfte dabei. In der Regel sind das deine Englischlehrerin bzw. dein Englischlehrer und noch eine zweite Fachlehrkraft.

▶ Die Prüfung besteht aus drei Teilen, nämlich der Präsentation, einer kommunikativ-situativen Aufgabe und einer Sprachmittlung.

▶ Als Einzelprüfung dauert die Prüfung etwa 15 Minuten, als Tandemprüfung rund 30 Minuten.

▶ Jeder Prüfungsteil dauert in etwa fünf Minuten.

Prüfungsteile

Präsentation

▶ Zu Beginn der Prüfung steht die **Präsentation** eines von dir gewählten und selbstständig vorbereiteten Themas. In der Prüfung hast du etwa fünf Minuten **Zeit**, dein Thema vorzustellen. Es bietet sich an, die Präsentation z. B. mithilfe einer PowerPoint-Präsentation, Flipchart oder mit Postern zu veranschaulichen. Auch Realien sind zur Veranschaulichung geeignet. Bei der Präsentation kommt es darauf an, dass du frei sprichst und dein Thema so darbietest, dass deine Zuhörer*innen deinem Vortrag gut folgen können.

Spätestens drei Monate vor der Kommunikationsprüfung solltest du mit deiner Lehrerin oder deinem Lehrer das **Thema** für deine Präsentation vereinbaren. Wähle es sehr sorgfältig aus; es sollte ein Thema sein, über das du wirklich gut Bescheid weißt und das dich interessiert – deine Begeisterung dafür wird deine Lehrkraft nämlich auch in der Prüfung spüren. Inhaltlich muss dein Thema dem Stoff von Klasse 7–10 entsprechen.

Mögliche Themen sind z. B. ein englischsprachiges Land (England, Irland, Neuseeland, Südafrika...) oder eine historische Persönlichkeit bzw. eine Person des öffentlichen Lebens (Rosa Parks, Queen Elizabeth II, Malala Yousafzai, George Washington, Mahatma Gandhi, Barack Obama...). Du kannst aber auch ein spannendes Buch oder ein Musikinstrument vorstellen. Darüber hinaus eignen sich natürlich auch Themen wie die Ureinwohner*innen eines englischsprachigen Landes, geschichtliche Ereignisse oder aktuelle politische Entwicklungen. Hast du dich für ein Thema entschieden, musst du auf die **Suche nach Informationsmaterial** gehen. Vor allem, wenn du online recherchierst, solltest du darauf achten, nur verlässliche Quellen zu verwenden. Erstelle danach zunächst einmal eine Ideensammlung.

Beginne rechtzeitig mit der Ausarbeitung und plane dafür ausreichend Zeit ein, denn du musst nicht nur die Gliederung deines Vortrags im Kopf haben und das Vokabular und dessen Aussprache beherrschen, sondern auch das Anschauungsmaterial vorbereiten und ggf. die Technik im Griff haben. Bei der Prüfung muss alles klappen!

Du kannst dir ein paar **Stichpunkte** oder eine Mindmap als Gedankenstütze für deinen Vortrag **notieren**. Diese Stichpunkte sind hilfreich, falls du einmal den „roten Faden" verlieren solltest. Achte aber in jedem Fall darauf, dass du frei, flüssig und zusammenhängend sprichst – du darfst also nicht an deinen Aufzeichnungen „kleben". Außerdem solltest du es vermeiden, dass dein Vortrag wortwörtlich auf dem von dir vorbereiteten Anschauungsmaterial wiederzufinden ist, denn das gibt Punktabzug.

Übe deine Präsentation so oft, bis du dich ganz sicher fühlst – das ist das beste Mittel gegen Aufregung. Deine Präsentation solltest du zuerst alleine üben, dann aber auch jemandem vorsprechen, der dir Feedback gibt und deine Zeit stoppt, damit du nicht zu lange redest. Fünf Minuten können lang sein – oder auch viel zu kurz. Bedenke, dass du bei der tatsächlichen Prüfung oft schneller sprichst, weil du aufgeregt bist. Beim Sprechen vor „Publikum" kannst du die Prüfungssituation simulieren und deine Nervosität in den Griff kriegen. Außerdem bekommst du Rückmeldung zum Aufbau und Inhalt deines Vortrags, zum Sprechtempo, zu Gestik und Mimik sowie zum Gebrauch von Grammatik und Wortschatz. Versuche, die Aufmerksamkeit deiner Zuhörer*innen aufrechtzuerhalten, indem du immer wieder Blickkontakt mit ihnen aufnimmst.

Entscheidest du dich für die Tandemprüfung, können du und dein Mitprüfling zwei unterschiedliche Präsentationen machen oder eine Präsentation zum gleichen übergeordneten Thema, wobei klar sein muss, wer für welchen Teil verantwortlich ist.

Im Anschluss an die Präsentation werden themenbezogene **Rückfragen** oder Verständnisfragen gestellt.

▶ Der zweite Teil der Prüfung ist eine **kommunikativ-situative Aufgabe**.
In einer vorgegebenen Situation sollst du zeigen, dass du frei sprechen und einen echten Dialog führen kannst. Das bedeutet, dass du der jeweiligen Situation angemessen – auf dem Niveau der Bildungsstandards – spontan agieren und reagieren kannst. Grundlage des Gesprächs können z. B. Bildimpulse oder Rollenspiel-Kärtchen sein. Mithilfe dieses Materials sollst du dich mit deinem Gegenüber unterhalten, Informationen austauschen und Meinungen und Gefühle ausdrücken. Am Ende soll eine Entscheidung getroffen werden (z. B. Planung eines Reiseziels, Entscheidung für einen Nebenjob) bzw. die Aufgabe erfüllt worden sein (z. B. Buchung eines Hotelzimmers oder Kauf einer Fahrkarte). Wichtig ist, dass du auf die Äußerungen der anderen Person eingehst und nicht einfach etwas sagst, was nicht zum vorangegangenen Redebeitrag passt. Rückfragen, wenn du etwas nicht verstanden hast, sind völlig in Ordnung und spiegeln einen natürlichen Gesprächsverlauf wider. In einer Tandemprüfung findet das Gespräch zwischen dir und deinem Mitprüfling statt. Wirst du alleine geprüft, übernimmt deine Lehrkraft die zweite Rolle.

Kommunikativ-situative Aufgabe

Sprachmittlung

▶ Der dritte Teil der Prüfung ist eine **Sprachmittlung**. Deine Aufgabe ist es, zwischen zwei Parteien in einer Alltagssituation zu vermitteln, wobei eine der Personen kein Englisch und die andere kein Deutsch kann. Diese beiden Rollen werden von den zwei prüfenden Lehrkräften übernommen. Hier ist es wichtig, dass du nicht wörtlich übersetzt, sondern sinngemäß Informationen von der einen in die andere Sprache überträgst. Achte darauf, dass du alle relevanten Aspekte weitergibst und dass diese auch verstanden werden. Unwichtige Details solltest du weglassen. Bei der Sprachmittlung ist es außerdem wichtig, adressatengerecht und situationsangemessen zu handeln, denn es macht einen großen Unterschied, ob du z. B. zwischen zwei dir unbekannten Erwachsenen vermittelst oder zwischen deinem kleinen Bruder und deinem Austauschschüler.

Bei der ins Englische übertragenen Äußerung kommt es vor allem auf die Verständlichkeit an. Wenn du beim Sprechen jedoch den einen oder anderen kleinen sprachlichen Fehler machst, ist das nicht so schlimm. Konzentriere dich, damit du die Informationen immer in der richtigen Sprache weitergibst.

6.3 Hilfreiche Wendungen zum Bereich „Speaking"

Die folgenden Wörter und Ausdrücke helfen dir in Gesprächen. Du solltest sie auswendig lernen. Die Wendungen sind übrigens auch als digitale „MindCards" verfügbar, mit denen du am Smartphone oder Tablet üben kannst.

Die eigene Meinung ausdrücken

I would prefer … *Ich würde lieber …*	↔ I would prefer not to … *Ich würde lieber nicht …*
I would like … *Ich würde/möchte gern …*	↔ I don't like … / I dislike … *Ich mag … nicht.*
I think / believe / expect / imagine / suppose (that) … *Ich glaube, (dass) …*	↔ I don't think / believe / expect / imagine / suppose (that) … *Ich glaube nicht, (dass) …*
I doubt (that) … *Ich bezweifle, (dass) …*	↔ I don't doubt (that) … *Ich bezweifle nicht, (dass) …*
I'm for … *Ich bin für … / dafür, (dass) …*	↔ I'm against … *Ich bin gegen … / dagegen, (dass) …*
I would … *Ich würde …*	↔ I wouldn't … *Ich würde nicht …*
I'm sure / certain … *Ich bin sicher …*	↔ I'm not sure / certain … *Ich bin nicht sicher …*
In my opinion … *Meiner Meinung nach …*	↔ That's not my opinion. *Das ist nicht meine Meinung.*

Andere nach ihrer Meinung fragen

What's your opinion / view (about / on) …?	*Was ist deine Meinung zu …?/ Was denkst du über …?*
How do you view the situation? / How do you see this?	*Wie siehst du die Situation?/ Wie siehst du das?*
Could you explain something / your ideas / your feelings / to me?	*Könntest du mir etwas/deine Vorstellungen/deine Gefühle erklären?*
What would you say about …?	*Was würdest du über/zum Thema … sagen?*
How do you (personally) feel about …?	*Was hältst du (persönlich) von …?*
(stark) What about (no smoking in public places)? Do you think that's right?	*Was denkst du über (das Rauchverbot in der Öffentlichkeit)? Glaubst du, dass das richtig/in Ordnung ist?*
(stark, eine Antwort fordernd) I don't suppose you'll / you would agree, will you / would you?	*Du wirst sicher nicht zustimmen, oder?*

> **Tipp**
> Du kannst auch Fragen mit Verneinungen stellen, um deine*n Gesprächspartner*in zu einer Meinungsäußerung zu bringen:

Don't you think that …?	*Glaubst du nicht, dass …?*
Wouldn't you like to see …?	*Hättest du nicht auch lieber …?*
Shouldn't we …?	*Sollten wir nicht …?*

Zustimmen und widersprechen

I agree (with you). *Ich bin deiner Meinung.*	↔	(I'm sorry but) I disagree (with you). *Ich bin nicht deiner Meinung.*
Yes, of course. *Ja, natürlich.*	↔	No, not at all. *Nein, ganz und gar nicht.*
That's a good idea. *Das ist ein guter Vorschlag/eine gute Idee.*	↔	Excuse me but I think that's a bad idea./That's a bad idea. *Das ist kein guter Vorschlag/keine gute Idee.*
I'm for that. *Ich bin dafür.*	↔	(I'm afraid) I'm against that. *Ich bin dagegen.*
You're right (about … / to say that …). *Du hast recht (mit …/wenn du sagst, dass …).*	↔	I'm sorry, but you're wrong about … /You're wrong to say that … *Das stimmt nicht./Es stimmt nicht, wenn du sagst, dass …*

Speaking – Kommunikationsprüfung

> **Tipp**
> Wenn du entsprechende Adverbien vor „right", „wrong" und „understand" stellst, wird deine Antwort sehr deutlich.

You are absolutely right. *Du hast völlig recht.*	↔	You are totally wrong. *Du liegst völlig falsch.*
You fully understand. *Du verstehst vollkommen.*	↔	I think you don't really understand (the problem). *Ich glaube, du verstehst (das Problem) überhaupt nicht.*

> **Tipp**
> Wenn du dir mit deiner Meinung nicht sicher bist, kannst du dies z. B. folgendermaßen ausdrücken:

I'm not sure / certain.	*Ich bin mir nicht sicher.*

Jemanden unterbrechen

Can I ask you something?	*Kann ich dich etwas fragen?*
Can / May I (just) say something, please?	*Kann ich bitte etwas sagen?*
Excuse me, but …	*Entschuldige, aber …*
I don't wish to interrupt you but … / I'm sorry to stop you but …	*Ich möchte dich nicht unterbrechen, aber … / Ich unterbreche dich ungern, aber …*
I'm sorry, I don't agree with …	*Ich bin anderer Meinung (als) …*
I'm sorry, that's not right / fair.	*Das ist nicht richtig / fair.*
I'm sorry, but (I'd just like to say) …	*Es tut mir leid, aber (ich möchte gerne sagen, dass) …*

> **Tipp**
> Manchmal möchtest du jemanden unterbrechen, weil du eine ausgeprägte Meinung zu dem hast, was gesagt worden ist. Die „Nettigkeiten" werden dann meist weggelassen und die Ausdrucksweise ist sehr viel direkter. Denke aber daran, dass du nicht zu emotional oder wütend werden darfst, denn sonst besteht die Gefahr, dass du die Kontrolle über deine Äußerungen verlierst und dann vielleicht Fehler machst, die dir sonst nicht unterlaufen würden.

(*stark*) You're wrong there.	*Du hast nicht recht. / Da hast du mit Sicherheit nicht recht.*
I don't think you're right. / That's not right.	*Ich glaube nicht, dass du recht hast.*
(*wütend*) Oh, come on! You don't really believe that.	*Das glaubst du doch selbst nicht.*
How can you say that?	*Wie kannst du das sagen?*

Darum bitten, dass etwas wiederholt wird

Excuse me, could you say that again, please?	*Könntest du das bitte noch einmal sagen?*

Sorry, can you repeat that, please? / Could you please repeat what you said about …?	*Kannst du das bitte wiederholen? / Könntest du bitte wiederholen, was du über … gesagt hast?*
I'm sorry I didn't quite hear what you said. Could you say it again, please? / I'm afraid I didn't quite catch / understand you. Could you repeat it, please?	*Es tut mir leid, aber ich habe nicht genau gehört, was du gesagt hast. Könntest du es bitte noch einmal sagen? / Es tut mir leid, aber ich habe dich nicht genau verstanden. Könntest du es bitte wiederholen?*
I'm sorry / I'm afraid, I missed / forgot what you were saying (about …). Could you explain it again / once more, please?	*Leider habe ich nicht verstanden / vergessen, was du (über …) gesagt hast. Könntest du mir das bitte noch einmal erklären?*
I'm sorry / I'm afraid, you were talking a bit too fast for me. Could you say it again more slowly, please? / Would you mind repeating what you said, please?	*Es tut mir leid, du hast für mich etwas zu schnell gesprochen. Könntest du das bitte etwas langsamer wiederholen? / Das war leider ein wenig zu schnell für mich. Könntest du bitte wiederholen, was du gesagt hast?*

Ein bereits behandeltes Thema aufgreifen

You said earlier …	*Du hast vorhin gesagt …*
You mentioned / talked about …	*Du hast … erwähnt.*
A few minutes ago you said …	*Vor ein paar Minuten hast du gesagt …*
As you said before …	*Wie du vorhin / schon gesagt hast, …*
Can we go back to … for a minute?	*Können wir noch einmal auf … zurückkommen?*

Das Thema wechseln

We've talked a lot about … Could we look at … now?	*Wir haben viel über … geredet. Könnten wir jetzt über … sprechen?*
Can we move on and talk about …?	*Können wir weitergehen und über … reden?*
We should really talk about … too.	*Wir sollten wirklich auch über … reden.*
That's what I think about (tennis). But what about (football)? What do you think about it?	*So denke ich über (Tennis). Aber was meinst du zu (Fußball)?*
Can we talk about … now?	*Können wir jetzt über … sprechen?*
Perhaps we should also talk about …	*Vielleicht sollten wir auch über … reden.*
Can / May I say something at this point?	*Kann ich an dieser Stelle etwas sagen?*

Speaking – Kommunikationsprüfung

Andere zum Reden bringen

Direkte Fragen mit Fragewörtern, wie z. B. „what", „where", „when", „who", „which", „how":

What do you think, (Anne)? *Was meinst du, (Anne)?*

Entscheidungsfragen (Fragen ohne Fragewort):

Are you interested in …? *Interessierst du dich für …?*

Bestätigungsfragen:

The weather is terrible today, isn't it? *Das Wetter ist schrecklich, oder?*

Tipp

> Manchmal musst du kurz überlegen, bis du weißt, was du sagen möchtest. Damit das Gespräch dennoch nicht unterbrochen wird, kannst du folgende Füllwörter benutzen: *Well, … / Let me see … / I see … / I'm not sure, but … / What I'm trying to say is … / Actually, I think … / I guess …*

6.4 Übungsaufgaben zum Bereich „Speaking"

Präsentation – monologisches Sprechen

1. **Australia** – Talk about everything you know about Australia and what makes it special. What makes it worth travelling to?

2. **Martin Luther King**
   a) Put the information on Martin Luther King Jr. (**A–K**) in the right order.

A	He won the Nobel Peace Prize in 1964.
B	He married in 1953.
C	He became a minister and civil rights activist.
D	He and his wife had 4 children.
E	He became the president of the SCLC[1].
F	Martin Luther King Jr. was born in 1929.
G	He died in Memphis.
H	He studied at Crozer Theological Seminary.
I	He led the Montgomery Bus Boycott.
J	He organised and led the March on Washington.
K	He was assassinated in 1968.

   1 SCLC – Southern Christian Leadership Conference

Early life and education	Family	Career	Important political events	Achievement(s)	Death

   b) With the help of the information you gathered in task a), prepare a presentation about the life of Martin Luther King. Add further details too.

Speaking – Kommunikationsprüfung | 175

3. You and your partner want to do something special after the exams. You have collected several ideas. Together, discuss them and decide afterwards what you are going to do.

   These are your ideas:
   ▶ a weekend at the lake
   ▶ a rock-climbing course
   ▶ a bike tour
   ▶ a camping weekend in the wilderness
   ▶ a city trip
   ▶ a trip to the beach
   ▶ a weekend on a farm, …

Kommunikativ-situative Aufgaben – dialogisches Sprechen

4. **Teacher:** After our summer fête last year the school raised €2,500 to give to a charity. Which charity do you think we should give it to? Here are some we have selected, but of course you may have other ideas too. Discuss carefully the reasons for or against each charity and try to come to a decision about what to do with the money.

€ 2,500 for charity

sponsor a child in the developing world, providing education

help AIDS awareness

toys and things for a local kindergarten

animal hospital

to support Green, a new environmental group

Speaking – Kommunikationsprüfung | 177

Bei den folgenden kommunikativ-situativen Aufgaben gibt es zwei Varianten, damit du dich sowohl auf eine **Tandemprüfung**, in der du ein Gespräch mit deinem Mitprüfling führst, als auch auf eine **Einzelprüfung**, in der deine Englisch-Lehrkraft die zweite Rolle übernimmt, vorbereiten kannst.

5. Choose either task a) or task b).
   a) You want to buy a new smartphone, but your mum thinks it is too expensive. She suggested that you pay half of it. You agreed, but you need to look for a part-time job.
   Now you are talking to your mother about different possibilities of how to earn money and the advantages and disadvantages of each job. — Einzelprüfung

   b) You want to buy a new smartphone, but your mum thinks it is too expensive. She suggested that you pay half of it. You agreed, but you need to look for a part-time job.
   Now you are talking to one of your friends about different possibilities of how to earn money and the advantages and disadvantages of each job. — Tandemprüfung

   Here are some jobs you can discuss:
   ▶ babysitting
   ▶ tutoring younger students
   ▶ doing the shopping for older people
   ▶ waitressing in a café
   ▶ doing a paper round
   ▶ walking someone's dog
   ▶ helping people in the garden
   ▶ …

Speaking – Kommunikationsprüfung

Einzelprüfung

6. Choose either task a) or task b).

   a) **A trip to London**

   You are a tourist in London. Read role card ❶. Act out the dialogue with a partner.

   In the oral exam, your teacher would be the clerk at the tourist information centre (role card ❷).

   Role card ❶ – tourist

   You have just arrived in London and you want to stay for one week. You go to the tourist information centre, because you need some information to make the most of your stay. Talk to the clerk and try to find out about …

   ▶ different means of transport
   ▶ three interesting and fun activities that you can do for free
   ▶ three sights (opening hours, price …)
   ▶ places where you can get tasty food

   Role card ❷ – clerk at a tourist information centre

   You work at a tourist information centre in London. A teenager from Germany asks you a lot of questions about the following points. Answer all the questions he or she might have.

   You can use the following information, but feel free to include other things you know about London.

   ▶ **means of transport** → public transport (Tube, buses – get "Oyster card" for visitors); rental bikes; hop-on hop-off buses
   ▶ **interesting and fun activities** that you can do for free → e. g. free London walking tour, picnic in Hyde Park, deer-spotting in Richmond Park, Changing of the Guard, Platform 9¾ at Kings Cross Station, watch Tower Bridge open …
   ▶ **sights** (opening hours, price …) → some museums and art galleries are free (e. g. British Museum, National History Museum, Tate Modern) …
   ▶ **food** → restaurants and cafés nearby, supermarkets, Chinatown …

Speaking – Kommunikationsprüfung | 179

b) **Two days in London**

Work with a partner. Choose either role card ❶ or ❷ and only read your card. Start the conversation with some small talk before you plan your trip. In the end, you need to **agree** on the following points:

- means of transport
- free activities
- sights
- food

Tandemprüfung

Role card ❶ – German tourist

You have just arrived at the youth hostel in London, where you want to stay for one week. You start talking to another tourist from the United States and you decide to spend the next two days together. Talk about the following things:

- **means of transport** –
  your idea: "Oyster card" for visitors → public transport
- three **interesting and fun activities** that you can do **for free** –
  your ideas: Changing of the Guard, picnic in Hyde Park, watch Tower Bridge open …
- three **sights** you want to visit together –
  your ideas: Madame Tussauds and London Eye (discount with Oyster card) …
- places where you can get **tasty food** –
  your ideas: bakeries, cafés and restaurants nearby

Role card ❷ – American tourist

You have already been in London for two days. At the youth hostel where you are staying for another three days, you start talking to a tourist from Germany, who has just arrived. You two decide to spend the next two days together. Talk about the following things:

- **means of transport** – your ideas: rent a bike; hop-on hop-off bus
- three **interesting and fun activities** that you can do **for free**
  – your ideas: deer-spotting in Richmond Park, free London walking tour, Platform 9¾ at Kings Cross Station …
- three **sights** you want to visit together –
  your ideas: British Museum, Tate Modern or National History Museum (all free), Tower of London …
- places where you can get **tasty food** –
  your ideas: Chinatown, not eat out, but buy food at supermarket and cook at hostel

Speaking – Kommunikationsprüfung

Sprachmittlung

7. **At a Tea Room**

You are on holiday in Brighton with your grandma. She doesn't speak English at all, but she has heard so much about typical English tea rooms that she wants to visit one with you. Help her to communicate.

grandma (teacher)	mediation (candidate)	waitress (teacher)
		Hello and welcome to Rosie's Tea Room. I'm afraid we don't have a table for you at the moment. If you don't mind, you can certainly wait – it shouldn't take too long until a table is free.
	a) …	
Aber der Tisch da vorne am Fenster ist doch frei, vielleicht hat sie ihn nicht gesehen. Kannst du sie bitte fragen, ob wir den Tisch nehmen können?		
	b) …	
		I'm terribly sorry, that table is reserved, but the guests at table 10 at the other window are about to pay the bill. You can have their table in a few minutes.
	c) …	
Ach, das ist ja auch ein sehr hübscher Tisch. Wie schön, dass es doch so schnell klappt. Bedank dich bitte bei der netten Dame dafür.		
	d) …	
		I'm glad that you like it. Please follow me to your table and have a look at the menu. I'll be right back to take your order.
	e) …	
Solche freundlichen Menschen hier. Das ist genau, wie ich es mir vorgestellt habe. Ich hätte gerne einen Schwarztee und du willst doch sicher auch einen Tee, oder? Bestellst du bitte für uns beide?		
	f) …	
		Would you like milk with your tea? And can I get you anything to go with your tea?

	g) ...	
Ja natürlich, wenn man das in England so macht, nehmen wir Tee mit Milch. Kannst du bitte fragen, was sie empfiehlt, dazu zu essen?		
	h) ...	
		We usually have sandwiches with ham or salmon or scones[1] with strawberry jam.
	i) ...	
Das hört sich alles toll an. Lass uns von allem etwas bestellen. Ich habe sowieso großen Hunger ...		
	j) ...	
		Excellent. Thank you. I'll be back with your tea soon.
	k) ...	

[1] scones – typisches, englisches Gebäck. Du brauchst den Ausdruck hier nicht zu übersetzen.

8. An exchange student

Emma ist eine Austauschschülerin aus Irland. Leider spricht sie noch fast kein Deutsch. Euer Rektor, Herr Fischer, kann leider auch nicht wirklich gut Englisch und bittet dich, ihm beim Erklären des Ablaufs zu helfen.
Vermittle jeweils für den Rektor ins Englische und für Emma ins Deutsche.

headmaster (teacher)	mediation (candidate)	Emma (teacher)
Kannst du Emma bitte in meinem Namen willkommen heißen und ihr sagen, dass es uns freut, dass sie für einige Zeit unsere Schule besuchen wird. Sie ist die erste Austauschschülerin, die aus Irland kommt.		
	a) ...	
		Thank you so much, I'm really happy to be able to go to your school for the entire school year. I haven't met many people yet, but everybody I've talked to has been very nice.
	b) ...	

Das ist schön, zu hören. Jetzt habe ich noch ein paar wichtige Informationen für Emma. Kannst du ihr bitte sagen, dass bei uns die Schule um 7.30 Uhr anfängt und außer donnerstags um 12.45 Uhr endet?	
c) ...	
	Oh, school days in Germany are really short. That's nice. But what about Thursdays? And where do I have to go tomorrow morning at 7.30?
	d) ...
Donnerstags gibt es in der Mensa um 13 Uhr Mittagessen. Der Unterricht startet wieder um 14 Uhr und geht bis 15.30 Uhr. Emma soll morgen einfach zum Lehrerzimmer kommen. Frau Müller wird ihr dann ihr Klassenzimmer zeigen.	
e) ...	
	All right, I'll be there. What shall I do if I don't understand the teachers? My German marks at school are good, but I seem to have some problems understanding spoken German.
	f) ...
Sag ihr, sie soll sich einfach von ihren Mitschülerinnen und Mitschülern helfen lassen. Das wird sicher kein Problem.	
g) ...	
	All right. Are there any school rules I should know about?
	h) ...
Ja, die gibt es tatsächlich. Man muss freundlich mit Mitschülerinnen und Mitschülern und allen Lehrkräften umgehen, man darf keinen Kaugummi kauen und das Rauchen ist verboten. Hier ist eine Kopie unserer Hausordnung. Du kannst Emma ja vielleicht helfen, wenn sie die anderen Punkte nicht versteht.	
i) ...	

9. At a hotel in Florida

Du bist mit deinen Eltern im Urlaub in Florida. Ihr habt gerade eingecheckt und seid sehr enttäuscht von eurem Zimmer und dessen Zustand. Da das Englisch deiner Mutter etwas eingerostet ist, bittet sie dich, bei der Rezeption anzurufen.

mother (teacher)	mediation (candidate)	receptionist (teacher)
		Beach Holiday Hotel, Linda Jones speaking, how may I help?
	a) …	
Sag ihr bitte, dass wir vor 10 Minuten eingecheckt haben, wir aber mit unserem Zimmer überhaupt nicht zufrieden sind. Unsere Zimmernummer ist die 425.		
	b) …	
		Oh, I'm sorry about that. What's the problem with your room?
	c) …	
Das Zimmer ist für eine Familie nicht geeignet. Außerdem ist es schmutzig und wir haben keinen Meerblick, obwohl wir Meerblick gebucht haben. Wir möchten sofort ein anderes Zimmer.		
	d) …	
		We're fully booked, so I don't have another room for you. If you open the window and look left, you can see the ocean though. I can send the cleaners to you and they'll clean again.
	e) …	
Sag ihr bitte, dass das wohl ein Witz ist mit dem Meerblick und dass das Zimmer einfach zu klein ist für drei Leute. Die Dusche im Bad funktioniert auch nicht richtig und es kommt nur kaltes Wasser. Sie soll jemanden schicken, der das repariert.		
	f) …	
		All right, that is a problem. I'll send you our caretaker to repair the shower right away. I hope you'll still have your dream holiday.

Speaking – Kommunikationsprüfung

g) …

Von wegen Traum-Ferien. Da ist wohl eher Albtraum-Ferien der passende Ausdruck … Frag sie bitte noch, ob es eine vegetarische Alternative beim Abendessen gibt.

h) …

Of course there is a vegetarian option. You can eat as much as you want from our salad bar.

i) …

Unglaublich. Sag ihr bitte, dass wir uns sofort nach einem anderen Hotel umsehen werden und wir eine komplette Rückerstattung unseres Reisepreises erwarten.

j) …

Good luck with that. Have a nice day.

k) …

Darauf brauchen wir nichts mehr zu antworten. Lass uns gleich unseren Anwalt anrufen.

▶ **Aufgaben im Stil der Abschlussprüfung**

Baden-Württemberg – Realschulabschluss
Aufgaben im Stil der Abschlussprüfung

♪ 187

A. Listening Comprehension

1. A survey on the use of video platforms

5 pts

You will hear a radio report about a survey on the use of video platforms. You will hear the report twice. Take notes and fill in the table.

a)	who carried out the study	
b)	number of students in the study	
c)	average time per week students spend watching videos online	
d)	favourite kinds of videos for boys (top 2)	❶ ❷
e)	favourite kinds of videos for girls (top 2)	❶ ❷

2. Different ways of travelling

5 pts

You will hear a radio show about travelling trends. What do Roger, Rachel and Jason say about their favourite type of holiday? Listen to the radio show twice and write the correct name (Roger, Rachel, Jason) next to the statement, but be careful: one statement does not fit. Mark this statement with a cross (✗).

a) _____ I really hate sport.

b) _____ I love the feeling of sand under my feet.

c) _____ I don't need a bed when I'm on holiday.

d) _____ The heat is not my thing.

e) _____ Meeting new people is great.

3. Cyberbullying

6 pts

You will hear a radio interview about cyberbullying. You will hear the interview twice. Take notes and fill in the missing information.

how the victims were bullied

a) Kevin:
_____
_____
_____

Jenny:
nasty anonymous messages on her phone

Emma:
online poll in which people were asked to rank her looks

how they felt

Emma:
depressed

b) Jenny:
_____
_____
_____

c) Kevin:
_____
_____
_____

CYBERBULLYING

who they talked to

Jenny:
her best friend Zoe

d) Kevin:
_____
_____
_____

Emma:
nobody at first / later to a teacher and her parents

how the bullying ended

Kevin: brother told the principal about the bullying / talked to the bullies / bullies were suspended from school for a while

e) Emma:
_____
_____
_____

f) Jenny:
_____
_____
_____

4. Eye movement 4 pts

You will hear a report about eye movement. One ending to each of the following sentences is correct.
Tick (✓) the correct ending to finish the sentences.
You will hear the recording twice.

a) Lie detectors are used by the police and the FBI but they are ...
   A ☐ frequently unreliable.
   B ☐ very expensive and complicated.
   C ☐ only used for men.

b) Even innocent people who are very nervous might have ...
   A ☐ fast moving eyes.
   B ☐ a fast heartbeat and sweaty hands.
   C ☐ a slow heartbeat and dry hands.

c) If you see a picture of a familiar face ...
   A ☐ your eyes stay longer on a few features.
   B ☐ your face relaxes.
   C ☐ your eyes dance from one feature to the next.

d) Even if tracing eye movement is promising, ...
   A ☐ you can't tell whether a person is lying.
   B ☐ you need a special course to be able to do it.
   C ☐ more research is needed.

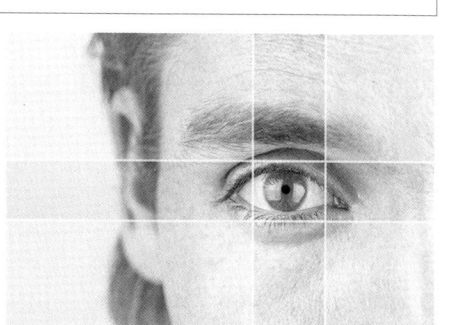

B. Text-based Tasks

Global hunger stable, but obesity on rise

The United Nations says more than 820 million people around the world are hungry while at same time obesity is hitting record levels.

A report recently released by five U.N. agencies dealing with food, nutrition and health says that while hunger levels have mostly stabilized, more people around the world are anxious about where their family's next meal will come from. The report also listed several different reasons for these anxieties. "People that feel insecure because they are in areas under conflict, insecure because they are in countries with high levels of inflation, insecure because they are very low paid that they will not have money to buy their food – this number reached 2 billion people around the world," José Graziano da Silva, director-general of the Food and Agriculture Organization (FAO) said at the report's launch. "This is really a big, big number. We were surprised when we found this figure."

The report notes the highest hunger rates are in Africa and growing steadily in almost all parts of the continent, where climate and conflict, economic slowdowns and downturns have driven more than 256 million people into a state of food insecurity. Not knowing whether you will have enough food for yourself and your family makes life a hardship. Children in particular are the most at risk and starve to death. In Asia, the lack of food is a big problem too: more than 500 million people, primarily in the southern part of the continent, are suffering from malnutrition. This sort of hunger has lasting impacts on its victims and their development, especially children, who suffer from stunting[1] and wasting[2]. As a result, children don't grow as they should and are often very weak and get ill.

"So the question is what are we going to do about it?" asked World Food Program Executive Director David Beasley. "Because if these were your little girls and your little boys, I guarantee you, you'd be doing everything you could to do something about it." Beasley appealed to parents all over the world who never have to worry about the next meal for their children. He also stressed that the problem of world hunger is solvable, but is not achievable without ending war and conflicts, which consume a huge portion of the global economy that could be used for development. Therefore, ending wars and conflicts should be the focus.

For the first time, the U.N. agencies were also able to gather data on world obesity rates, which are skyrocketing. "We have about 830 million obese people in the world," said the FAO's Graziano da Silva. He said trends indicate that the numbers of overweight and obese people in Africa and Asia would soon exceed those who are hungry. Graziano da Silva said obesity rates are rising by 6.3 % and 7.5 % per year respectively in Africa and Asia, while the global average is 4.8 %. "It's really a global epidemic issue the way obesity is rising and how fast it is rising," Graziano da Silva said and went on to explain that the cost of obesity is very high, some $ 2 trillion a year in related illnesses and other side effects.

In order to prevent this global epidemic from spreading any further, Graziano da Silva urged better labelling of foods, reducing the levels of salt, fats and sugars in processed foods and restricting advertising for some products geared toward children. He noted healthy and fresh foods also need to be promoted and access to them needs to be increased for some populations.

That there is a growing number of obese people in the world at large is shocking. Watching people fighting hunger while others struggle with unhealthy eating habits is depressing. The changes Graziano da Silva suggested are steps in the right direction, but it will take time to convince the governments to take action and to make the food industry implement³ them. *(660 words)*

Adapted from: Margaret Besheer, Voice of America – Science and Health, July 15, 2019.

1 stunting – *Unterentwicklung*
2 wasting – *Marasmus (Krankheit, die durch Unterernährung entsteht)*
3 (to) implement – *umsetzen, einführen*

1. Match the headings with the parts of the text. There are two more headings than you need.   5 pts

Example: ❽ – f

❶ Ways to prevent obesity
❷ War in Africa
❸ Facts and figures about food insecurity worldwide
❹ How to solve the problem of world hunger
❺ Tips on healthy eating
❻ Hunger and its consequences in Africa and Asia
❼ Obesity around the world

a) lines 3–13
b) lines 14–24
c) lines 25–33
d) lines 34–43
e) lines 44–48

2. Decide whether the following statements are true, false or not in the text.   3 pts

Example: g) – not in the text

a) Many people are insecure about feeding their family.
b) José Graziano da Silva expected the number of people who are anxious about their next meal to be as high as in the report.
c) There are various reasons for the high hunger rates in Africa.
d) The number of wars in Asia and Africa is increasing.
e) Soon fewer people in Africa and Asia will be obese rather than hungry.
f) Healthy food, fresh fruit and vegetables play an important part in preventing obesity.

6 pts

3. Finish the sentences using the information from the text.

Example: g) – C

a) According to the text, strong inflation and low wages can cause ...
- A anxiety.
- B depression.
- C anger.
- D obesity.

b) Two billion people ...
- A want to get a better job.
- B think about moving to a safer country.
- C are afraid they cannot feed their family.
- D live in an area under conflict.

c) Beasley said all the conflicts and wars have to stop so that ...
- A fewer people are killed in fights.
- B fewer soldiers are needed.
- C less money is needed.
- D fewer children lose their parents.

d) U.N. agencies found out that ...
- A people want to go into space.
- B there are more overweight people in the world than there are people who suffer from hunger.
- C only Africa and Asia have a problem.
- D the number of obese people is going up slowly, but steadily.

e) It is a worldwide problem that more and more people ...
- A do not care about the environment.
- B weigh too much.
- C in Africa are starving to death.
- D are afraid of wars.

f) Graziano da Silva wants ...
- A food to be labelled more clearly.
- B processed food to be banned.
- C advertising for fast food to be prohibited in general.
- D companies to make more kid-friendly advertisements.

| 4. Find three measures that can help to stop obesity. | 3 pts |

| 5. Answer the questions in complete sentences by using the information from the text. | 8 pts |

a) What are the reasons for food insecurity according to the text?
b) Why are the hunger rates in Africa steadily rising?
c) What consequences does malnutrition have?
d) How will the problem of obesity develop?

C. Use of Language

| 1. Find words or expressions in the text which mean more or less the same. | 3 pts |

a) not long ago   (lines 3–13)
b) shortage   (lines 14–24)
c) diseases   (lines 34–43)

| 2. Find the opposites. | 3 pts |

a) weak   (line 24)
b) rising   (line 39)
c) better   (line 45)

| 3. Choose two of the following words and give a definition. | 4 pts |

a) obesity   (line 2)
b) solvable   (line 30)
c) (to) reduce (line 45)

| 4. Vocabulary – Grammar | 6 pts |

Complete the text by using suitable forms of the words. Find words of your own to replace the question mark.

Nelson Rolihlahla Mandela _____ the Nobel Peace Prize in   a) to receive
1993 after he _____ 27 years in prison. He was one of the   b) to spend
political leaders _____ fought for the rights of black people   c) ?
and against apartheid. He is the founding father of _____   d) peaceful
in South Africa.
If you take the time to read his book *Long Walk to Freedom*,
you _____ a lot about this great _____ leader, who can be   e) to learn   f) politics
described as a special person with a _____ mind.   g) beauty
Nelson Mandela _____ president of South Africa in 1994   h) to elect
after _____ the country's first democratic election.   i) to win

He is one _____ the most important figures in history. j) from/of/off
Since 2009, on 18th July, his birthday _____ as Nelson k) to celebrate
Mandela International Day. It is a day to take action and
make the world a better place. Can you make a _____ in l) different
your community too?

5. Ask questions.

You are talking to John, who has just returned from his trip around South Africa.
Ask him three questions about his trip.
Use different question forms or tenses.

6. Paraphrasing

Complete the second sentence so that it means the same as the first sentence. Use between two and five words including the word in brackets.

Example:
Brad: I have tons of stuff to throw away.
(get rid)   I need to … of junk.
→ … get rid of a lot …

a) **Penny:** I can't wait to celebrate my birthday. I'm so excited!
   (look forward)   I'm … birthday this year.

b) **Brad:** Listening to people can make a big difference.
   (important)   It's … have someone who listens to them.

c) **Penny:** I've never heard such a sad story.
   (ever)   It's the … heard.

d) **Ben:** The activity I like best is reading biographies.
   (pastime)   Reading biographies …

D. Writing

1. Write a comment.

Choose **one** of the following statements. Discuss the pros and cons and give your own opinion. Write about 100 words.

A   Homework should be abolished.
B   Social media destroy communication.
C   Schools should switch to e-books.

2. Choose task **A** or task **B**. 18 pts

You only have to do **one** of the following tasks.

A Write a story with **one** of the following endings in about 160 words.
Ending ❶ ... and that's why I got a huge cake from my neighbour.
Ending ❷ ... and that's why I'm on YouTube now.

B Write a letter of complaint.
Your family spent a week at a hotel in Sydney. It was the worst stay at a hotel you have ever had. Write a letter of complaint and explain why you weren't satisfied. Write about 160 words.

E. Interpreting

1. You have found an interesting article about baby elephants on the internet. Answer the questions in **German**. You need not write complete sentences. 6 pts

UN bans sending baby elephants from wild to zoos and circuses

1 Delegates at a U.N. wildlife conference in Geneva voted to ban the practice of taking baby elephants from their natural habitat and placing them in zoos and circuses.

5 Forty-six countries at the UN Convention on International Trade in Endangered Species (CITES) voted to outlaw the practice. While 18 voted against it, including the United States, nineteen abstained.

The ban proclaims entertainment venues to be "unacceptable and inappropri-
10 ate destinations" for elephants. "This decision will save countless elephants from being ripped away from their families in the wild and forced to spend their lifetimes imprisoned in substandard conditions at zoos," the Humane Society International said. "The capture of baby elephants is horribly cruel and traumatic to both the mothers, their calves and the herds that are left behind."

15 Sunday's decision specifically targets Botswana, Namibia, South Africa, and Zimbabwe. CITES says Zimbabwe has sent more than 100 baby elephants to China since 2012, traumatizing the animals who it says are beaten, kicked, and treated cruelly by their handlers. Several have died.

Adapted from: Voice of America – Science and Health, August 18, 2019

a) Was sollte bei der Konferenz beschlossen werden? (1 pt)
b) Wie war das Abstimmungsergebnis? (1 pt)
c) Warum ist ein solches Verbot wichtig? (1 Angabe) (1 pt)
d) Wer ist traumatisiert, wenn Babyelefanten eingefangen werden? (1 pt)
e) Was passierte mit den Babyelefanten aus Simbabwe? (2 Angaben) (2 pts)

Aufgaben im Stil der Abschlussprüfung

9 pts

2. School rules

Your school is taking part in an exchange programme with an Irish school. Your headteacher wants you to inform the Irish students about the school rules. Write down the rules for the exchange students in English.

a) Um gut lernen zu können, haben die Schüler*innen stets alle Unterlagen dabei, die sie an diesem Tag benötigen, und erscheinen rechtzeitig zum Unterricht.

b) Alle elektronischen Geräte (z. B. Smartphones) dürfen im Schulhaus nicht benutzt werden. Jede*r ist selbst dafür verantwortlich, dass sie sicher verwahrt werden.

c) Ein freundliches und höfliches Miteinander ist selbstverständlich. Hilfsbereitschaft wird an unserer Schule großgeschrieben.

d) Die Schüler*innen gehen fair und respektvoll miteinander um und achten auf das Eigentum anderer. Gewalt in jeder Form ist verboten.

e) Jede*r soll sich an unserer Schule wohlfühlen. Die Schüler*innen zeigen Verständnis füreinander, akzeptieren kulturelle Unterschiede und respektieren andere Meinungen. An unserer Schule ist kein Platz für Mobbing.

f) Auch außerhalb der Schule – z. B. auf dem Schulweg und in der Freizeit – verhalten sich alle Schüler*innen verantwortungsbewusst und achten auf eine angemessene Sprache.

Bildnachweis
S. 189: © Gajus. Shutterstock
S. 195: © Claudia Paulussen. Shutterstock

► Original-Aufgaben der Abschlussprüfung an Realschulen in Baden-Württemberg

Baden-Württemberg – Realschulabschluss
Englisch 2021

2021-1

A. Listening Comprehension

1. Yoga

5 pts

You will hear a radio interview with the yoga instructors Lisa, Peter and Dr Sing. You will hear the recording twice. Write the correct name (Lisa, Peter, Dr Sing) next to the statement. Some names must be used twice.

a) _____ Yoga was first practised in Asia before it travelled around the world.

b) _____ In yoga you practise specific body postures and forms of breathing.

c) _____ Yoga is good for people who are stressed and physically harmed.

d) _____ Yoga is a very old form of physical and spiritual exercise.

e) _____ Yoga lovers meet to practise yoga outdoors.

4 pts

2. Vikings

You will listen to a guided museum tour on Vikings. You will hear the recording twice. Take notes to complete the cluster.

a) places they came from:
- _____
- _____

b) reasons for leaving their homelands:
- _____
- _____

Vikings

c) swords:
- _____
- _____

d) ships:
- _____
- _____

5 pts

3. The Prom

You will hear a voice message from Lena's American exchange partner Mary-Lou about last night's prom. You will hear the recording twice. One ending to each of the sentences is correct. Mark the correct ending.

a) Mary-Lou went dress shopping downtown …
- ☐ yesterday.
- ☐ two weeks ago.
- ☐ two months ago.

b) The dress …
- ☐ could not be rented.
- ☐ was too expensive.
- ☐ fell apart.

c) The poster had been put on Mary-Lou's school locker …
- ☐ by Derek.
- ☐ by the other girls.
- ☐ by Tiffany.

d) Tiffany's dress ...
- [ ] was the same as Mary-Lou's.
- [ ] was stolen.
- [ ] fell on the dance floor.

e) Derek ...
- [ ] drove Mary-Lou home.
- [ ] danced with Tiffany.
- [ ] called Mary-Lou's dad.

4. Digital footprint

6 pts

You will hear a podcast about your digital footprint. You will hear the recording twice. Take notes to fill in the table.

a)	two examples of leaving a digital footprint	• _____ • _____
b)	what employers check out about candidates	• _____
c)	what to do when you find something upsetting	• _____
d)	how to protect your identity online	• _____
e)	advantage of your digital footprint	• _____

B. Text-based Tasks

How online shopping is changing the world

1   In the past, there were only a few things delivered to our homes like newspapers, pizza or Asian food. Nowadays, there is a universe of products like DVDs, video games, Spanish oranges, clothes, books, groceries or medicine and
5   you can order them all online. Even more exotic is ordering insects to feed your tarantula. Or do you need help around the house? So why not order a plumber or a carpenter online to help you. This new experience of shopping is known as e-commerce or e-business.

Most home deliveries still consist of the familiar brown cardboard parcels
10 from retailers[1] such as *Amazon*, which is responsible for half of all the packages delivered in the US each year. Jeff Bezos, *Amazon's* founder, never wanted his customers to worry about shipping – about how much it costs, or about how long it takes. "Time is money. Save both.", is the slogan which shows that *Amazon's* main goal is to deliver their products as quickly as possible. *Ama-*
15 *zon's* emphasis on speed forced other retailers to hurry, too, and shoppers started to believe that something that cannot be received quickly is not worth having at all.
In 2005, *Amazon* created *Prime*, a club for shoppers paying a fixed fee every year, so that they got free two-day shipping on everything they bought. *Prime*
20 now has more than 100 million members. A market analysis firm found that 93 per cent of *Prime* members keep their subscription after a year, and 98 per cent after two years. "Not for patient people," runs a *Prime* slogan, and it is right: one out of every three *Prime* members has deleted items from their shopping baskets after learning that they could not arrive in two days. Mean-
25 while, *Amazon* halved *Prime* shipping time down to a day.

A lot of attention has been paid to problems such as how best to pack a box, how to beat traffic and what to do when a delivery driver rings the doorbell and no one is home. The cardboard box is the most obvious symbol of e-commerce and stands for the conflict of choosing between our unlimited con-
30 sumption and the health of the planet. A heavier box costs more to buy and it also uses more fuel to ship, for example. Like every company, *Amazon* has been trying to design boxes that are both light and strong. But still many companies use packaging materials excessively.

However, the environmental impact of all that paper and plastic is just one
35 part of the overall carbon footprint of online shops. In addition, vans and trucks of companies such as *FedEx*, *UPS* and *DHL* increase traffic. The great trick of online retail is to get us to do more shopping without thinking about it for too long. So, when ordering online some people buy far more than they need, send unwanted items back and order new ones, forcing drivers to come
40 back. Some people live so far out in the countryside that delivery drivers must make an effort to find them. Especially the cities struggle with home delivery because they were not designed to handle this amount of transport activity.

Delivery drivers block the side of the road to load and unload their packages. Streets are jammed and citizens suffer from air pollution.

How will e-commerce handle the challenges in the next decade? Different ideas are being discussed: using drones, parachutes, autonomous vehicles or robots. Obviously, there is still a long way to go to make e-commerce more efficient and more eco-friendly.

(591 words)

Adapted from: Samanth Subramanian: How our home delivery habit reshaped the world, The Guardian, 21.11.2019, https://www.theguardian.com/technology/2019/nov/21/how-our-home-delivery-habit-reshaped-the-world

1 retailers – Einzelhändler

---

1. Decide whether the following statements are true, false or not in the text. — 3 pts

Example: B 1 g) – not in the text

a) The majority of products sold online are delivered in brown cardboard boxes.
b) Many *Prime* members end their membership within a year.
c) In the future *Amazon* will reduce shipping time to less than a day.
d) Because of the carbon footprint of their companies, *FedEx*, *UPS* and *DHL* now use alternative fuel.
e) Finding customers' homes in rural areas is sometimes difficult for delivery drivers.
f) Online sellers are discussing using only drones to deliver their products.

---

2. Match the headings with the parts of the text. There are two more headings than you need. — 5 pts

Example: B 2 h) – 6

a) Importance of delivery speed
b) Jeff Bezos' biography
c) Consequences of home delivery
d) Trip to the shops
e) Unsolved issues
f) Changes in the way of shopping
g) Ideal packaging

1. lines 1–8
2. lines 9–25
3. lines 26–33
4. lines 34–44
5. lines 45–48

---

3. Finish the sentences using the information from the text. — 6 pts

Example: B 3 g) – C

a) DVDs, video games and groceries …
  A are the most popular things ordered online.
  B arrive in plastic boxes.
  C are available online.
  D are only delivered by *Amazon*.

b) Being an *Amazon Prime* member ...
   A you need to pay an annual fee.
   B makes you patient.
   C you have to wait for the ordered goods for more than two days.
   D you only have to pay for shipping.

c) More than 100 million people ...
   A do online shopping at least twice a week.
   B regret their subscriptions as *Prime* members.
   C have deleted items from their shopping baskets.
   D have joined *Amazon Prime*.

d) Returning unwanted products ...
   A is cheap for *Prime* members.
   B costs *Amazon* several million dollars per year.
   C demands revisits of couriers.
   D costs an extra fee.

e) In cities ...
   A inhabitants struggle with ordering online.
   B there is too much competition.
   C packaging materials pollute the streets.
   D transport activity has increased because of e-commerce.

f) To cope with e-commerce in the future you will have to ...
   A reduce it.
   B improve eco-friendliness.
   C concentrate on longer shipping distances.
   D get rid of the packaging.

4. Answer the questions in complete sentences using the information from the text.

a) How can e-commerce help you with your jobs around the house?
b) What should not be a problem for Jeff Bezos' customers?
c) How does *Amazon* influence other retailers?
d) Why do cardboard boxes have to be light? (2 items)
e) What adds to the carbon footprint of online shops?

C. Use of Language

| 1. Find words or expressions in the text which mean more or less the same. | 5 pts |

a) assistance (lines 1–8)
b) money you pay for something (lines 18–25)
c) sign which represents something (lines 26–33)
d) struggle of opposing ideas (lines 26–33)
e) people living in a city or town (lines 34–44)

| 2. Find the opposites. | 5 pts |

a) never (line 11)
b) bought (line 19)
c) more (line 20)
d) halved (line 25)
e) different (line 45)

| 3. Explain two of the following words in complete sentences. | 4 pts |

a) to hurry (line 15)
b) member (line 20)
c) strong (line 32)

| 4. Vocabulary – Grammar | 5 pts |

Complete the text by using suitable forms of the words. Write them down.

Scientists warn: Insects will disappear

Global warming is not the only serious _____ to humans.   a) to threaten
Another one is the falling numbers of insects and the
many species _____ have already died out. Scientists say   b) ?
that half of all insects worldwide _____ since the 1970s.   c) to disappear
A new warning is that over 40 per cent of insect species
could die out in our lifetime. One researcher said the
number of insects was decreasing by 2.5 per cent every
year. Many species of _____, bees and other insects are   d) butterfly
now extinct. This can trigger a catastrophic collapse of
the _____ ecosystems.   e) Earths / Earth's / Earths'

Professor Dave Goulson said a lot of insects _____ by   f) to kill
pesticides used for farming and gardening. He said lower
numbers of insects might mean we would not have
enough _____ for people. He told reporters: "Three-   g) feed
quarters of our crops depend _____ the help of insects.   h) from / on / of

Crops will begin to fail. If this happens, we _____ things like strawberries any longer. One of the most worrying trends is the decline of honeybees. In the USA, the number of honeybee colonies _____ from six million in 1947 to just 2.5 million in 2014." Professor Goulson warned: "We can't wait another 25 years before we do anything because it will be too late."

i) not have

j) to drop

Sean Banville: Breaking News English – Lesson: Insect Apocalypse,
https://breakingnewsenglish.com/1911/191117-insect-apocalypse.html

5. Ask questions.

Ask four questions. Use different question forms or different tenses.
You are talking to Peter Harris, a swimming pool attendant.
Ask him about his job.

D. Writing

1. Write a comment.

Choose **one** of the following statements. Discuss the pros and cons and give your own opinion. Write about 100 words.

A People should use public transport only.
B Young people can only enjoy their spare time when spending money.
C Life is boring without a computer.

2. Choose one of the following tasks.

A Write an email of application. Write about 160 words.

> **Computer Support for Seniors**
>
> We, the Sutherland Court Care Home, are offering a computer club for our residents.
> We are looking for young people who are skilled with the computer and will be able to support our seniors once a week.
> Please send your application to: recruitment@hc-one.co.uk

B Write a story. Write about one of the following pictures in about 160 words.

C Write a diary entry. Complete the diary entry in about 160 words.

Dear Diary,
You won't believe it. This morning something really strange happened to me. ...

E. Interpreting

> 1. Read the text about the Tours of Dublin and answer the questions in **German**. You need not write complete sentences.

7 pts

Tours of Dublin

1 When visiting the Irish city, you want to take in the best sights and attractions of Dublin – and you have several ways to explore the city to pick from.

It begins with the easiest and cheapest option, which would be a self-guided tour of Dublin on foot. Of course, you could use Dublin's public transport
5 system. Or you could also use a rental car to get around, but we do not recommend driving in Dublin as a tourist.

The best and most comfortable way to get to know Dublin is one of the many pre-organised bus tours. On our Hop-on-hop-off Tours you see all the major sites at your own pace and so they are actually the most flexible Dublin tours
10 of all. They usually go in circles around the city centre, but the flexibility for you comes with the opportunity to get off, and later re-enter the buses at any stop.

On another tour, called Viking Splash Tour, you will be driven around the city streets and the Grand Canal in an amphibious vehicle, while mainly being in-
15 formed about Dublin's Viking heritage. This is a fun tour and you take in most of the important sites, but you cannot get off at any point.

There is even a tour in the evening. It follows the trail of Dublin's ghosts and grave-robbers on a specially designed double-decker bus and with a performance of live actors. It is only for the brave ones, definitely not covering the
20 main tourist spots, but a good evening entertainment.

It is also possible to see Dublin from the water on our Dublin river tour. You cruise up and down the river Liffey in a modern boat, which allows for panoramic views of the Quays and the Docklands area. It is a big plus to see Dublin from a different point.

Bernd Biege: Tours of Dublin – How to Visit Dublin's Main Attractions Without Major Effort, TripSavvy vom 29. 06. 2019, https://www.tripsavvy.com/tours-of-dublin-1542304

a)	Warum bietet es sich an, Dublin auf eigene Faust zu erkunden?	(1 pt)
b)	Was sind die Vorteile der Hop-on-hop-off-Tour? (2 Angaben)	(2 pts)
c)	Warum fährt man bei der Viking Splash Tour in einem Amphibienfahrzeug?	(1 pt)
d)	Was ist das Besondere an der Abendtour? (2 Angaben)	(2 pts)
e)	Was erwartet uns bei einer Bootstour auf dem Liffey?	(1 pt)

2. Mediation: German – English

9 pts

Your school's movie club takes part in an international film project. Your partner school is in Slovenia and your contact person is Lara. There is a team meeting.

(2 pts) a) *Patrick:*
Wir müssen ihr unbedingt mitteilen, dass sich zwei Gruppen verkleinert haben. Sarah und Selina sind aus dem Projekt ausgestiegen.

(2 pts) b) *Leila:*
Wir sollten nicht vergessen, ihr zu schreiben, dass eine Gruppe bereits das Video über die wichtigsten Sehenswürdigkeiten von hier fertiggestellt hat. Häng doch die Datei gleich mit an.

(2 pts) c) *Jana:*
Der Skype-Termin nächsten Mittwoch muss wegen eines Fußballturniers ausfallen. Einige Jungs nehmen daran teil. Wir müssen fragen, ob die slowenische Gruppe am Donnerstag Zeit hat und wir den Skype-Termin verschieben können.

(2 pts) d) *Uli:*
Wie sieht es denn jetzt eigentlich mit der Unterkunft beim Austausch in Slowenien aus? Haben sie schon geklärt, ob die Unterkunft der deutschen Schüler in Gastfamilien sein wird oder in einer Jugendherberge? Ich finde Stockbetten ätzend.

(1 pt) e) *Frau Krauß:*
Und am Ende dürft ihr nicht vergessen zu schreiben, dass sich unser Schulleiter, Herr Bender, schon sehr freut, die Mitglieder der slowenischen Gruppe kennenzulernen.

Inform Lara. You need not write complete sentences.
a) …
b) …
c) …
d) …
e) …

Bildnachweis
S. 2021-4: Lkw © philia. Shutterstock; Kreditkarte © nrt. Shutterstock;
Umschlag © julynx. 123rf.com; Geschenk © Verkhozina Ekaterina. Shutterstock
S. 2021-8: Task B Photo 1: U.S. Coast Guard photo by Petty Officer 3rd Class Ali Flockerzi
Task B Photo 2: dlohner/pixabay

Baden-Württemberg – Realschulabschluss
Englisch 2022

Um dir die Prüfung 2022 schnellstmöglich zur Verfügung stellen zu können, bringen wir sie in digitaler Form heraus.

Sobald die Original-Prüfungsaufgaben 2022 freigegeben sind, können sie als PDF auf der Plattform *MyStark* heruntergeladen werden (Zugangscode vgl. Farbseiten vorne im Buch).

Prüfung 2022

www.stark-verlag.de/mystark